JESUS

A VISUAL HISTORY

THE DRAMATIC STORY *of the*
MESSIAH *in the* HOLY LAND

JESUS

A VISUAL HISTORY

DONALD L. BRAKE SR. | *with* TODD BOLEN

ZONDERVAN

Jesus, A Visual History
Copyright © 2014 by Donald L. Brake

This title is also available as a Zondervan ebook. Visit www.zondervan.com/ebooks.

Requests for information should be addressed to:

Zondervan, 3900 *Sparks Dr. SE, Grand Rapids, Michigan* 49546

Library of Congress Cataloging-in-Publication Data

Brake, Donald L., Sr., 1939–
    Jesus, a visual history: the dramatic story of the Messiah in the Holy Land / Donald L.
Brake, with Todd Bolen.
      p. cm.
    Includes bibliographical references and index.
    ISBN 978-0-310-51537-1 (softcover)
    1. Jesus Christ—Biography. 2. Palestine—Description and travel. 3. Israel—Description
and travel. I. Title.
BT301.3.B725 2014
232—dc23   2014003705

Published in association with the literatry agency of Credo Communications LLC., Grand Rapids, Michigan 49525; www.CredoCommunications.net.

Cover design: *Studio Gearbox*
Cover photography: *top: ramzihachicho/www.istockphoto.com; bottom left: D. Brake; bottom middle: Todd Bolen/www.BiblePlaces.com; bottom right: © Alex Gulevich/www.123RF.com*
Interior design: *Matthew Van Zomeren*

Printed in China

14 15 16 17 18 19 20 /CTC/ 22 21 20 19 18 17 16 15 14 13 12 11 10 9 8 7 6 5 4 3 2 1

To my wife, Carol, the original "Wonder Woman."
From a blind date to life partner, mother of my children,
grandmother of my grandchildren,
and love of my life for sixty years.

CONTENTS

ACKNOWLEDGMENTS

IT MUST HAVE BEEN SAID SOMEWHERE, "It takes a village to publish a book." Books published in the modern age are not just facts and information. They present the author's message and intention in a readable style and graphic format. For this reason, a book produced today requires the efforts of many gifted men and women who spend a great deal of time practicing their art. This book is no exception. Authors are bolstered by generations of accumulated knowledge and expertise by authors of the past. The bibliography in *Jesus, A Visual History* recognizes many of these men and women who have gone before in the quest for knowledge and the desire to make it known to later generations.

I am pleased to acknowledge a number of specially gifted people who have made this book possible. To them I am deeply grateful.

WRITING AND VISUAL AIDS

My thanks to Todd Bolen, a scholar, historian, and professor experienced in firsthand knowledge of the Holy Land, for his scholarly contributions and suggestions in history, biblical knowledge, and insight. The photos in this book, unless otherwise acknowledged, were provided by Todd Bolen from his *Pictorial Library of Bible Lands* (www.bibleplaces.com). They are a great resource for teachers and students alike. Additional black-and-white photos from the early twentieth century are freely available to the public from the US Library of Congress's Matson Photograph Collection (www.loc.gov/pictures/collection/matpc/) and in an improved edition, *The American Colony and Eric Matson Collection* (www.lifeintheholyland.com).

Thanks to award-winning author Shelly Beach for editing for style and offering valuable suggestions on writing and presentation.

Thanks also to artist and illustrator Ron Waalkes, who has faithfully and joyfully labored in producing original artwork that has made a major contribution to the visual appearance of this book.

Thanks to Multnomah librarian, Pam Middleton for her help in tracking down rare and unusual sources.

Thanks to my wife, Carol, for her editing and helpful suggestions—not sparing any area of the book from her sharp editorial scalpel.

Bill Schlegel, geographer, historian, teacher, and Holy Land guide, was the first to introduce me to the specific places and events in the life of Jesus. His willingness to share maps from his scholarly and graphic atlas of the Bible, *Satellite Bible Atlas: Historical Geography of the Bible*, visually enhances the journeys of our Savior.

Book Publication

Literary agent Tim Beals of Credo Communications showed tenacity and persistence in finding an acceptable publisher. He continually encouraged my resolve to see this book published.

My friend David Sanford has encouraged me for several years to write, write, and then write some more.

Zondervan Personnel for Editing and Design

Thanks to acquisitions editor Madison Trammel for getting this project running and to senior editor Nancy Erickson, for her efforts in accuracy and overall editing expertise. Thanks also to the composition and marketing team for their skill in design and excitement for the project.

A WORD . . .

"Faith comes from hearing the message, and the message is heard through the word about Christ."

—*Romans 10:17*

WE KNOW ABOUT THE LIFE OF JESUS primarily from what we read in the gospels of Matthew, Mark, Luke, and John. As early as AD 170, Tatian wove the stories of the four gospels into one continuous narrative called the **Diatessaron**. Since that time, readers have used harmonies of the gospel accounts to get a complete picture of the life of Jesus. Modern English harmonies were introduced with the work of J. J. Greisbach in 1776. The Gospels were placed side by side in parallel columns where synoptic material was recorded. This format allowed the reader to see the accounts together, even though the format at times interrupted an individual writer's timelines, clarity, and writing purposes.

When the writers of the Gospels composed their accounts, each author utilized source material[1] and then arranged the stories and details to portray Jesus from each author's unique perspective. The gospel of Matthew focuses on Jesus' major dissertations. Mark concentrates on Jesus' ministry in Galilee. John's record centers almost entirely on Jesus' story while he was in Jerusalem. Luke forms a bridge between the others, describing what happened after Jesus' travels and recording his sermons, as well as detailing his Perean ministry.[2] The different perspectives of the gospel writers are usually described theologically.

The Hebrew name Jesus (Yeshua) written on a Jerusalem ossuary dating from Jesus' time.

Indeed, the four accounts are not just unbiased news reports but theological documents written to instruct and encourage believers and so convince them of the truth presented within.

While the four accounts of Jesus' life are often chronological, the authors did not necessarily desire that every event be presented in sequence; nor did they record a complete biography of Jesus in the sense we use the term today, or explain geographical locations of events. For this reason, a full chronological tracing of Jesus' footsteps can be challenging. The most comprehensive story line of the life of Jesus may be found when comparing the four gospels in harmony.

For the purposes of this book, the author has chosen to rely on the *NIV Harmony of the Gospels*, edited by Robert L. Thomas and Stanley N. Gundry (Harper Collins, rev. ed., 1988), to follow as closely as possible a basic chronological order. Consulting a harmony makes it easier for readers to follow the "where and when" of Jesus' life. (Please note that other versions of harmonies are available and suitable.) The presentation here will provide citation of the gospel accounts in each section and the paragraph number associated with Thomas and Gundry's *NIV Harmony of the Gospels* (noted as T&G.) Because their volume includes the complete texts of the gospel accounts, it is a helpful companion to this work. The *Visual History* will then provide a unique presentation in chronological fashion on the geographical aspects of the gospel accounts.

PREFACE

GOD'S PLAYING BOARD

HE SPOKE AS ONE WITH AUTHORITY — calm and confident, with a delivery that inspired the soul. My first encounter with the life of Christ at Dallas Theological Seminary came under the teaching of Professor Dwight Pentecost, a man who profoundly shaped my thinking and life's work. He taught with a conviction and passion for his subject, and his students rarely saw him consult his notes. The moment I walked into his classroom, I fell in love with the Jesus of the Gospels and yearned to walk where he walked.

Years later my dream became a reality as our El Al airliner touched down at Ben Gurion Airport with a squeal of tires. I held my wife's hand as we scanned the world that lay beyond our tiny window. Israeli soldiers — both men and women — stood armed and ready to spring into action. A rush of excitement ran through us. We were in the Holy Land for the first time, and our anticipation overshadowed the disappointment and tensions of the past year.

We arrived in Israel from Ethiopia, where a military coalition had overthrown Emperor Haile Selassie. The coup d'état had replaced his monarchy with a military government, and the change came through violence. We spent nearly a year in 1976–77 enduring the harassment of roadblocks and military searches, home invasions, weapons searches, and even a period of house arrest. Thus, our second term as missionaries with the Sudan Interior Mission ended in anguishing heartache.

But our feeling changed as we landed in Tel Aviv. New excitement surged through us. We were in the Holy Land. Our stay in Jerusalem at the Institute of Holy Land Studies (now Jerusalem University College) helped us transition from a painful and disappointing final year in Ethiopia to a new ministry in Portland, Oregon, at Multnomah School of the Bible (now Multnomah University).

For three weeks, we studied the varied terrain of the sacred land. Professor Jim Monson introduced students to the wonders of studying in a land he called "God's playing board of biblical history." Clad in khaki clothes, with a well-worn and tattered straw hat tied under his chin, he joyfully prepared for another tour. His canvas knapsack stuffed with a *Student Map Manual*, Bible, and papers flapping against his hip, Monson led the charge up one tel (or tell, a mound with the ruins of multiple civilizations) and then another, covering the land from Dan to Beersheba. Along the way, he spoke in our bouncing bus, as if we were riding an Egyptian chariot, explaining the ridge routes, the valleys below, the soil types, the rock formations, and the agriculture. At the end of our twelve-hour day, we collapsed in our bus seats, exhausted and hungry, and many students fell asleep — but Jim never missed a beat, making sure we were instructed about every corner of the land. His enthusiasm for the nation and the Scriptures infected everyone, causing us to fall in love with the land.

I returned to the institute a decade later as a guest lecturer for a semester when I was taking a sabbatical from my teaching responsibilities at Multnomah. Then in 1990 I became president of the Institute of Holy Land Studies and was given a front-row seat to the first Gulf War. I returned to the United States as pastor of North Carrollton Baptist Church in Texas and then went back to Multnomah in 1999 to continue building the school I opened in 1986.

I still have an insatiable love for Israel and desire to share my enthusiasm for the land and my love for the biblical Jesus. It has been one of my dreams for many years to share my love of the Holy Land and for Jesus, my Savior, in a book. This book is the fulfillment of that dream.

I hope that as you journey with me through the land of Jesus, you will experience the singe of the desert's hot breath, be refreshed by the cool evening breezes, feel the stir of the wind stroking the waves of the Sea of Galilee, and follow the scents and sounds of the crowded markets that draw you into the life of the Middle East. Most of all, I pray all these experiences will deepen your love for the Savior whose life story is explored in the pages that follow.

INTRODUCTION
THE HOLY LAND UNDER SIEGE

THE CHILLING WAIL OF AIR RAID SIRENS woke me from a deep sleep. It was 3:00 a.m., and the Gulf War had begun. Israeli authorities had warned us for days of an impending attack on Iraq. For months world powers stood poised to invade Kuwait and drive Saddam Hussein from his occupation of that tiny sovereign nation. In Israel we prepared for the possibility of a retaliatory strike, but we did not think it would ever come. Analysts tried to calm Israeli citizens by pointing out that Saddam would not dare take such a bold step. They could not have been more wrong.

My wife, Carol, and I bounded out of bed in a dead run to the dorms to awaken the students as sirens echoed through the Kidron Valley and reverberated through the streets of Jerusalem. As a first-year president, the responsibility for the safety of the students lay heavy on my heart. Although the Israeli Defense Forces prepared us for how to seal rooms, distribute gas masks, and perform injections against mustard gas, the students' faces revealed their panic.

Authorities forecast the Scud missiles would strike five minutes from the time the sirens sounded. We quickly herded the students into our bedroom and adjoining guest room. One handicapped student was carried to the room in her wheelchair. We had prepared the room by sealing the windows and doors with plastic and tape, storing bottled water and food, preparing unopened gas masks, and tuning the radio to the Hebrew station.

The tension was so palpable over the next few minutes you could have cut it with a knife. Military advisers had emphasized that a biological or mustard gas attack would be odorless. Gas masks were to stay on our faces until the all-clear siren sounded. Men with beards quickly began dry shaving to assure an airtight fit. But when we placed the masks over our faces, we noticed a strange smell. Some people imagined the smell was from the residue of an exploding Scud. Relief swept the room when we realized the smell came from the rubber masks—not mustard gas. Soon the radio announced in Hebrew that the Scuds had landed in Tel Aviv—all was clear in Jerusalem. We had survived the first of many alarms.

Saddam's "mother of all battles" was under way—the first Gulf War. The invasion of the coalition forces occurred at 3:00 a.m. Israeli time January 17, 1991. The Scud attacks began to rain down on Israel from Iraq in the early hours the following day. The land of Israel was under siege—again!

Over the next several days, we entered the sealed rooms when the sirens sounded. By the twenty-eighth time or so, students often stayed outside to watch the sky for the battle between the Scuds and the Patriot missiles and to listen for the cheering of the Arabs as the missiles flew over Jerusalem. Forty Scud missiles were shot into Israel between January 17 and February 23, 1991. While most Scuds were fired at the heavily Jewish populated city of Tel Aviv, it was reported that on February 2 two Scuds hit outside Jerusalem. The war ended on February 27 when President Bush declared a suspension of offensive combat and laid out the conditions for a permanent cease-fire.

The attacks on Israel were unprovoked. Israeli forces did not participate with the coalition forces in the invasion of Kuwait; in fact, their closest allies strongly recommended they should not make any effort at retaliation. Saddam was, very simply, trying to provoke the Israelis to respond.

The Arab/Israeli conflict rages on in the twenty-first century. Even within the territory of Israel itself, the struggle continues. The Arabs want the Jews to leave the land of Israel; the Jews want the Arabs to accept them. Jews want Jerusalem as their capital; the Arabs want Jerusalem as their capital. The question that lingers is when it will stop. When will these neighbors learn to coexist in peace? And when will the prayers for the peace of Jerusalem be answered?

A STRATEGIC LOCATION

Israel sits like an island in the midst of the Rift Valley, with fertile plains, rolling hills, mountain ranges, and desert oases stretching from snow-capped Mount Hermon to the sunbaked Negev, and from the living Mediterranean Sea to the Dead (Salt) Sea. Israel has played a central role in world history for more than three thousand years due to its coveted location. Bordered on the south by Egypt, on the west by the Mediterranean Sea, on the north by Syria and Lebanon, and on the east by Jordan, the name given to this tiny strip of land is the "Bridge of God" or the "Land Between."

The rich history of Israel's land began over four thousand years ago when God gifted it to Abram and his descendants. Throughout biblical history, the land was conquered, settled, and fought over continuously. Its capital was established in the Judean hills by King David, who conquered the existing Jebusite city and called it Jerusalem. At the end of the Old Testament period, the Persians were in control of Israel. Yet as the New Testament began, Rome governed the land. In between these ruling powers, the political struggles of the Jews shaped the landscape of the Holy Land. The figure below records the political landscape of Israel from Alexander The Great to the New Testament period.

POLITICAL FORTUNES OF ISRAEL
The Land Between

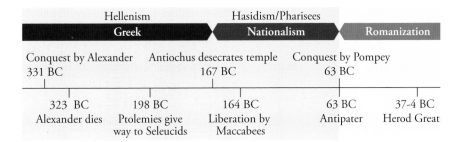

A BRIEF HISTORY OF THE LAND FROM ALEXANDER THE GREAT TO KING HEROD

Alexander the Great's conquest of the Western world brought an end to Persian domination and introduced a period of Hellenization (the adoption of Greek culture) to the Holy Land. The Greek language became the lingua franca of the entire empire. Greek domination was weakened, however, with the new division of the Greek Empire among the generals who survived Alexander. His failure to mentor an heir to the empire gave entry to the Seleucids (Antigonus) in Syria, Cassander in Macedonia, Ptolemy in Egypt, and Lysimachus in Western Turkey. Syria's attempt to Hellenize the Jews sparked the Maccabean revolt that led to one hundred years of liberation of the Holy Land. Jews successfully ruled the land of Israel[1] under the Hasmonean dynasty until the mighty Romans conquered them in 63 BC.

During these one hundred years of independence (167–63 BC), the role of king was blurred with the role of priest (Aristobulus I was the first to

HASMONEAN DYNASTY 167–63 BC

Matthias Maccabaeus

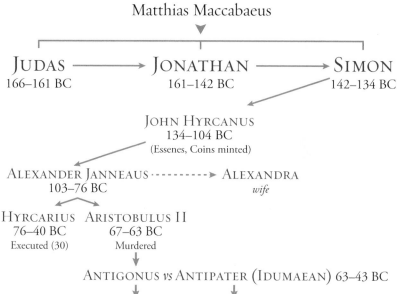

JUDAS ⟶ JONATHAN ⟶ SIMON
166–161 BC   161–142 BC   142–134 BC

JOHN HYRCANUS
134–104 BC
(Essenes, Coins minted)

ALEXANDER JANNEAUS ·········▸ ALEXANDRA
103–76 BC   *wife*

HYRCARIUS   ARISTOBULUS II
76–40 BC   67–63 BC
Executed (30)   Murdered

ANTIGONUS *vs* ANTIPATER (IDUMAEAN) 63–43 BC

assume the dual role). The confusion ultimately contributed to the downfall of the Hasmonean dynasty. Wealth, misuse of power, and perceived status provided the basis for corruption. Rome's eventual destruction of the Hasmonean dynasty and subsequent subjugation of the Holy Land fertilized the soil that produced discontent and later bore the fruit of the corrupt Herod the Great.

This Hasmonean fortress of Hyrcania is located eight miles southeast of Jerusalem. It was originally built by Alexander Janneaus about 100 BC and named Hyrcania in honor of his grandfather, Hyrcanus. Herod the Great rebuilt Hyrcania, perhaps to protect his borders.

Herod's father, Antipater, held a powerful office under the Jewish Hasmonean kings. His assistance to Julius Caesar in Alexandria, Egypt, gave him the right to preside over and collect taxes in Judea. Antipater was an Idumean (a descendant of the Edomites of

Masada from above with view of the siege ramp. Herod's massive and decadent palaces were constructed between 37 and 31 BC. Below, the outlines of the Roman encampments are visible.

the Old Testament) by birth. Though he later converted to Judaism, he was never fully accepted by the Jews.[2] His position as *epitropos* (governor) of Judea led the way for his son Herod's succession.

Herod became governor of Galilee in 47 BC following the poisoning assassination of Antipater in 43 BC. He remained in that position until appointed king of Judea by Rome in 40 BC. Octavian, nephew of Julius Caesar, gave Herod oversight and portions of the profits from the Cyprus copper mines. In addition to this territory in the land of Israel, he also gave Herod mixed parts of modern Jordan, Lebanon, and Syria.

Herod's appointment by Rome sparked heightened controversy in Israel. The new king claimed only partial Jewish heritage. He was an Idumean[3] who married a Hasmonean wife, Mariamne, and gave his children Hasmonean names. Rome believed Herod's mixed background would help him rule a seemingly difficult and stubborn people.

Though Rome crowned Herod, the Jewish population crowned Antigonus, a member of the royal Jewish line and the last of the Hasmonean rulers. Herod's paranoia prompted him to flee to Masada for safety. He later left Masada for Rome, hoping to garner Rome's support. He returned to Judea shortly thereafter with two legions of Roman soldiers. After a five-month

Roman siege catapult reconstruction

Masada siege tower reconstruction

Masada catapult balls

siege in the summer of 37 BC, he took Jerusalem and beheaded Antigonus. Herod was king, but his subjects hated him as an outsider, an animosity that would haunt him his whole life.

It was under Herod's rule that reconstruction of the Jewish temple began. Its completion and the expansion of the Temple Mount were among his crowning achievements. Herod's love for building extended to the various lands under his control, and his accomplishments became legendary. The city and harbor at Caesarea, his opulent palaces in Masada and Jericho, and the fortress at Herodium,[4] are among his most well-known endeavors.

Herod's prolific career of building water systems, fortresses, and cities was overshadowed, however, by heavy taxation and brutality, a Roman practice that continued to the time of Jesus.[5] On April 1, 4 BC, Herod died. His slaughter of his favorite wife, Mariamne, twenty-five years earlier and his two sons (by Mariamne) in the last three years of his life reveals his utter cruelty.

In an early will, Herod named one of his sons, Archelaus, as his successor.

THE STORY OF MASADA

Masada boasts a vibrant history. Not only did Herod build his elaborate palace on its northern end, but the stories of later Jewish revolt are legendary. In AD 66 Judea had no king, and the ruling Romans controlled the fortress of Masada. That year the Jews revolted, as they had done on many prior occasions. This time, however, the seriousness of the rebellion led Rome to eventually stamp out the revolt once and for all. Once Galilee was destroyed, the Roman machine destroyed Jerusalem, and finally attacked the stronghold of Masada.

Fleeing from Jerusalem, a Zealot, Eleazar Ben Yair, and his followers attempted to over-run the Romans at Masada and so began a long fight to free Judea from Roman rule. About one thousand men, women, and children defended Masada. In the fall of 72, Rome decided to subdue the fortress. The task proved enormous. They began by building fortified camps along a perimeter wall around the foot of the mountain to prevent escape. Then they built a large ramp of earthen materials, stone, and wood.

On top of the mountain, living conditions were very simple, and fortified walls protected the inhabitants. A ritual bath and a synagogue attest to the devotion of the residing families. Excavators later uncovered coins and fragments of scrolls used by the Jewish defenders, including portions of Leviticus, Deuteronomy, Psalms, and Ezekiel.

A legion of five thousand or more foot soldiers, several thousand auxiliaries, mounted warriors, archers, stonemasons, and engineers equipped with battering rams and catapults advanced toward Masada. The approaching Romans created a fearsome sight. As the invaders proceeded to prepare for their final assault, the Zealots fought back by hurling stones down the mountainsides, launching surprise attacks, and employing other defensive tactics. Finally, at nightfall in the spring of AD 73, the attacking forces breached the wall. They then retreated to prepare for the next morning's attack.

Eleven ostraca (pieces of pottery with inscriptions) were found near the inner gate of the northern complex at Masada. The inscriptions attest names or nicknames that seem to fit Josephus's account. Remains of a man, woman, and child were found on the lower level of the northern terrace. Yadin believed they were Jewish rebels who committed suicide in AD 73.

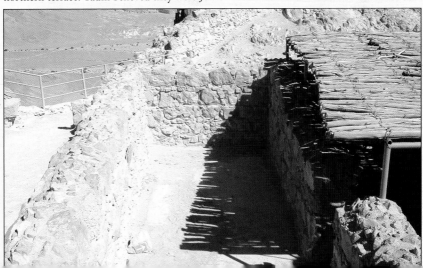

The early morning mist gave the advancing army a glimpse of an epic view: the mountaintop was in flames and no one was in sight. While searching for the Zealots, the soldiers found two women and five children, who told the Romans that rather than die at their hands, everyone had committed suicide.[7]

In 1963 Yigael Yadin began the Masada Archaeological Expedition. Several thousand volunteers applied for the dig. Camp was set up next to the site of General Silva's camp during the siege of AD 72–73.[8] Today a visit to Masada boasts breathtaking views, and while walking atop, one can still feel the grandeur and mystique of the site.

In his fifth will, he named Antipas as his sole successor. In his final (sixth) will, Herod divided his succession in three ways, naming Archelaus as king, Antipas as tetrarch of Galilee and Perea, and Philip as tetrarch of Gaulanitis, Trachonitis, Auranitis, Batanea, and Paneas. Archelaus called upon Rome to confirm his position, but Rome was conflicted by the various claims to the throne. Rebellion broke out in Judea, and the Jews insisted that neither of Herod's sons be given the throne and that Israel be given independence. Rome finally succumbed to Archelaus's claim, and the emperor Augustus appointed him as *ethnarch*[6] of Judea, Samaria, and Idumea.

CHAPTER ONE

MESSIAH IN A "CRIB": A BABY CHANGES EVERYTHING*

Matthew 1:1 – 2:12; Luke 1:1 – 2:38; John 1:1 – 18 (T&G 1 – 14)

THE MESSIAH OF THE OLD TESTAMENT BECOMES JESUS OF THE NEW TESTAMENT (Luke 1:57 – 66; T&G 8a)

God's final recorded words in the Old Testament book of Malachi were followed by four hundred years of silence. When God spoke again through an angel, it was to a priest named Zechariah (whose name means "Yahweh remembers"): "Do not be afraid, Zechariah; your prayer has been heard" (Luke 1:13).

From the time of David, the priesthood was divided into twenty-four divisions to accommodate about twenty thousand priests. The duties of the honored course called "Abijah" offered the incense in the temple.[1] Zechariah, an older priest living in the hill country,[2] traveled to Jerusalem to perform his duty. When Zechariah saw the angel, he was gripped by fear, but the angel calmed him and prophesied that Zechariah's wife, Elizabeth, would bear him a son who would be called John. Zechariah, however, was doubtful and faced the consequences of his skepticism: the Lord rendered him unable to speak.

Mary is first introduced to us shortly after she arrived in Nazareth. She and Joseph became engaged, or *betrothed*. Customs of the day suggest that Mary was thirteen or fourteen years of age. The Mishnah—the authoritative teachings

---

* Author's Note: While the author has taken liberty by embellishing the biblical narratives, he has retained the intent of the literal account.

Ein Kerem village; traditional birthplace of John the Baptist

LC-matpc-00964/www.LifeintheHolyLand.com

embodying the oral tradition of Jewish law and forming the first part of the Talmud—mentions that sexual activity between betrothed couples occasionally occurred in the Jewish community, but such intercourse was considered unacceptable. Pregnancy during a betrothal would bring great shame.

Mary's early life was in Sepphoris, a thriving community in Galilee. Her mother, Anna, had moved to Nazareth, a more religious, conservative town, to raise her family when her husband died.[3] At the time, Joseph lived in Nazareth, just over three and a half miles from Sepphoris. Both Mary and Joseph traced their ancestry to King David, a critical detail in Jesus' lineage.

During the months of her engagement, Mary busied herself with preparing for the many details of the wedding. Like any young girl her age, she was undoubtedly excited, but she was also separated from Joseph. One day as young Mary sat meditating about her future life, an angel appeared before her.

Sepphoris from the east

Why was an angel appearing to *her*? She had no reason to believe she was anyone special. But before Mary had time to be overwhelmed, the angel spoke words that would not only change Mary's own life but the course of history: "You will conceive and give birth to a son, and you are to call him Jesus. He will be great and will be called the Son of the Most High.... His kingdom will never end" (Luke 1:31–33).

Mary responded to the angel not out of unbelief but with a question that demonstrated her thought process. The idea that she was pregnant seemed unbelievable because she and Joseph were not intimate. However, Mary's questions were answered when the angel told her of the baby's divine origin. Immediately she was flooded with unbounded joy and she erupted in praise: "My soul glorifies the Lord and my spirit rejoices in God my Savior, for he has been mindful of the humble state of his servant. From now on all generations will call me blessed" (Luke 1:46–48).

God honored Mary in a unique way, but what about the reaction of her family and friends to the news of a new baby on the way—to an unwed mother! What would her mother, Anna, think? How would Joseph react to such shocking and horrifying news? What might he do? What would her friends say about her faithfulness to Joseph and to God?

And how did Joseph respond to a situation that threatened to brand him as a social outcast? He obediently accepted the instruction of the angel who was sent to him, and he was filled with joy and humility at the thought of providing the

The Church of the Annunciation is a Franciscan Catholic church built in the 1960s over the remains of older structures that date back to AD 356. The previous Byzantine church was supposedly built on the site of Mary's house, precisely where Gabriel announced the birth of Jesus to the Virgin Mary.

earthly home for the Messiah. He lovingly cared for Mary and encouraged her. He may have even provided for Mary's expenses to visit her cousin Elizabeth, who was living in Judea. It is likely that he sought advice from the rabbis and attended synagogue, where he asked for Scriptures telling about the promised Messiah, then repeated them to Mary when he came home. His excitement over the birth of a son was intoxicating. He, too, felt a great responsibility to respect God's instruction and lead his family in the faith of their fathers.

The miracle of Mary's conception by the Holy Spirit didn't exempt her from the discomforts of pregnancy: mood swings and a cumbersome body. However, before her pregnancy became noticeable, Joseph sent her to visit Elizabeth and Zechariah in Judea. Word had arrived that God wonderfully and miraculously granted them grace in their old age — they were expecting a child. When Mary arrived and Elizabeth heard her greeting, the baby in Elizabeth's womb leaped for joy.

The three months with Elizabeth sped by, with mother and baby growing, while Mary and Elizabeth joyfully and lovingly stitched baby clothes. They continually rejoiced in the Lord's goodness and the honor he bestowed on them.

JOURNEY TO BETHLEHEM (Luke 2:1 – 7) (T&G 10)

According to Roman law, everyone was required to report to their tribe's place of birth for tax registration. When Joseph told Mary they must travel from Nazareth to Bethlehem, their "hometown," for the census, Mary expressed

Bethlehem. The Church of the Nativity is the oldest standing church in the Holy Land. Originally built by Constantine in the fourth century, the current structure was built by Emperor Justinian in the AD 530s. In AD 614 empathetic Persian invaders spared its destruction when they saw depictions of Persian magi on the walls. Local Muslim-Christian friendship prevented its destruction during Al-Hakim's rule in 1009. Today Bethlehem is controlled by the Palestinian Authority and has a population of about twenty-two thousand, not including the suburbs of Beit Jala and Beit Sahour.

concern. The baby was due soon. Could she endure the long distance alternately walking and riding the donkey? Regardless, necessity required that they prepare for the long, hard trip.

Travel was difficult and dangerous. Weary travelers faced health concerns, the dangers of armed bandits, a shortage of safe lodging, and the continuous search for food and water. The movement of people for taxing purposes in Jerusalem meant that crowds overflowed into the surrounding areas, including Bethlehem. At this time of year, it was nearly impossible to find lodging outside family contacts.

Library of Congress, LC – 10170/www.LifeintheHolyLand.com

Couple traveling by ancient mode of transportation near Bethlehem (suggestive of the trip to Egypt to avoid Herod's deadly plot)

As Mary and Joseph traveled south toward Bethlehem, they watched travelers scrambling for accommodations, shoving and shouting to secure a place for themselves. Weary families searched for the homes of welcoming relatives to take them in as they traveled for the census.

Mary and Joseph hoped or assumed that they would find lodging with a distant relative they barely knew. As was the custom, he certainly would provide shelter for them if space was available, but they also knew his house would be sought out by other relatives coming to take part in the census.

Mary and Joseph arrived at the relative's home, exhausted from the long trip. He may have warmly welcomed the couple into his home, but he told them other family members occupied the guest quarters. However, Mary and Joseph were welcome to stay in the stable. He cleaned it and laid down fresh straw.

THE BIRTH OF THE MESSIAH, THE SAVIOR
(Luke 2:1 – 7) (T&G 10)

Imagine for a moment the day of Israel's greatest historical event. An orange glow creeps across the limestone floor, gradually illuminating every corner of the cave with a golden aura until its beams fall across a manger.

THE "INN" IN HISTORY

Luke's nativity account states that Mary gave birth and laid Jesus in a manger because there was no room for them in the inn. Traditional Christmas pageants depict Mary and Joseph arriving at Bethlehem only to find the local motels (inns) full. But to accommodate the young family and the pregnant mother, the kind innkeeper offered Mary and Joseph a place in the stable with the livestock, where the baby Jesus was born.

However, the text leaves us to ponder an interesting question: Why were the shepherds attending their flocks in the fields in the cold and rainy winter season? Luke notes that there were "shepherds living out in the fields nearby, keeping watch over their flocks at night" (2:8). A careful investigation of the facts gives us the likely answer.

Common houses in Bethlehem were often composed of several rooms that included a main living area, guest room, private family room, and a storage room to house the animals. The storage room was often a cave with a shared entrance by the main house. It is reasonable to assume that in Mary and Joseph's case, the guest room was already occupied by others, so Mary and Joseph were offered the cave room.

Justin Martyr first suggested in the second century that Jesus' birthplace was a cave. The limestone in the hill country of Bethlehem made it easy to carve caves out of the hillside or to incorporate existing caves into building structures, sometimes with multiple stories. This housing style was very different from that of Capernaum, where living quarters were usually constructed in an *insula*, a large communal living area with bedrooms placed around an open courtyard for social meetings or dining.

The King James Bible is a revision of earlier sixteenth-century versions, from Tyndale to the Bishop's Bible. These versions consistently use the term *inn*. However, *inn* is not the best translation, given the use of the word. Shakespeare, writing in the KJV period, also uses the term *inn* in his play *The Tragedy of King Richard II* to mean "habitation or lodging." The King James translators of the day intended to translate the Greek term *kataluma* (Luke 2:7)

Traditional place of the manger in the Church of the Nativity

to refer to a "lodging house of some sort."

The Greek term is general. Its broad meaning could include the traditional use of the term *inn*. Luke 22:11, the only other place where it is used in the New Testament, translates this Greek word as "guest room" (where Jesus and the disciples eat the Passover supper). This guest

Interior of a peasant home located partially in a cave near Bethlehem

room may have been the guest room in the Essene community that inhabited an area inside the southern wall of the city. If the original writer, Luke, wanted to refer to a separate *habitation* or *lodging* he could have chosen *pandocheion* ("inn"), as in Luke 10:34, which refers to the place the good Samaritan took the victim of robbers.[4]

Mary and Joseph undoubtedly traveled with a large group for safety from bandits and access to food. It is most likely that Mary and Joseph expected to stay not in a hotel ("inn") but in the homes of their Bethlehem relatives, only to find that other relatives had arrived for the census and occupied the "guest room." The only room available was the room reserved for the animals. Although we cannot be sure, these facts lead us to speculate that the animals were out grazing in the fall fields that night because it was *prior* to the winter season that required the cave's warmth and protection. Indeed, it was not likely a cold and rainy night as is so often presumed.

Handwoven blankets, cradled in mounds of fresh straw, swaddle the form of a newborn child. Outside, the streets of Bethlehem surge with activity. The world is oblivious to the wonder that deity lay among them, breathing in the first scent of a sin-cursed world in a common stable.

Wonder of wonders, this helpless infant was the Son of God. Not descending to earth with the glory and pomp of a world leader, but as a body-bound, earth-anchored human child.

All Israel had been praying for and anticipating this day for centuries. Yet they were busy, looking elsewhere when their Savior came.

But Mary knew.

The anguish of her labor pains faded as the child snuggled into her breast. The tiresome journey from Nazareth faded into a distant memory as she looked into her child's beautiful face and watched him stretch and squirm. Like any mother, she felt as if her heart would burst with love and joy.

Prophecies from the Scriptures foretelling the life of the newborn Son of God likely raced through Mary's mind. He would grow, play, develop, and finally endure conflict as he sought to bring salvation to the world. The words were too much to comprehend. For the moment, one thought captivated her heart: her desire to care for him, to protect him, and to prepare him for the destiny God had ordained for him. Together she and Joseph pledged to dedicate their lives to raising him to obey the laws of God. And as Gabriel had instructed, they named him Jesus.

DATE OF JESUS' BIRTH

Although the Western church traditionally celebrates Jesus' birthday on December 25 and the Eastern church celebrates it on January 6, we cannot know the date with certainty. The gospel accounts provide evidence that suggests fall or spring is more likely. Room in the stable indicates that perhaps not all of the animals were present as they would have been in the cold of winter. Further, flocks of sheep were grazing in the fields.

Grapes are harvested from September to November; figs are harvested in August and September; pomegranates are harvested during September; and green and black olives are harvested from September through early November. Wheat and barley are sown in November, anticipating a spring harvest. Thus, the months of August through October would provide the sheep and goats time to graze in the fields without destroying the cash crops. Sheep like to graze among the fig trees in the fall. Allowing sheep to freely graze among the barley and wheat crops in the spring would be senseless. But animals grazing among the fall foliage would leave the stable empty for weary family travelers looking for a place to stay.

It is possible, however, that Jesus' birth occurred in the spring, in March or early April. The fields would have been plentiful with spring foliage, barley (March), wheat (May), and natural grass. The cold of the winter would have given way to the warmth of spring and a field with pasture. The law required Jews to go up to Jerusalem for the Passover festival (March/April). This, along with Caesar's census, would doubly explain the crowds in Jerusalem and Bethlehem.

Whichever explanation best represents the facts, a winter birth seems to be the least plausible explanation in light of grazing habits and the gospel accounts. Our current attachment to December may be explained by early Christians wanting to celebrate Jesus' birth in place of the pagan holiday Saturnalia, observed December 17–25.

Perhaps the true Christmas season is not a winter wonderland and gentle snow but a season of pleasant fall evenings, with the breezes singing in harmony in anticipation of the birth of God's Son.[5]

He will be called
> Wonderful Counselor, Mighty God,
> Everlasting Father, Prince of Peace.

Isaiah 9:6

WORSHIP OF THE HUMBLE (Luke 2:8 – 20) (T&G 11)

After the stress of giving birth, Mary dozed off to sleep. She awakened to a small band of shepherds at the entrance of the cave—so excited that they could hardly contain their enthusiasm. In their excitement, they kept

THE GENEALOGY OF JESUS

Jesus' divinity rests, in part, on the miracle of the virgin birth. The miracle is more accurately a miracle of *conception*, not of birth. To qualify as the Redeemer for the sins of humankind, Jesus needed to be a sinless human. According to the Bible, the virgin birth was also physically necessary in order for Jesus to circumvent the cursed line of Jeconiah.[6] The genealogies of Matthew and Luke both trace Jesus' lineage. Luke's account affirms the virgin birth with the phrase, "He was the son, so it was thought, of Joseph" (Luke 3:23). Luke traces Jesus' genealogy from Adam through Mary's line. Matthew traces Joseph's genealogy from Abraham with emphasis on Israel's king David, to whom the promise of a future kingdom was given. While Matthew's list emphasizes Jesus' legal right to the throne of David, Luke's account shows Jesus' human line of descent. Together they emphasize that Jesus was both human and divine.[7]

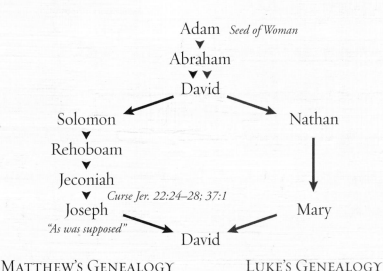

Adam *Seed of Woman*

Abraham

David

Solomon — Nathan

Rehoboam

Jeconiah *Curse Jer. 22:24–28; 37:1*

Joseph *"As was supposed"* — David — Mary

MATTHEW'S GENEALOGY   LUKE'S GENEALOGY

interrupting one another to give the young parents the details about how they came to the birthplace of the Messiah. A star had beckoned them. And while they followed, the most beautiful music they ever heard surrounded them. Their words tumbled out as the young mother adoringly stroked the face of her sleeping child.

"The night began as any other night; we were looking after our fathers' flocks. . . ."

Excitedly, the shepherds strung out the threads of their stories.

"The cold, damp air was chilling, and we were huddled around a small fire in our rock shelter. Suddenly a blinding light illuminated the darkness. We were terrified. We are God-fearing boys who attend synagogue. What had we done? Was God angry with us? We aren't perfect, of course, but we couldn't think of anything truly bad we had done. All these things were racing through our minds. Then the angel spoke, calmly reassuring us, 'Do not be afraid. I bring you good news that will cause great joy for all the people. Today in the town of David a Savior has been born to you; he is the Messiah, the Lord.'

"You can imagine how startled we were when a mighty choir of angels began to sing God's praises. That huge star kept blinking and beckoning and moving in the direction of Bethlehem. We wanted to follow in the worst way, but we knew how angry our father would be if we left the flock alone. What if a wild beast attacked the sheep while we were away? And there were reports of thieves on the road taking advantage of travelers.

Shepherds with flock. The area to the east of Bethlehem is traditionally believed to be where the shepherds were in the fields keeping watch over their flocks. Even today local shepherds can be seen tending their flocks in this area.

"But in the end, it didn't matter. Nothing could keep us from following the light to the promise of the coming of the Messiah."

Despite their weariness, Joseph and Mary listened intently to each shepherd's story. They felt humbled by the significance of the birth of their child. And with the joyful thought in their minds that Jesus was their King, and with the soft straw pillowing their heads, God's earth-appointed parents of the Messiah fell asleep.

MARY OBSERVES JEWISH PURIFICATION RITES
(Luke 2:22–38) (T&G 13)

Mary and Joseph set off from Bethlehem for Jerusalem to perform purification rites in accordance with the law of Moses. Every firstborn male was considered "holy to the Lord," and a sacrifice had to be made to redeem him. After the birth of her child, Mary, as a Jewish woman, was also required to go through a purification ritual. For new parents, the excitement of going to the beautiful temple for the ritual and visiting the city brought enormous joy.

An elderly man at the temple named Simeon had asked God to see the Messiah before he died, and God granted his prayer that day at the temple. As the baby Jesus gazed at him, Simeon fell to his knees in thankfulness for being in the presence of the long-promised Messiah. After worshiping in Jerusalem, the family returned to Bethlehem.

Over 150 *mikvot*, or purification baths, have been found in Jerusalem. Sixty of these are in the Upper City (western hill) where the priestly families lived. Forty were found in the excavations on the southern side of the Temple Mount.

Daniel Frese/BiblePlaces.com

THE WISE MEN OFFER GIFTS (Matthew 2:1–12) (T&G 14)

Outside the Bethlehem family's comfortable house, a brightly shining star[8] beckoned yet another group. Wise men, magi who studied the heavens, joined together in the conviction that the star would lead them to the Messiah.

Fear gripped them greater than any they had encountered on their long journey, when they sought the location of the new king from the cruel and unpredictable King Herod. He was an evil man who lived in constant fear of a Jewish uprising in which the Jews would remove him from the throne.[9] Once he heard Jesus would be a king, Herod became furious, assuming his rule would be put in jeopardy. Herod's paranoia led to his cruel order to kill all of the baby boys in Bethlehem, whom he saw as threats to his throne. But God protected Jesus by sending an angel to warn Joseph of the danger, and they escaped to Egypt.

THE VISIT OF THE WISE MEN

The popular nativity scene displayed in department store windows and reenacted in schools and church plays portrays the shepherds and the wise men visiting the babe in the manger together. However, in Matthew 2:11, the wise men came to a "house," not a manger or to an "inn," suggesting that some time had passed since Jesus' birth. The fact that Herod sought to kill all male children under the age of two years indicates that some time had transpired since the Magi saw the star and Herod realized that the Magi had disregarded his command. Joseph and Mary could have been in Bethlehem for up to two years before they fled to Egypt. After the death of Herod, they chose to return to Nazareth because Herod's son Archelaus was reigning in Judea (Matt. 2:23).

Three men on camels near Bethlehem (suggestive of magi). The tradition that there were three magi comes from the number of gifts presented. No doubt the caravan was much larger.

LC-matpc-06282/www.LifeintheHolyLand.com

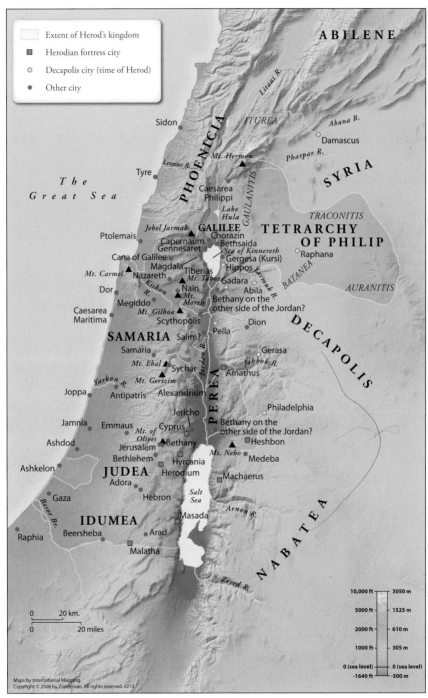

Legend:

- ☐ Extent of Herod's kingdom
- ■ Herodian fortress city
- ○ Decapolis city (time of Herod)
- ● Other city

ABILENE

The Great Sea

Sidon

PHOENICIA

ITUREA

Litani R.

Abana R.

Damascus

SYRIA

Tyre

Leontes R.

Mt. Hermon

Pharpar R.

Caesarea Philippi

GAULANITIS

Lake Hula

TRACONITIS

Ptolemais

Jebel Jarmak

GALILEE

Chorazin

Bethsaida

TETRARCHY OF PHILIP

Capernaum

Gennesaret

Sea of Kinnereth

Gergesa (Kursi)

Raphana

Cana of Galilee

Magdala

Tiberias

Hippos

BATANEA

Mt. Carmel

Nazareth

Mt. Tabor

Gadara

AURANITIS

Dor

Kishon R.

Nain

Mt. Moreh

Abila

Bethany on the other side of the Jordan?

Caesarea Maritima

Megiddo

Mt. Gilboa

Scythopolis

Dion

DECAPOLIS

SAMARIA

Salim?

Pella

Samaria

Mt. Ebal

Sychar

Jabbok R.

Gerasa

Yarkon R.

Mt. Gerizim

Amathus

Joppa

Antipatris

Alexandrium

Jordan R.

PEREA

Jericho

Philadelphia

Jamnia

Emmaus

Mt. of Olives

Cyprus

Bethany on the other side of the Jordan?

Ashdod

Jerusalem

Bethany

Heshbon

Bethlehem

Hyrcania

Mt. Nebo

Medeba

Ashkelon

JUDEA

Herodium

Machaerus

Adora

Salt Sea

Gaza

Hebron

Arnon R.

NABATEA

IDUMEA

Masada

Raphia

Besor Br.

Beersheba

Arad

Malatha

Zered R.

Scale:

0   20 km.
0   20 miles

10,000 ft	3050 m
5000 ft	1525 m
2000 ft	610 m
1000 ft	305 m
0 (sea level)	0 (sea level)
-1640 ft	-500 m

Holy Land in the Time of Jesus

YEAR OF JESUS' BIRTH

We are certain that Jesus was not born in AD 1 (*Anno Domini*— "In the year of the Lord"), for Herod died in March or April 4 BC, and Jesus was born while Herod still ruled Judea (Matt. 2:1). Augustus ordered a census while Quirinius was governor of Syria. This may have been the census of 8 BC in Egypt and perhaps a year or so later in Israel. This places Jesus' birth between 6 BC or, as some suggest, as late as 4 BC.

In AD 525 Pope John I asked Dionysius to develop a Christian calendar that would celebrate Christianity rather than a pagan Roman ruler as the basis for the calendar. Prior to this, the calendar was based on the date of the founding of Rome. Dionysius modified the Alexandrian calendar, which used the persecutor Diocletian to reckon the dating.

The Christian calendar, denoting Christ's birth as AD 1, was based on the date of January 1, 754 AUC (*ab urbe condita*— "from the year of the founding [of Rome]").[10] According to the first-century biographer Josephus, Herod died in 750 AUC. Christ had to have been born before Herod died, so Christ could have been born no earlier or later than 6–4 BC. By the time the error was recognized, it was too late to change all of history's calendars.[11]

AGRICULTURAL CALENDAR
CYCLE OF FEASTS, AND HARVESTS

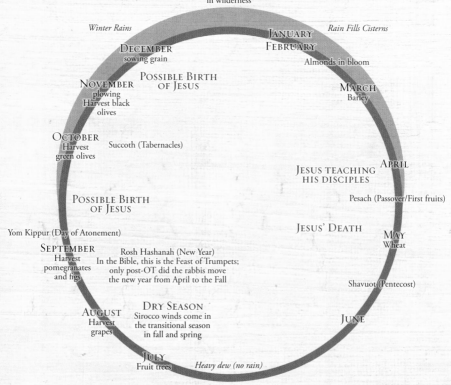

PEAK OF RAINY SEASON
heaviest rain fall in the
mountains to lightest
in wilderness

Winter Rains   JANUARY   *Rain Fills Cisterns*
FEBRUARY

DECEMBER
sowing grain

Almonds in bloom

POSSIBLE BIRTH
OF JESUS

NOVEMBER
plowing
Harvest black
olives

MARCH
Barley

OCTOBER
Harvest
green olives   Succoth (Tabernacles)

JESUS TEACHING   APRIL
HIS DISCIPLES

POSSIBLE BIRTH
OF JESUS

Pesach (Passover/First fruits)

Yom Kippur (Day of Atonement)

JESUS' DEATH

SEPTEMBER
Harvest
pomegranates
and figs

Rosh Hashanah (New Year)
In the Bible, this is the Feast of Trumpets;
only post-OT did the rabbis move
the new year from April to the Fall

MAY
Wheat

Shavuot (Pentecost)

AUGUST
Harvest
grapes

DRY SEASON
Sirocco winds come in
the transitional season
in fall and spring

JUNE

JULY
Fruit trees   *Heavy dew (no rain)*

MODERN IDENTITY OF ANCIENT HOLY LAND SITES

Although churches and monuments in the Holy Land have been designated to memorialize events in Jesus' life, we cannot be absolutely certain of the identity of these places. Tradition, Scripture, and reason guide us in identifying potential sites. For Christians, these "holy sites" are not places to be worshiped but can be used as aids to understanding the events and teachings of the Bible. We worship God alone, not sites, locations, or relics.

Those taking part in actual gospel recorded events did not leave messages written on pillars or stones or commemorative objects to designate the location of an event.[12] Nevertheless, knowledge of the background and context of Scripture is important for our interpretation of the events and historical context of Scripture.

Just how then are biblical locations from so long ago identified with any degree of certainty? Can tourists to the Holy Land be assured they are visiting real, identifiable sites, as opposed to unsubstantiated locations perpetuated to satisfy those seeking a spiritual experience?

Various sources for research are used to identify traditional biblical sites.

1. Literary sources, such as Josephus and the church fathers, often record distances from one location to another. These references are invaluable for archaeological discovery.

FLAVIUS JOSEPHUS, JEWISH HISTORIAN

The most extensive information available today for the life and history of the Jewish people comes from the first-century Jewish writer Josephus. He wrote two major works: *Wars of the Jews* (circa AD 75–79) and *Antiquities of the Jews* (circa AD 93/94).

Josephus was born into a wealthy priestly family about AD 37. His propensity for survival led to his label as "Traitor."[13] After a trip to Rome on behalf of priests being tried in Rome, Josephus returned with an exalted view of Roman splendor and power. This trip shaped the rest of his life.

As war loomed in Israel at the beginning of the Jewish revolt in AD 66, Josephus was placed in charge of the Jewish forces in Galilee. Under questionable circumstances, he surrendered to Vespasian at Jotapata in AD 67, and he predicted Vespasian would become emperor. When Vespasian did become emperor, he granted Josephus citizenship as an act of gratitude. Josephus adopted the emperor's family name of Flavius and became a history writer. The Jews considered Josephus their "Benedict Arnold."

Josephus's mention of John the Baptist, James the Just, and Jesus are the earliest non-Christian references to Christianity.[14]

BETHLEHEM, THE CITY OF DAVID
(Matthew 2:1; Luke 2:4 – 7; cf. 1 Samuel 20:6)

An impressive church built over the traditionally celebrated birthplace of Jesus marks one of the holiest locations in Christianity. Early tradition identifies a cave in Bethlehem as Jesus' birthplace, and both Justin Martyr and Origen (third century) acknowledged this as the correct location.

The Byzantine emperor Constantine built a church over this same spot in AD 327. Today the original floor of Constantine's church is preserved beneath the current floor in the entryway of the church. The emperor Hadrian (AD 135), in an attempt to eradicate the memory of Christianity, had planted a grove of olive trees there dedicated to the god Adonis, lover of Venus, and established a worship center. This act demonstrates the site was acknowledged even before Hadrian and guaranteed the lasting memory of Jesus, whom he so wanted to destroy.

The deterioration of the church built by Constantine led Emperor Justinian in the sixth century to raze the church and build a new one. This is the same church visited today. The present structure survived the Persian invasion (AD 614) because the invaders saw a mosaic depicting the magi as Persians. Impressed by the symbolism, they did not destroy the Bethlehem church.

The conquering Crusaders came in 1099 and added a monastery on the north side while they were fortifying the compound. On Christmas Day in 1100, Baldwin's coronation as the first king of Jerusalem took place in Bethlehem by the Byzantine (Greek Orthodox) patriarch.

Over the years, control of the church and its functions became a tug-of-war between the Roman Catholics and the Greek Orthodox. Fires in 1834 and 1869 added to the deterioration, and under the British mandate repairs were made to help preserve this holy site. Recently, conflicts occurred between Jews and Arabs in the church and some damage occurred. Today the Greek Orthodox, the Armenians, and the Franciscans (Catholics) each control certain portions of the property they use for worship services.

2. Toponomy (study of place names): ancient place names are often preserved in modern Arabic names.
3. Archaeology can confirm the occupation of sites at the time described in a biblical account.
4. Tradition, while it may be flawed, can be reliable. Sites became "holy" very early because eyewitnesses remembered significant events and where they took place.

Jesus' birthplace is clearly identified in the New Testament. It is a small village called Bethlehem and the City of David (Matt. 2:1; Luke 2:4–7; cf. 1 Sam. 20:6). The modern city of Bethlehem is built over the ruins of the ancient town where Jesus was born.

Jesus' birth changed world history in a way no one else's entry into the world ever has. Galatians 4:4 tells us, "But when the set time had fully come, God sent his Son, born of a woman, born under the law." But his entry into the world was only the beginning. You are about to embark on the "greatest story ever told." The life of the Messiah changed the history of the world and prepared the way for eternity.

EARLY LIFE OF JESUS
(5/4 BC–AD 28)

Bethlehem:
  Birth of Jesus (Luke 2:1–7)
  Visit of shepherds (Luke 2:8–20)
  Circumcision on 8th day (Luke 2:21)
  Visit of Magi (Matt 2:1–12)
  Flight to Egypt (Matt 2:13–18)
  Journey to Nazareth (Matt 2:19–23)
Jerusalem:
  Birth of John foretold (Luke 1:15–25)
  Presentation at Temple (Luke 2:22–38)
Nazareth:
  Betrothal of Joseph and Mary (Matt. 1:18–25)
  Annunciation of birth of Jesus (Luke 1:26–38)

CHAPTER 2

MESSIAH IDENTIFIED BY DIVINE PROMISES: THE NAZARENE FROM GALILEE

Matthew 2:13 — 3:17; Mark 1:1 — 11; Luke 2:39 — 3:23 (T&G 15 — 24)

FAMILY LIFE: FROM ANTIPAS TO ARCHELAUS
(Matthew 2:13 — 23; Luke 2:39; T&G 15 — 16)

Herod's death relieved the Jewish community, for his reign had caused much misery. However, all Israel soon realized there was little to be encouraged about when they heard the news of the cruel Archelaus's appointment to rule over Judea.[1]

An angel told Joseph in a dream that his young family must return to Israel. Mary would not have been disappointed, for they had many friends and relatives in Nazareth, which was under Herod Antipas's jurisdiction.

Mary and Joseph agreed that the community would be a great place to raise Jesus. The Nazareth neighborhood provided the security of family life, and the hamlet was off the heavily traveled international highway between Egypt and Syria. As Jesus grew, he was content to work alongside his father.

The writers of the Gospels give us very few details about the way Jesus spent the next thirty years of his life.[2] The family, including Jesus' brothers and sisters (Matt. 13:55 – 56; Mark 6:3), lived seemingly normal lives.

Nazareth

HEROD ARCHELAUS (23 BCE – AD 18)

Following the death of Herod the Great, the kingdom was divided into three parts as his will stipulated. Antipas was to rule over Galilee and Perea as tetrarch, and he selected the centrally located Galilean city of Sepphoris as his capital. Antipas launched a huge building project that lasted throughout Jesus' lifetime. As the largest and most beautiful city in Galilee, Sepphoris greatly influenced Nazareth, even though the Gospels do not mention it by name.

Archelaus was the ethnarch of Samaria, Judea, and Idumea from 4 BC to AD 6. He was the son of Herod the Great, brother of Herod Antipas, and the half-brother of Herod Philip who ruled the Transjordan region. Archelaus received the tetrarchy of Judea by the last will of his father, although a previous will bequeathed it to his brother Antipas. He was proclaimed king by the army but declined to assume the title until he was granted permission from Caesar Augustus.

Archelaus's cruelty was legendary. His slaying of nearly three thousand Pharisees instilled fear among the Jews. Nevertheless, in 4 BC Augustus awarded him control of Samaria, Judea, and Idumea. In AD 6 his kingdom was stripped from him and placed under the direct control of Rome.

When Herod the Great died, Joseph was told by an angel in a dream to return to Israel. However, upon hearing that the cruel Archelaus succeeded his father as ruler of Judea, Joseph was afraid to return to Bethlehem and was again warned in a dream to go to Galilee.

LC-matpc-06282-t/www.LifeintheHolyLand.com

A carpenter at work with tools similar to Qatzrin construction tools

Construction tools at Qatzrin (from the fourth century)

Jesus grew into manhood as he developed in wisdom and stature. Sadly, Joseph seems to have passed away sometime before the family moved to Capernaum.[3] No doubt, Mary missed Joseph terribly. He had been her protector and provider and the father who guided and taught her children. And during those years, Joseph had taught Jesus the building trade.

As the eldest son, Jesus assumed the seat of family authority. When he determined it was time to be about his heavenly Father's business, he moved his family to Capernaum, a pleasant town and good place to make a family home, and began his public ministry. Many devout Jews lived there, and

NAZARETH OF GALILEE

Nazareth is a thriving city today, but in Jesus' time it was a small village with a population of about 400–500. Capernaum was larger, with a population of 1,500–1,700. The nearby Herodian cities of Sepphoris and Tiberias were consumer cities. The large building projects of the period provided a lively economy for farmers, builders, and fishermen. Herod Antipas's building projects demanded basalt and limestone quarrying, agricultural products, fish, and meat. Joseph, and his son Jesus, may have had jobs in Sepphoris or Tiberias. Capernaum was near enough to profit from the expanding economy as well. Builders used tesserae for mosaics that covered the floors in affluent private homes and public buildings, as well as limestone for frescoes and plaster. Local non-Herodian cities lacked these amenities and stood in stark contrast. Their roofs consisted of a mixture of mud and straw and floors of packed mud as opposed to those in the cities. This meant the building profession flourished in the larger and wealthier towns.

it was in close proximity to other major towns. However, the antagonism of the synagogue's elite toward Jesus would grow and threaten his earthly future.

THE HOMESTEAD OF JESUS: NAZARETH OF GALILEE
(Matthew 2:19 – 23; Mark 1:1; Luke 2:40 – 3:2; T&G 16 – 20)

City life differed vastly from life in rural villages. City dwellers looked to shopkeepers for their food. Their diet consisted of fish, barley and lentil porridge, nuts, olives, and various fruits. Normally, meat appeared on the table only on special occasions. The wealthy priests, traders, landowners, and government officials who occupied the cities feasted on extravagantly catered meals with the finest wine. The wealthy aristocracy viewed mealtime as a social event and an opportunity to display their finest clothing.

JOTAPATA

Jotapata was the site of Josephus's surrender to the Romans. The Jewish general led the revolt in Galilee. In July AD 67, the Romans captured the city. Josephus convinced the Jews of the city to kill each other, and the last two alive would commit suicide. When Josephus was one of the last two, he surrendered instead. Brought before General Vespasian, Josephus predicted Vespasian would one day be emperor, so Vespasian allowed him to live.

Jotapata, site of Josephus's surrender to the Romans

SEPPHORIS

Josephus mentions this town for the first time during the reign of Alexander Jannaeus (103 BC), but archaeological remains were identified from Iron Age II. Gabinius, proconsul of Syria in 55 BC, made it the district capital.[4] The city surrendered to Herod the Great in 37 BC after Herod attacked the city in the midst of a snowstorm.[5]

After riots following Herod's death in 4 BC, Varus, the legate of Syria, conquered Sepphoris and sold its inhabitants into slavery. Antipas rebuilt and fortified Sepphoris after Galilee came under his rule. He made Sepphoris his capital until he built Tiberias in AD 19.[6] Some scholars suggest that Joseph and Jesus helped in the reconstruction of Sepphoris. Since Herod Antipas rebuilt the city, and since stone is the main building craft of the area, Joseph, living in nearby Nazareth, would have been a builder in stone as well as wood.[7]

According to Josephus, Sepphoris was almost entirely Jewish during the days of Herod Antipas. Sepphoris became the "Sanhedrin" of Galilee and an important military post. The city supported Vespasian in the Jewish revolt, surrendering to the Romans and thus preventing the destruction of the city.[8] They even minted coins in honor of Vespasian as the "peacemaker."[9]

Sepphoris with theater

In light of the archaeological discovery of Sepphoris, as well as indications from Josephus, scholars have revisited the traditional view of Jesus working as a carpenter alongside Joseph in Nazareth. The term describing Jesus as a "carpenter" actually describes the more general occupation of a "building contractor." In a land where the primary building material was stone, the career of a building contractor included stonework. Hand-carving stones and fitting them in buildings was an honorable and profitable business. Sepphoris, the district capital, was located just three miles north of Nazareth, perhaps an hour's journey. Herod's desire to arrest Jesus may be the reason the Gospels never mention Jesus visiting Sepphoris.

The wealth Herod developed in Galilee led to economic woes and challenges to Jewish values in many smaller villages. Jesus spoke of the blessings to the poor; he empathized with the hungry and supported release from debt. And yet Jesus did not single out Sepphoris or Tiberias for condemnation, but rather Capernaum, Bethsaida, and Chorazin.[10] Jesus was more concerned with what people did with his messianic claims than with rulers' social abuses.

The residents of Nazareth, like the residents of other small villages, were basket weavers, tanners, shepherds, carpenters, farmers, and, of course, masons. Nazareth was an insignificant country town characterized by conservative Jewish practices. Nathanael, testifying to Nazareth's poor reputation, asked, "Nazareth! Can anything good come from there?" (John 1:46)

Matthew 2:23 records that Jesus "would be called a Nazarene."[11] Early in Christian history, Jerome associated the fulfillment of this prophecy with Isaiah 11:1: "A shoot will come up from the stump of Jesse; from his roots a branch (*netzer*) will bear fruit." Revelation 22:16 reads, "I, Jesus, have sent my angel to give you this testimony for the churches. I am the Root and the Offspring of David, and the bright Morning Star." The beggar Bartimaeus, when he heard Jesus was from Nazareth, shouted, "Jesus, Son of David, have mercy on me!" (Mark 10:47).[12]

During excavations in Caesarea in 1962, archaeologists found an inscription listing priestly families who settled in Galilee during the Roman period. Bargil Pixner suggests that sometime around 100 BCE, a clan of David returned from the Babylonian captivity and settled in Nazareth. According to Pixner, the name of the town came from the Davidic clan known as *netzer* ("shoot/branch"; Isa. 11:1).[13] This suggests that Jesus, as the branch, was called "the Nazarene" in reference to his Davidic lineage (as the branch or *netzer*) rather than a Nazirite.[14]

Jesus' life in Nazareth had minimal impact on his ministry when compared to his ministry in Capernaum, and yet he is not called a "Capernaumite." Most likely Jesus was known as one from Nazareth because that is where he was reared from childhood to adulthood.[15] Jesus was a Nazarene as the offspring/branch of David and a man from the Davidic town of Nazareth. Many pilgrims to Galilee today have the opportunity to visit a unique reconstruction of first-century life at the attraction known as Nazareth Village. Basd on New Testament scholarship, Nazareth Village brings to life a farm and Galilean village, re-creating Nazareth as it was two thousand years ago. The experience helps visitors visualize daily life in the Nazareth of Jesus' day.

JOHN'S MINISTRY FOR THE MESSIAH
(Matthew 3:1 – 6; Mark 1:2 – 6; Luke 3:3 – 6; T&G 21)

God had blessed Mary's cousin Elizabeth with a son named John. When he grew up and began his ministry, the people called him the "Baptist" because of his work in purifying his followers through a ritual form of bathing. Although baptism is different from self-immersion in the Jewish tradition of

John the Baptist's cave near Tsuba in Judea. Recent excavations of this site, under the direction of Shimon Gibson, indicate the site may have been identified with the ministry of John the Baptist. However, the authenticity has come under attack.[17]

cleansing in a mikveh,[16] many men and women came to John in preparation for the impending arrival of the kingdom of God.

Although Elizabeth was proud of John's dedication, she may have worried about his itinerant lifestyle of wandering in the desert and subsisting on a diet of locusts and honey. Her son was of priestly birth — the son of the priest Zechariah — but he gave up his right to wear priestly robes and instead chose to shed the trappings of his former life for the humble role of preparing the way for the Messiah and his kingdom.

John the Baptist's food, locusts and wild honey. Some people, finding the thought of John chasing locusts around the desert odd, favor the view that the "locust" referred to the carob pod, a food fed to pigs (Luke 15:16).

John's message resonated with the fervor of the ancient prophets Elijah, Elisha, and Isaiah. His call to preach

AN ETHIOPIAN BAPTISM

I gripped the steering wheel tightly and held off on the accelerator as I guided my Land Cruiser through the Ethiopian mountains. Despite my excitement, I deferred to safety on the treacherous dirt roads. I was on my way to an area of southern Ethiopia to observe my first baptism in a church that numbered in the thousands. During the Italian occupation prior to World War II, the church there had grown from fifty believers to ten thousand. And as the church grew, baptisms became common but certainly not ordinary. And not at all like the baptisms I witnessed and participated in while living in America.

Here in America, baptismal services are performed with dignity and decorum. In my circles, seminary students often practice immersion baptisms, attempting to follow their professors' instructions not to disturb the water any more than necessary. Reverent hymns are played as participants are immersed and quietly emerge from the water. But nothing had prepared me for how different an Ethiopian baptism would be.

I sat on a hill overlooking a shallow lake formed by damming up a small mountain creek, eagerly awaiting the ceremony. To my amazement, hundreds of people crowded along the shore waiting to be baptized. *How in the world can all of these Christians be baptized before darkness overtakes us?* I wondered. What happened next moved me spiritually and brought me to a state of suppressed hilarity at the same time.

Eight or ten local elders walked into the knee-deep lake as the men and women waiting to be baptized sang, danced, and jumped up and down. So much for a solemn, reverent event! And there was no sign of a line or a system for taking turns. Elders used eucalyptus tree switches to drive back the enthusiastic crowd from the lake's edge, trying desperately to maintain some sort of order. Their task was futile. The people were so eager to follow Jesus in baptism that they couldn't wait, even for a few minutes.

The ceremony began when a baptizing elder grabbed a candidate and, without saying a word, dunked him in the shallow water. Sputtering, the candidate emerged from the water, jumped up, and ran into the arms of cheering, exuberant relatives and friends. The sight was priceless. At the conclusion of the event, all participants, family members, and guests joined hands and sang their way through the nearby villages as a testimony to unbelievers. The joy and celebration of God's people at an event many American churchgoers take for granted was an inspiring experience for me.

That day I gained a new appreciation for a "baptismal service." It was a time of rejoicing and worshiping. The power of this experience gave me insight into the baptisms of the New Testament.

An Ethiopian baptism

D. Brake

THE SITE OF JOHN'S BAPTISM MINISTRY

John baptized in the river Jordan, "Bethany on the other side of the Jordan" (John 1:28).[18] The precise location is impossible to identify. To follow John's baptizing ministry, one must look carefully at the gospel accounts.

John's gospel presents a day-by-day account of the first week of Jesus' ministry (John 1:29, 35, 43; 2:1).[19] This would suggest that "Bethany [Bethabara] on the other side of the Jordan" refers to a region east of the Sea of Galilee[20] identified with Batanea, Herod Philip's territory, rather than the area called "Bethany/Bethabara" on the east side of the Jordan just north of the Dead Sea.[21] The disciples Andrew, Peter, and Philip were from Bethsaida, a territory near Batanea. Jesus' call of these men to discipleship (John 1:43–50) was likely near Bethsaida (Nathanael lived in Cana; John 21:2).[22]

Another site for John's later baptisms is Makhadet 'Abara, just one mile north of the mouth of the Harod Valley. John 3:23 says John baptized "at Aenon near Salim, because there was plenty of water." This site may be near the Harod River south of the Sea of Galilee, about twenty miles downstream from the Yardenit baptismal site where modern pilgrims often seek to be baptized.

Recent discoveries also claim a long-standing site just north of the Dead Sea on the Jordan side of the border as the site of "on the other side of the Jordan" and associate it

with John's baptism of Jesus.[23] This small village is in a ford near Bethabara, which is claimed by some as the correct understanding for "Bethany on the other side of the Jordan." Archaeologists discovered a cave seven miles north of the Dead Sea near Jericho, and in their early excitement, they claimed it to be the spot where John the Baptist baptized his early converts. Scholars soon pointed out the late date of the cave and denied it had any association with John.

However, explorations from 1996 have uncovered a Byzantine church and have determined that this site is quite possibly the area where John baptized Jesus

Hajlah ford in the vicinity of Wadi Gharrar with baptismal area. Wadi Gharrar is a small tributary of the Jordan River fed by five springs. Tradition holds that these springs provided the water that was used by John the Baptist for baptizing. Those who support this tradition note that (1) "Bethany on the other side of the Jordan" was not necessarily a location on the river itself, (2) this site is closely connected with the river, and (3) it was unlikely that a swiftly flowing river like the Jordan was used for frequent baptisms.

(Matt. 3:13–17). In AD 530 the pilgrim Theodosius described a church built on the east side of the Jordan as the site of John's baptizing. An early Christian tradition associated the crossing of the Jordan by Joshua and the place of Jesus' baptism as the same location.

The evidence favors John's early baptizing ministry taking place in this area of Perea near the Jordan River at a site easily accessible to those dwelling in Judea and Jerusalem (Matt. 3:7; Mark 1:5; John. 1:19) and probably not "Bethany on the other side of the Jordan."[24] John baptized in a similar small hamlet alongside a small ford situated on the Jordan River. Geographer and historian Carl Laney notes that the Pilgrim of Bordeaux (AD 333) identifies the site of Jesus' baptism as five Roman miles (four and a half miles) north of the Dead Sea and five miles east of Jericho. On the

Fifty yards from the Jordan River the Byzantines built three churches to commemorate John's baptism of Jesus. The earliest church was built on stilts to keep it from being flooded.

far side of the river at this location is the Wadi el-Kharrar, which is fed by a spring and flows westward into the Jordan River.[25]

Theodosius (AD 550) is the first to make mention of a church built at this venerable site by the emperor Anastasius (AD 491–518), apparently east of the Jordan. The Hajlah ford, just east of Qasr el-Yahud ("the fort of the Jews"), believed to be the ruins of the monastery built by Anastasius, has been favored as the site of Jesus' baptism.[26]

Jesus was probably baptized by John in the area just north of the Dead Sea (at Hajlah ford; Matt. 3:5). John continued his baptizing ministry "on the other side of the Jordan" in the area of Batanea in the Jarmuk River at Bethany, east of the Sea of Galilee in Herod Philip's territory (John 1:28). Then later he was baptizing at Aenon near Salim just south of Scythopolis (John 3:23). While John's baptisms are usually associated with the Jordan (Mark 1:5), he clearly baptized "on the other side" or "beyond" the Jordan River.

("The word of God came to John," Luke 3:2) is reminiscent of God's call to the prophets Haggai, Zechariah, and Malachi. He proclaimed the nearness of the day of judgment and thundered, "You brood of vipers! Who warned you to flee from the coming wrath? Produce fruit in keeping with repentance.... The ax is already at the root of the trees, and every tree that does not produce good fruit will be cut down and thrown into the fire" (Luke 3:7–9). The image must have caused great angst among the people. But John's real message was intended to prepare the way for Jesus. His baptism did not proclaim purification for Judaism or the Essenes but symbolized cleansing for those wishing to repent of their sins. His voice in the wilderness prepared the way for Israel's King and Messiah.

NEW TESTAMENT HISTORY

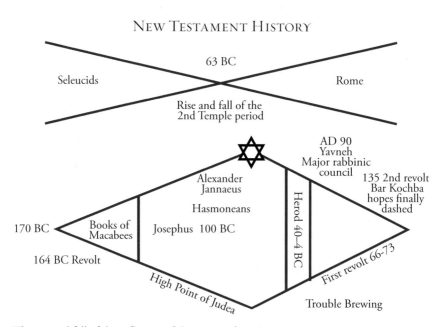

The rise and fall of the influence of the nation of Israel

CHAPTER 3

MESSIAH'S DIVINE AUTHORITY: CERTIFIED BY OBEDIENCE, TESTING, AND MIRACLES

SUMMER/FALL AD 29 – SUMMER 30
Matthew 4:1 – 12; Mark 1:12 – 14; Luke 3:21 – 4:13 (T&G 24 – 36)

JESUS CERTIFIED FOR MINISTRY: ARMED IN THE JORDAN AND THE DUEL IN THE DESERT
(Matthew 3:13 – 4:11; Mark 1:9 – 13; Luke 3:21 – 4:13; John 1:19 – 34; T&G 24 – 27)

As the son of the priest Zechariah, John was entitled to all the perks that accompanied his father's favored priestly status. But instead, John chose humble clothing, a humble diet, and a revolutionary message that signaled a new day had come that would break down established religion and its corrupt value systems. John's baptism signified that those who participated were submitting to the God of Israel.[1] His baptism was radical because it called for true repentance. He demanded that people confess their sins and turn to God in obedience. Baptism did not grant forgiveness, but it prepared its recipients for the coming of a Savior who would forgive sin. John prepared the way for the Messiah and warned that the kingdom of heaven was near (Matt. 3:2 – 3).[2]

John's baptism of Jesus, however, had nothing to do with confession of sin or repentance on Jesus' part, as evidenced by John's initial reluctance to baptize Jesus. Jesus' baptism was performed in order to "fulfill all righteousness." But what does that mean? John's baptism did not set Jesus apart as a priest; Jesus, from the tribe of Judah, did not qualify for the Levitical priesthood.[3] As a Jew born under the law, Jesus also had already been circumcised. He paid taxes as required by the law. In every way he fulfilled the law of Moses. Instead, Jesus' baptism introduced him to Israel as their Messiah, with God's anointing to fulfill the functions of the messianic office (Acts 10:38), including proclamation of the coming kingdom.

Immediately after Jesus' baptism, the Spirit led him into the desert to be tempted by Satan. As Jesus wandered amid barren rocks and made his way through the hills and valleys without food and water, the devil began his work.

Perhaps temptation came as a threatening roar or with a barely audible hiss. We do not know. But we do know that the father of lies always chooses his best disguise when he twists God's truth.

"Hungry, Jesus? Then turn these rocks to food and drink — you know you have the power to do it!"

"You say you will be King? Prove it. Throw yourself off the temple and let the angels save you."

Satan continued his relentless attack: "Look at the kingdoms before you. Say the word, and I will give them all to you. There is no need to suffer and die. Worship me and all your wishes will be fulfilled — now."

Scripture doesn't tell us what Jesus thought. But we can speculate that as God he knew the intent of Satan's heart and saw through his plan. Jesus chose

JESUS' AGE

The gospel of Luke puts Jesus' age at the beginning of his ministry at "about thirty years old" (3:23). Jesus was born somewhere between October and March 5 BC/4 BC. If Jesus' baptism occurred prior to Passover in AD 28, he was about thirty or thirty-one years old. If John baptized him early in AD 29, he was thirty-one or thirty-two years old. Harold Hoehner suggests Jesus' baptism was more likely sometime prior to Passover AD 30. This means his age ranged between thirty-two and thirty-three. The former calculation allows for a more acceptable timetable for John's ministry, allowing for Jesus' ministry to occupy at least three years, and it still allows for his age to be "about thirty years."[4]

The Jordan River at Yardenit, a popular site for pilgrims to be baptized today.

the weapon of war that promises defeat of God's enemy — Holy Scripture. He said, "It is written ...," and Satan slinked away in defeat, plotting his next battle with the Son of God.

Jesus passed Satan's test and proved his moral right to the throne of King David. By resisting the devil's temptation, Jesus also proved himself superior to Adam, who had given in to Satan's temptation and eaten the fruit in the garden. By honoring God in the wilderness, Jesus proved himself not only faithful but sufficient to provide for the penalty for our sins.

FROM WELL WATER TO FINE WINE
(John 2:1 – 12; T&G 29 – 30)

Almost immediately after Jesus was baptized, he began gathering his team to proclaim God's message. John brought Andrew and his brother Simon into the group. Jesus wasted no time in changing Simon's name to Peter. The next day, Jesus chose Philip and Nathanael. Scripture reveals later that Nathanael became the first of the disciples to accept Jesus as the Son of God (John 1:49). Once these men learned Jesus' true identity, they dropped everything and followed him.

Water jar. John 2:6: "Nearby stood six stone water jars, the kind used by the Jews for ceremonial washing, each holding from twenty to thirty gallons."

Jesus' work as a carpenter came to an end as he began his ministry. His responsibilities to his family changed. Joseph had passed away while his young family was living in Nazareth, so Mary's eldest son, Jesus, was responsible to provide for her financial needs. Presumably, in the years Jesus had followed his father's occupation after Joseph's death, he had accumulated savings that would provide for his mother. While the ages of her sons James, Joseph, Judas, and Simon (Mark 6:3) are not known, it is possible some were teenagers or younger. Mary and Joseph also had daughters (Matt. 13:56), and the age span between Jesus, who was the oldest to Simon or one of the sisters was perhaps wide. If these siblings were productive adults, perhaps they helped Mary financially as well. Later, while dying on the cross, Jesus entrusted the care of his mother to John, who was not a sibling.

Jesus did not need to convince Mary of his divine identity. She brought him into the world, nursed him, nurtured him, and protected him from birth through childhood. Once Jesus attained adulthood, she freed him to give his attention to his ministry while she attended to the needs of the rest of her family. Jesus left his family and his mother, but she understood that he must be about his Father's business as he performed his first miracle.

The gospel account holds us in its grips as we await the first of Jesus' miracles of changing water into wine. The disciples had already observed Jesus' all-powerfulness as he answered Nathanael's question, "How do you know me?" Jesus responded, "I saw you while you were still under the fig tree before Philip called you," and he went on to say, "You will see greater things than that" (John 1:48 – 50).

We know little about Jesus' brother Joseph. He is referenced in Mark 6:3 and Matthew 13:55. We do know, however, that Jesus' family, unlike Mary, did not readily accept him as the Messiah. We are not told if Joseph ever believed or if he wrestled with his doubts about his brother's identity until the day he faced Jesus in eternity. But let's view the wedding feast as perhaps a skeptical brother might have interpreted Jesus' first miracle.

Sure, I'd heard about the big wedding feast at Cana, and I wasn't about to miss out on the chance for a little partying with my friends. Of course Jesus showed up. And the night ended up being all about him—the way it always was.

At first I was excited about the free-flowing wine and the dancing. Everyone was there. After all, Cana is a small village. We were all enjoying ourselves when the party hosts figured out they were going to run out of wine and be humiliated. My mother confidently looked to Jesus for a solution—after all, he was her oldest son. I'm not really sure what she expected him to do about it, and he didn't seem pleased that she'd asked him.

I've never really figured out what happened next—it all happened so suddenly. But Jesus ordered the caterers to fill with water six jars that were reserved for ritual cleansings. We all thought it was a strange request, but the servers complied. And to our amazement, instead of water pouring from the jars, we were all served the finest wine we had ever tasted.

The people in the room that day saw what happened. *I* saw what happened. And I can only say I do not have an explanation. Jesus' disciples, many people at the wedding, and my mother, of course, pronounced what happened a 'miracle.' In fact, I heard it said that for many, this was the day they believed in him. As for me, I got a glimpse of something that caused me to reevaluate my skepticism.

Once the disciples saw this miracle, they began to understand that they sat at the feet of the Messiah. "His disciples believed in him" (John 2:11).

UNDERSTANDING BIBLE MIRACLES

The Bible has much to say about miracles and their purpose. What is a miracle? We sometimes refer to an unusual or implausible event as a miracle. The use of *miracle* in the Gospels refers to an event that is more than implausible or unusual. It is an act or event that is beyond explanation by natural reasoning. It is an event that injects a supernatural element into the natural order and defies scientific explanation.

The main purpose of a miracle is to reveal truth in a persuasive manner and often in response to the exercise of faith. Miracles are not performed just for the comfort of people. If miracles were designed solely to relieve suffering or repair brokenness, Jesus would simply heal everyone.[5] Miracles also authenticate the messenger. When Jesus walked the earth, his miracles confirmed that he was who he said he was. Jesus not only declared that he was the King of God's coming kingdom, but he did miracles that were consistent with that coming kingdom. Because wine was a symbol of the messianic kingdom (Isa. 25:6), by changing the water into wine, Jesus was demonstrating that he was able to bring in God's kingdom.

CANA[6] OF GALILEE

There are four modern sites that may be the location of the biblical Cana: Kanah, Ain Kanah, Kefar Kenna, and Khirbet Cana. Only the last two are likely candidates for the New Testament location of Cana.[7]

Kefar Kenna (village of Kenna) is four miles northeast of Nazareth, where a Greek Orthodox Church marks the traditional site with a presentation of ancient storage vats, supposedly jars like those used by Jesus. A Franciscan Catholic church in the same village displays a jar claiming to be the one used by Jesus.

Kefar Kenna (village of Kenna) is just four miles northeast of Nazareth.

LC-matpc–07007-t/www.LifeintheHolyLand.com

Khirbet Cana (ruin of Cana) lays eight and a half miles north of Nazareth along the depression known as the plain of Bet Netufa on the ancient road from Ptolemais to Magdala. Adrichomius, writing near the close of the sixteenth century, placed Cana three miles north of Sepphoris and described it as having a mountain on the north and a broad, fertile plain toward the south. This description fits Khirbet Cana very well. Anselm, in AD 1507, also assigned this site as the ruin of Cana.

The support for Khirbet Cana outweighs the evidence for Kefar Kenna. In 1321 Marinius Sanutus described Cana as north of Sepphoris, adjacent to a high round mountain on the north

The undisturbed site of Khirbet Cana from the west (the mound in the center of the photo). The village was repopulated in the Hellenistic period after Tiglath-Pileser III destroyed it in 732 BCE. Josephus's army camped near here. Vespasian destroyed the city in AD 67 during the Jewish revolt. Most scholars prefer Khirbet Cana (ruin of Cana) as the site of Jesus' first miracle. Khirbet Cana lies 8.5 miles north of Nazareth along the depression known as the plain of Bet Netufa and on the ancient road from Ptolemais to Magdala. It is a short distance from Jotapata and down a ridge within walking distance.

Aerial view of Kefar Kenna

and having the same broad, beautiful plain on the south extending to Sepphoris. At that time, the place where the six water pots stood had a triclinium[8] for the feast in a crypt underground, like that in the Church of the Nativity. Saewulf, in 1103, described Cana as six miles north of Nazareth on a hill with a monastery called Architriclinium. In the eighth century, St. Willibald found a large water pot there and claimed it as one of the six pots from the wedding feast.

Khirbet Cana is the best option as a fortress used by Josephus. The location was isolated on all sides, with slopes that could easily be defended. In fact, it is one of the most defensible positions in the area.

Jesus' goal in performing miracles was not to become "the life of the party" but to gather men and women who were committed to him and to reaching their world with his message.

JESUS GOES TO JUDEA AND JERUSALEM
(John 2:13 – 25; T&G 31 – 32a)

Jesus, with his first public miracle (John 2:11) behind him and after a short stay in Capernaum, set out for the Passover in Jerusalem (John 2:12). While there are differing opinions as to which feast Jesus attended in Jerusalem, scholars believe the Passover of April 7, AD 30, is most likely.

John reports that Jesus cleansed the temple during this Passover feast. This cleansing should not be confused with his similar act during the Passion Week. The precise wording of the accounts and the differing chronological contexts make it clear that these are two distinct events (Mark 11:15 – 18; Luke 19:45 – 48).

Imagine Mary's conversation with Jesus and John about the cleansing of the temple when they returned to Galilee from the Jerusalem trip (John 4:43 – 45). Although Jesus was exhausted from long days and the pressure of debating in the Holy City and his trip through Samaria, he took time to tell his mother about his trip. Later John filled in details that Jesus purposefully omitted, perhaps to prevent Mary from excessive concern. Earlier Mary expressed her anxiety over Jesus going to Jerusalem. The priests and authorities looked at Jesus with contempt, and she feared what they might do. Mary may have remembered Simeon's warning that a sword would pierce her own soul (Luke 2:35).

Her forebodings were confirmed as she quizzed John about Jesus' activities in the temple. His account may have gone something like this: "Jesus gave a tongue-lashing to the money changers and those selling sacrificial animals." These unscrupulous men were cheating worshipers by demanding they purchase Jerusalemite animals for sacrifice and refused to give honest exchange

Temple Mount model of Royal Stoa. The Temple Mount plaza was surrounded by covered colonnades on all sides. The largest one was on the south side and was known as the Royal Stoa. This area was used for monetary transactions and judicial activity. This may have been the place where Jesus chased out the money changers. "The Sanhedrin may have moved to the Royal Porch about the time of the death of Christ; according to the Babylonian Talmud it was 'forty years before the destruction of the temple' that the Sanhedrin moved from its former meeting place at the Chamber of Hewn Stone, which the Mishnah states was 'in the Temple Court.'"[9]

rates to those without temple-approved currency.

John continued, "Jesus became furious. He released their sacrificial birds from their cages, smashed their sheep pens, and flipped their tables. Animals were running through the temple, and money went flying everywhere. Everyone froze — and every eye was on Jesus." John's words were a mixture of pride and awe as he described the scene.

"And the priests? You wouldn't believe their rage. They could barely contain themselves. Something tells me this is just the beginning of their opposition to Jesus."

In spite of opposition from authorities, Jesus was pleased at the crowd's early response to his message.

Tyrian shekel hoard from Isfiye (Druze village in northern Israel on Mount Carmel), perhaps for temple tax (c. first century AD). The shekel, minted between 126 BCE and AD 56, weighed 14.2 grams of silver. The money changers in the temple converted all currency into the dependable silver shekel worth double a regular shekel. Their legendary dishonesty in exchange rates brought Jesus' wrath.[10]

Men and women saw his miracles and responded in belief (John 2:23–25). But was the message for common people only? Would any from the powerful ruling classes be included in the "good news"? That question was about to be answered.

A CLANDESTINE MEETING WITH A PHARISEE
(John 3:1 – 21; T&G 32b)

John's story of a Pharisee named Nicodemus gave evidence that some within the powerful Sanhedrin were accepting Jesus' message. Later, during Jesus' trial, Nicodemus would prove to be a loyal friend. When Jesus first told this aristocrat about the new birth, Nicodemus thought Jesus was talking about going back into the womb — but Nicodemus didn't understand how that could happen.

THE NEW BIRTH BRINGS A NEW OUTLOOK

The blackness of night gripped me as I tried to fall asleep in my basement apartment. Once again sleep eluded me. Night after night, I'd pondered the claims of Christianity. I wanted to believe Jesus was real and that he cared for me. I tightly closed my eyes and prayed, "Jesus if you are real, appear at the foot of my bed." I opened one eye, but to my disappointment, he was not there. Despair washed over me. Little did I know that this experience was the beginning of a journey of hard-fought faith questions I shared with Nicodemus.

A few months later, I married my high school sweetheart, and she began working for a jeweler. He thought it his duty to proclaim the gospel message to everyone he met. For weeks he worked on Carol as his semi-captive audience, trying to convince her that Jesus was real and the only way to God. Finally, one afternoon he asked permission to come to our apartment and talk to us together. By now Carol took Mr. Platt seriously, and she was concerned about his claims that Satan would pull out all stops to try to prevent me from hearing the gospel message. I mockingly reminded her that I was not under the influence of Satan and would not be afraid of anything Mr. Platt had to say to me.

The following night, Mr. Platt sat at our kitchen table and explained the message of the Bible, from the Old Testament to the New Testament. As he finished, he made a statement that haunted me. "You will one day meet Jesus as your Judge or as your Savior."

My quick response was, "I want to, but I just can't believe the claims of Jesus."

Mr. Platt bowed his head and rubbed his thumb and forefinger on his temples in thoughtful mediation. Then he raised his head and spoke, quoting Roman 10:17, "So then faith cometh by hearing and hearing by the word of God" (KJV). At the time, I thought he was speaking words directly from God, and I felt a huge burden tumble from my shoulders.

I didn't have to worry about finding faith. If I studied God's Word, *he would give me the faith* I was searching for. What a revelation!

Mr. Pratt did not press Carol or me for a decision that evening. But a few nights later, as we lay in bed, both Carol and I accepted Jesus Christ as our Redeemer and Savior.

Carol and I both found the new birth Nicodemus found. My new life in Christ changed my outlook, goals, and motives for the rest of my life. In my passion to know more about God and serve him, I soon joined a church and enrolled at Moody Bible Institute to begin a new life that would eventually take me to the Holy Land—to walk where Jesus walked.

Nicodemus clearly misunderstood Jesus' teaching about being born "of water and the Spirit" (John 3:5). These words did not refer to a physical birth a second time, but a spiritual birth from above. As Jesus later explained to the woman at the well in Samaria, "water" represents "eternal life." Jesus went on to explain to Nicodemus that water is associated with the gift of the Holy Spirit (John 7:37–39). Nicodemus already confused literal meaning with metaphorical meaning, so there is little wonder he misunderstood "Spirit" and "wind," the same word in both Hebrew and Greek used in John 3:8.

Water and wind are life in the semiarid climate of the Holy Land, and they are eagerly anticipated by the people (Isa. 44:3–5). The significance of the concept of wind, as we know from the Old Testament, serves as an image for the work of the Spirit (Ezek. 37:9–10). As soon as Nicodemus understood Jesus' meaning, Jesus declared the famous words to him: "For God so loved the world that he gave his one and only Son, that whoever believes in him shall not perish but have eternal life" (John 3:16).

JESUS SUPERSEDES JOHN (John 3:22–36; T&G 33)

While John was baptizing in Aenon near Salim,[11] onlookers questioned the disciples concerning his identity and message. Ceremonial cleansing topped the list of questions. John's baptism reminded them of Old Testament ritual cleansing. Crowds throughout the region were seeking the one who had been with John "beyond the Jordan." John quickly pointed out that he was not the Christ but the forerunner of the Christ. The message was successfully being proclaimed among the Jews, but what about those who were longtime

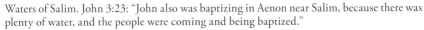

Waters of Salim. John 3:23: "John also was baptizing in Aenon near Salim, because there was plenty of water, and the people were coming and being baptized."

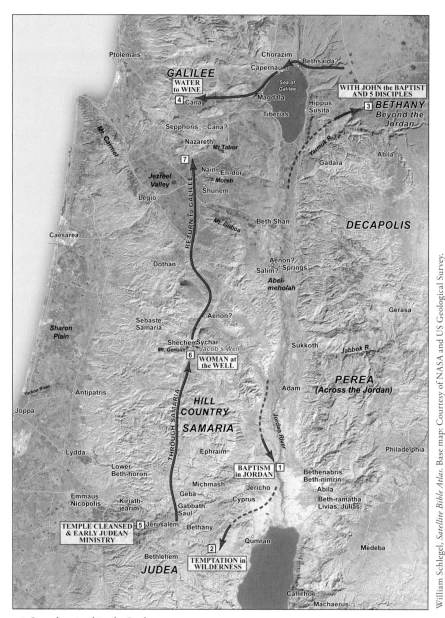

William Schlegel, *Satellite Bible Atlas*. Base map: Courtesy of NASA and US Geological Survey.

1. Jesus baptized in the Jordan
2. Jesus' temptation
3. John baptized at "Bethany on the other side of the Jordan" (John 1:28)
4. Water to wine miracle
5. First cleansing of the temple
6. Jesus confronted woman at the well and claimed to be the Messiah
7. Jesus' return to Galilee when hearing of John's incarceration (beginning of Galilean ministry)

enemies of the Jews? Would the message reach them? The gospel of John reminds his readers that the gospel is for everyone—yes, everyone.

JESUS' MESSAGE EXTENDS TO SAMARITANS
(John 4:1–45; T&G 34–36)

Jesus' message of eternal life was being developed. He clearly exhorted Nicodemus to be born from above by believing in him (John 3:16). The Samaritan woman at the well understood the message that everyone who drinks of the living water Jesus gives them will never thirst. She was so convinced that she wanted to spread the message to others, but the means of salvation, which included Jesus' death and resurrection, was not yet clearly understood. The Samaritans, who were hated by the Jews, came to believe when they heard the testimony of others: "This man really is the Savior of the world" (John 4:42). The gospel was for Jews, Samaritans (half Jews), and Gentiles.

JESUS' WORDS AND WORKS IN HIS EARLY MINISTRY
(AD 29–30)

First Year of Ministry

Jordan River area:
    Jesus' baptism (Hajlah ford) (Matt. 3:13–17)
    Jesus' wilderness temptation (Matt. 4:1–11)
    John's witness to Jesus (John 1:29–34)
    Jesus' first followers (John 1:35–51)
Cana:
    First miracle: water to wine (John 2:1–11)
    Healing a nobleman's son (John 4:46–54)
Jerusalem:
    Passover, first cleansing of the temple (John 2:13–22)
    Visit of Nicodemus (John 3:1–21)
Sychar:
    Woman at the well discourse (John 4:5–42)
On the other side of the Jordan (Batanea?):
    John baptizes (denied he was the Messiah) (John 1:28)
Aenon near Salim:
    John baptizes (John 3:22–36)

Jesus' ministry was well under way. He proclaimed his message of salvation in Galilee, Judea, and Samaria. Perhaps to his followers, Jesus' return to Galilee brought hope. But his message came into conflict with Jewish leadership's definition of the law of God. Instead of accepting Jesus' words, they increased their opposition. The common people were about to be participants in the great conflict: accept Jesus' message of salvation or reject it in favor of their religious leaders' interpretation of the law of Moses. Would the disciples continue to follow their Master, or would they too become disenchanted? We are about to find out.

CHAPTER 4

MESSIANIC MESSAGE DEFINED: THE KINGDOM OF GOD

SPRING – FALL AD 31

Matthew 4:17 – 9:17; 12:1 – 14; Mark 1:14 – 3:6; Luke 4:14 – 6:11;
John 4:46 – 5:47 (T&G 37 – 51)

JOHN GOES TO PRISON
(Matthew 4:12, 17; Mark 1:14 – 15; Luke 4:14 – 15; T&G 37)

Mary heard from her Son Jesus that Herod had cast Elizabeth's son, John (the Baptist), into prison for condemning Herod and his deviant relationship with Herodias, his brother's wife. The thought may have crossed Mary's mind to ask Jesus to go speak with the authorities to gain John's release, but she likely feared that he too would be arrested. After all, Jesus was already a source of controversy in his own right. Mary was concerned for his safety, thinking that perhaps it might be better if Jesus and John toned down their condemnation of the priests and their practices. However, both John and Jesus were doing the heavenly Father's bidding—and that assurance must have given some comfort to their earthly families.

A defining moment in Jesus' ministry came in late winter AD 31. Up to this time, Jesus' message focused on his person and ministry through miracles, with brief instructions on repentance and salvation, as seen in his encounter with Nicodemus and the woman at the well. At Jesus' baptism, God declared, "This is my Son, whom I love; with him I am well pleased" (Matt. 3:17).

Later Jesus demonstrated his moral authority as he resisted Satan's temptations. Jesus' early ministry centered on his person. He came to save the lost by their expressing faith in him (John 3:1–21). Beginning in Galilee and for the first time, Jesus preached, "Repent, for the kingdom of heaven [God] has come near" (Matt. 4:17), the same message John the Baptist had preached in anticipation of the Messiah's coming (Matt. 3:2). Now Jesus himself began to proclaim that the kingdom anticipated in the Old Testament was at hand.

Jesus' early message made no mention of the cross or his resurrection. His continuation of John's message would bring him into direct conflict with Herod Antipas, who saw any claim of a new kingdom as a threat to his authority. With John in prison, Jesus continued alone in proclaiming the kingdom message. "Jesus went throughout Galilee, teaching in their synagogues, proclaiming the good news of the kingdom, and healing every disease and sickness among the people" (Matt. 4:23). But he still had unfinished business in Cana.

JESUS' RETURN TO CANA (John 4:46–54; T&G 38)

Jesus hurried to Cana on his way back from Judea. He last visited Cana at the wedding feast. This occasion called for the healing of a Roman official's son. He knew doubters hesitated to believe unless they saw a miracle or sign. Nevertheless, some came to hear what he had to say, as well as to experience his healing. As Jesus healed, he took the awkward but necessary opportunity to rebuke the faithless citizens of Cana.

The Sea of Galilee, the Arbela cliff, and the plain of Arbela, looking to the northeast between Magdala in the north and Tiberias to the south. The plain of Arbela (Gennesaret) is noted for its production of wheat and durable, thick linen. In Jewish literature, the plain of Arbela is a site for messianic redemption of the Jews from foreign rule. Jesus may have visited the town of Arbela on his way from Nazareth to Capernaum or on his travels throughout the villages of Galilee.

Nazareth in the early 1900s

Unbelief plagued the Galileans. They didn't trust their Hebrew Scriptures, which demanded faith in God based on historic stories and events. But when a Roman official heard Jesus' message and saw his actions, he and his household believed. Jesus' own people turned him away again and again, yet he often found his most receptive hearing among Samaritans, Romans, and outcasts — the least likely to place their hope for salvation in a Jewish carpenter.

JESUS REJECTED AT NAZARETH (Luke 4:16–31; T&G 39)

Very little is known about Nazareth from ancient sources. Outside the New Testament, Nazareth is not mentioned until the Byzantine period (AD fourth century). Archaeological excavations confirm that the city existed as a small agricultural village during the Hellenistic and Roman periods.

When Jesus first entered the synagogue and began reading the daily Scripture lesson, people listened intently to his words and were impressed. Then he clearly presented his messianic credentials when he declared, "Today this Scripture is fulfilled in your hearing" (Luke 4:21).

You can almost hear the gasp of rage from the inhabitants of Nazareth

Nazareth. Jesus spent his boyhood years in Nazareth before beginning his ministry when he was about thirty. After moving his home to Capernaum, Jesus returned to teach in the synagogue of Nazareth twice but was rejected both times. This is the hill where tradition says Jesus was nearly thrown to his death by the angry Nazareth mob (Luke 4:28–30).

(Luke 4:28) as they cried out, "Of all the nerve! Isn't this Jesus, the carpenter Joseph's son?"

Then when Jesus threatened to stop performing miracles among them, as Elisha had done in the Old Testament among those in his community, the people in the synagogue attacked Jesus and attempted to throw him over a cliff on the edge of town.

Jesus' disciples were shocked by the hostile reception in Jesus' hometown. After all, he lived with his family in Nazareth for nearly thirty years, knew almost everyone in the close-knit community, and had many friends there. Imagine how Jesus' family and friends must have felt toward the men and women who sat at their table, worshiped with them in the synagogue, and sent their children to the same schools. These same people turned on Jesus and attempted to take his life.

Nazareth was Mary's hometown as well, and if she did not observe the outbreak in the temple that day, she certainly heard about it. She was ecstatic that Jesus escaped. Her mother's heart probably hoped that Jesus would never return to his hometown again at peril of his life.

But Mary was also a woman who "pondered" the things of God (Luke 2:19). Knowing this about her, we can also assume that she settled into the quiet assurance that Jesus entrusted his call, his future, and the persecution that would mark his life to his sovereign and loving heavenly Father, and that she would have to learn that same walk of faith in the difficult days ahead.

JESUS CHANGES HIS ADDRESS
(Matthew 4:13 – 16; T&G 40)

The people in Jesus' hometown of Nazareth rejected him. A permanent move to another town was inevitable, and Jesus was happy to establish his home in Capernaum for the remainder of his ministry. Unlike Nazareth, Capernaum welcomed him. Evidently the Jewish leadership did not feel threatened by Jesus or perceive danger associated with him. However, that was soon to change.

THE DISCIPLES GRADUATE FROM FOLLOWERS TO LEARNERS
(Matthew 4:18 – 22; Mark 1:16 – 20; Luke 5:1 – 11; T&G 41)

Jesus knew some of his disciples before he called them to become part of his ministry team. Their friendship and the time he invested in them are noted in John's gospel (3:22). Even before their "call" to discipleship, they were spending time with Jesus, learning about him, and gaining confidence in him. Many of the disciples were fishermen, and Tabgha was a fisherman's paradise. The coves at Tabgha produced an abundance of fish, and a spring provided a place for fishermen to clean their nets. This area was a community with strong personal values and the place where Jesus called James and John into his ministry. With the establishment of his ministry team, Jesus was ready to move forward in fulfilling God's plan.

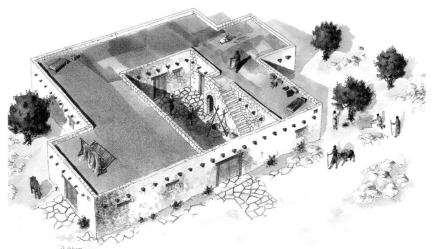

Ron Waalkes's concept of a typical first-century housing complex (Peter's or Jesus' home?). The house follows the same pattern as the other living quarters of the village of Capernaum. The various houses were clustered around a central courtyard. Peter, along with others, could have lived in the compound, perhaps Jesus' family as well. Imagine the front door leading to the room where Jesus was teaching when the roof was broken by men who lowered a paralytic on his mat down to Jesus' feet to be healed (Mark 2:1 – 12).

Capernaum from above. In existence from the second century BCE to the seventh century AD, Capernaum was built along the edge of the Sea of Galilee and had up to fifteen hundred residents. Today the ruins are owned by two churches: the Catholic Franciscans and the Greek Orthodox.

JESUS' MINISTRY IN FULL SWING
(Matthew 8:14 – 9:17; Mark 1:29 – 2:22; Luke 4:38 – 5:39; T&G 43 – 48)

Life shifted for Jesus once again when he moved into Peter's home in Capernaum.[1] Peter's mother-in-law was ill with a high fever, but she responded instantly to Jesus' touch and was completely healed. She rose from her bed and began serving Jesus and her household.

Synagogue in Capernaum. In this synagogue, a demon-possessed man recognized Jesus as the Holy One of God. In response, Jesus silenced the man and cast out the evil spirit (Mark 1:21 – 28).

Earlier Jesus dramatically healed a man in the synagogue (Mark 1:21–28), and his actions drew the attention of everyone in the district. Mark noted that the crowds came after sunset when the Sabbath was over and travel restrictions ended.

Jesus enjoyed living in Peter's house in Capernaum, where he could more easily go about his Father's business. Here Jesus was surrounded by his friends, and it is possible that Mary may have lived with him there as well. Typical first-century homes were arranged around a common courtyard in a compound. Archaeologists have identified a possible site for Peter's house and the synagogue referred to in the gospel accounts.

Jesus' ministry in Capernaum attracted multitudes of village residents as well as religious leaders. Everywhere Jesus went, he was pressed on all sides by inquiring and even adoring seekers. Jesus was an unusual preacher who presented an unusual message. Even more intriguing was that he demonstrated the authority of his message by performing miracles. It would seem that everyone would want to listen to him and give his message a fair hearing.

But that wasn't so.

Jesus' primary message was that all people needed to repent because God's coming kingdom as prophesied in the Old Testament was near. Since the kingdom would be preceded by judgment of the wicked, repentance was necessary lest one be excluded from the kingdom. As John had said, simply being born Jewish was not sufficient to enter the kingdom, for God could raise up sons of Abraham from the stones. The only way to be accepted into God's kingdom was to repent and produce fruit that demonstrated repentance.

During this time in his ministry, Jesus demonstrated his authority to be King. His realm of authority extended to demons, nature, sickness, defilement, the forgiveness of sins, taxation, and tradition. And yet controversy continued to follow his message.

THE BOILING POT OF CONTROVERSIES
(Matthew 8:2–12:14; Mark 1:40–3:6; Luke 5:12–6:11; John 5:1–47; T&G 45–51)

One day Jesus healed a leper who came to him. He was moved with compassion by the man's faith and healed him, then warned him not to tell anyone except the priests. But in his gratitude and excitement, the man began telling everyone what Jesus had done for him. At first the crowds thought the man had lost his mind, but they soon identified him as the leper they had shunned for years. Even though Jesus could no longer enter a town openly, people discovered where he was and came to him from everywhere (Mark 1:40–45).

CAPERNAUM (KEFAR NAHUM/TEL HUM)

On the northwest side of the Sea of Galilee lies the small village of Capernaum. Although not immediately identified as the biblical town of Capernaum, archaeological evidence has now marked it as the well-accepted biblical home of Jesus. Residents abandoned this ancient city a thousand years ago, but Arab families from the Semekiyeh tribe living there preserved it until the war of independence in 1948.

Biblical scholar Edward Robinson visited the site in the 1830s and was the first to identify the synagogue of Capernaum. In the late 1860s, another famous archaeologist, Charles W. Wilson, probed the same area for evidence of material culture. The Franciscans, custodians of much of the area, allowed a wall to be built around the compound to prevent looters from continuing to destroy the ancient remains. That wall is still visible today. In 1905 the Germans began to excavate the synagogue, and in 1921 a Franciscan from Nazareth restored the current synagogue structure. In 1968 another archaeologist, Father Virgilio Corbo, carried out extensive excavations that form the base of what is seen today.[2]

This small but well-developed fishing and agricultural village reinforces the fact that Peter and his brother Andrew left their hometown of Bethsaida to engage in a more productive fishing business in Capernaum. The village was structured fairly simply. Houses with basalt rock foundations and mud and straw roofs were all built around a common courtyard. Much of the daily activity, such as cooking, conversation, and artisan labor took place in the courtyard. In the heat of the summer, many residents made their beds outside as well. The lack of cisterns and latrines is no surprise for such a small community.

The importance of Capernaum lies in its relationship to the life and ministry of Jesus. This very small, insignificant fishing village became a standing symbol of nineteenth- to

Bedouin camp in Capernaum

First-century walls beneath Capernaum synagogue. A layer of basalt cobblestones that was obviously the floor of a yet earlier building has been found under the white limestone synagogue. The floor clearly dates to the first century AD or earlier. The floor connects to basalt walls like those found elsewhere in the region. The building plan of the earlier structure is the same as the later synagogue. The walls of the first-century building are underneath the later walls.

twenty-first-century pilgrim Christianity. Visitors stand in awe as they contemplate Jesus' very presence in this place. They can almost hear him preach in the synagogue, teach the disciples in Peter's house, or see him around the courtyard fire conversing with the villagers. They stand amazed to know they can view the same morning sunrise over the Sea of Galilee that Jesus and his disciples witnessed over two thousand years ago.

The synagogue

The synagogue that visitors to Capernaum view today is not the synagogue of Jesus' day. The Jerusalem Talmud describes the destruction of 480 synagogues in Jerusalem alone by the Roman general Vespasian during the conquest of Galilee. Historians believe the Roman invasion destroyed the Capernaum synagogue of Jesus' day.

Beginning in 1969, Franciscan archaeologists Stanislao Loffreda and Virgilio Corbo began cutting trenches inside the fourth-century synagogue and outside along the foundations in order to clarify the history of the various periods.[3] Surprisingly, structures (possibly private homes) were uncovered from the late Bronze Age (thirteenth century BCE), the Hellenistic, and the Roman periods. The large stone pavement uncovered beneath the main central nave is from the synagogue of Jesus' time, as are the basalt foundations.

PETER'S HOUSE

The New Testament refers to Peter's house (*Insula Sacra*)[4] as it relates to Jesus' ministry, and perhaps these ancient ruins are Jesus' and Peter's shared home. This structure formed a part of a typical village complex of private homes with small rooftop rooms surrounding a courtyard. This

Sunrise over the Sea of Galilee

Foundations of Peter's house. Excavations revealed one residence that stood out from the others. This house was the object of early Christian attention, with second-century graffiti and a fourth-century house church built above it. In the fifth century, a large octagonal Byzantine church was erected above this, complete with a baptistery. Pilgrims referred to this structure as the house of the apostle Peter. The remains of the church are from the fifth century AD and are located over the traditional location of the house of Peter, which evidence indicates is correct. Inscriptions mentioning Jesus and Peter were found in the house (in Aramaic, Greek, Latin, and Syriac).

traditional site for Peter's nearly square house and the western wall is still preserved today. The home was entered from a doorway preserved on the north flank near the northwest corner. An open L-shaped courtyard was entered through a well-preserved entryway.

The courtyard, shared by several other rooms, suggests that more than one family lived around a common courtyard. Peter's house was used for community gatherings as early as the end of the first century. In the late fourth century, new walls were constructed, plastered, and decorated with various floral motifs. This suggests a very early Christian church was built over what was recognized historically as the site of Peter's house. In the fifth century, architects built an octagonal church over the site.[5]

Peter's house was the setting of several biblical events: (1) the healing of Peter's mother-in-law (Matt. 8:14–15; the house was large enough to house three families: Peter's, Andrew's, and Jesus'); (2) the payment of the two-drachma temple tax (Matt. 17:24–27); (3) the healing of the paralytic lowered through the roof on a stretcher (Mark 2:1–12); and (4) the visit of Jesus' family, when he asked, "Who are my mother and brothers?" (Mark 3:31–35; cf. Matt. 12:46–50; Luke 8:19–21).

Tabgha. Ancient Heptapegon (modern Tabgha) was an excellent place for fishing in the first century, and this may explain why numerous traditions associate the ministry of Jesus and his disciples with the area.

The leper had approached Jesus during Jesus' visit to Tabgha. Falling on his knees, the leper begged Jesus to make him clean. His extraordinary confidence in Jesus' ability to heal him impressed the many onlookers. But even if Jesus did heal him, would his community confirm Jesus' miracle by suspending their shunning, or would they continue to treat him as a leper?

Pharisaical tradition dictated that on a windless day a leper must remain at least six feet away from a healthy individual, but on a windy day a leper must keep a distance of at least a hundred feet from the healthy. Jesus, while delighted to see the man so full of joy, instructed the leper first to go to Jerusalem to permit the priests to pronounce him clean according to the law.

Many people who observed the healing gasped at the idea that Jesus was deliberately confronting the Pharisees with his power and forcing them to acknowledge it. Jesus' power to heal a leper made them furious. They knew that only God had that power, and they weren't ready to give up their exalted positions to a rival power and king. Even Jesus' early ministry overwhelmed the people of Galilee.

Imagine that while sitting in the courtyard under the stars, Jesus' mother, Mary, couldn't help but be relieved when Peter's mother-in-law told her the healed leper did not go directly to Jerusalem. Again, Mary felt the tension between peace and fear tug at her soul. She cherished these days in Peter's house, serving Jesus and the disciples. Sometimes all of them gathered there: Simon, whom Jesus called Peter; his brother Andrew; the brothers James and John; Philip; Bartholomew (Nathanael); Matthew; Thomas; James, Alphaeus's son; Simon the Zealot; Thaddaeus (Judas), James's son; and Judas Iscariot. How long she could remain with them she did not know. But she prayed continuously for her son. And she prayed for peace.

Peace lasted scarcely a week. When the leper finally arrived in Jerusalem for cleansing, the Pharisees were livid. They hurriedly formed a caravan and set out for Capernaum, determined to discredit Jesus.

THE PARALYTIC HEALED
(Matthew 9:1 – 17; Mark 2:1 – 22; Luke 5:17 – 39; T&G 46 – 48)

Imagine that one evening Peter gathered his family and some neighbors around the fire and quietly spoke to them, saying, "Jesus healed a paralytic today and then announced to the Pharisees who witnessed the miracle that he forgave the man's sins. Of course, the Pharisees put a different spin on Jesus' actions and accused him of blasphemy. Imagine Jesus a blasphemer—unbelievable."

Peter, remembering the insults and accusations that were hurled at Jesus, grew more animated as he continued: "Of course, the Pharisees recognize that the Scriptures teach that only God can forgive sins. Jesus claiming an identity they have to accept or deny."

Kitchen at Qatzrin. Jews resided for centuries in this ancient Talmudic village until it was destroyed by an earthquake in the eighth century. The remains trace the village development from the Late Roman period (third–fourth centuries) to the Early Arab period (eighth century). The village features a magnificent, partially reconstructed synagogue and the ruins of residential buildings.

Those listening grew nervous. They knew that it was dangerous to take Pharisee opposition lightly. And they also knew Peter well enough to know that his blustering personality could often be his worst enemy. Who knew how God planned to use this mismatched band of disciples to do his work? And Jesus had yet to reveal his full plan. Who could know what would happen in the days ahead?

As the weeks passed, family members gathered often around the fire in the open court of Peter's house. They loved to listen to the events of the day when the disciples returned. One evening while Peter's mother-in-law was serving the evening meal, one of the men began to relate the story of how Matthew was recruited to become a disciple.

"Jesus was on his way to the Sea of Galilee and passed a tax office," he recalled.

PASSOVER/UNLEAVENED BREAD

Passover (*Pesach*) is one of the most widely celebrated Jewish holidays (March/April). It commemorates the biblical story of the exodus and freedom of the Hebrews from Egyptian bondage. Passover begins on the 14th of Nisan and marks the beginning of a seven-day celebration that includes the Feast of Unleavened Bread. The festival lasts for seven days in Israel and for eight days outside of Israel. Scripture commands Jews to retell the Passover story every year. This usually takes place during the Passover *seder* held in private homes on the first night of Passover. Sometimes the meals continue during the entire period of Passover and Feast of Unleavened Bread, but the meals on the first two nights are usually the ones considered *seder* meals.

Israel had seven major feasts: three in March/April — Passover, Unleavened Bread, and First Fruits/Passover (*Pesach*); three in September/October — Trumpets (known today as the Jewish New Year, *Rosh Hashanah*), Day of Atonement (*Yom Kippur*), and Tabernacles (*Succoth/ Booths*); and one in May/June — Pentecost (Feast of Weeks/Harvest/*Shavuot*). Every male was required to be in attendance for the three "grain" feasts: Unleavened Bread, Pentecost, and Tabernacles (Lev. 23).

The Feast of Unleavened Bread begins on the 15th of Nisan and lasts until the 21st. In preparation for Passover, all leavened food is removed from the house and must not be eaten during the festival. The unleavened bread symbolizes the haste with which the Israelites fled Egypt. Since they did not have time for the bread to rise in order to have provisions for the journey, they had to bake it without yeast (Ex 12:11; Deut. 16:3).[6]

Everyone knew that tax collectors often acquired a bad reputation because they could legally confiscate property for back taxes and that many accepted bribes to keep taxes low for the wealthy. No one liked tax collectors.

The disciple continued. "Jesus called on Matthew to join our group. To my surprise, Matthew got up from his table and immediately followed Jesus. When the Pharisees saw Jesus associating with a tax collector, they accused him of collaborating with thieves and robbers." The disciple shook his head. "Sometimes it doesn't make sense to me. Jesus keeps on doing things that irritate the Pharisees. Why can't he just choose to be silent once in a while?"

Heads nodded in agreement as the irritated disciple continued. "I've heard it with my own ears. Jesus told the Pharisees, 'If one is sinless, he has no need of repentance. I have come to heal those who recognize their sinful condition.'"

The fiery tirade finally gave way to drifting thoughts and weary eyes. The evening came to an end, and the call of much-needed sleep soon drew the disciples and their companions to the comfort of their rooms.

But the questions remained with many. Would Jesus choose to be silent? Or would he continue to call his followers to a life-and-death choice regarding his identity?

The day was dreary with the promise of rain as Jesus left the following morning for Jerusalem to celebrate his second Passover since the beginning of his ministry (April 25, AD 31). Mary wanted to go along to help with food and laundry, but Jesus thought the trip would be too strenuous for her. She

Synagogue in Capernaum. Jesus taught here following his confrontation with the demoniac (Mark 1:21–27; Luke 4:31–37), healed the daughter of the synagogue ruler Jairus (Mark 5:22, 35–43; Luke 8:41–42, 49–56) and the servant of the centurion who built this synagogue (Matt 8:5–13; Luke 7:3–10). Jesus gave his famous sermon on the Bread of Life from this synagogue (John 6:35–59).

surmised that the dangers of her association with him might be the reason he didn't want her to go along. The Pharisees continually tried to provoke her Son, and it was whispered that the paranoid Pilate feared Jesus planned to usurp his throne. Mary still lived with the horrible memories of how quickly Herod had arrested and executed Elizabeth's son, John.

James insisted on accompanying the group to Jerusalem even though he was skeptical about Jesus and his mission from God. He didn't say why he was going, but Mary was glad he was taking the time to be with his half-brother. Jesus had been a quiet and obedient child who kept to himself. But his quiet confidence caused some of his brothers and sisters to pull away from him. Although she never spoke her questions, Mary sometimes wondered what lay behind the steady gaze in her Son's eyes that seemed to look straight into her heart. She'd prayed relentlessly that James would come to understand that Jesus was the long-awaited Messiah and learn as much as he could from Jesus before he completed his earthly mission.

Mary heard the stories at the fireside. And at times she heard the disciples' whispers—stories of how the religious leaders constantly challenged Jesus' teaching and miracles. She knew they were looking for ways to use the law of Moses to charge him with a capital crime. Healing the paralytic was the first incident that could have resulted in a formal charge with the penalty of death. Jesus' popularity with the people had deterred the Pharisees—but that could only last so long.

With tears in her eyes, Mary hugged her sons good-bye, watching Jesus, James, and the disciples head south toward Jerusalem.

THE LAME MAN HEALED ON THE SABBATH

(Jerusalem) (Matthew 12:1 – 14; Mark 2:23 – 3:12; Luke 6:1 – 11; John 5:1 – 47; T&G 49 – 52)

Leaving Capernaum, Jesus headed for Jerusalem to celebrate his second Passover feast. Like all well-intentioned Jews, he wanted to be in Jerusalem for the Passover.

Again Jesus ignored concerns for his safety when he healed a lame man on the Sabbath by the Pool of Bethesda near the Sheep Gate. Sabbath law forbade carrying a burden on the Sabbath, as well as engaging in many other common duties. Mothers and servants were forbidden to light fires to cook and had to prepare all food for the Sabbath by sundown on Friday. But Jesus used this opportunity to explain to the Pharisees that their interpretation of Moses' law missed its true intent.

Wheat, a member of the annual grass family. Each stem of wheat has an ear at the end that contains seeds or grains.

Nevertheless, the Pharisees used Jesus' working of this miracle to accuse him—this time of working on the Sabbath[7] and equating himself with God.

The apostle John pondered the Pharisees' blindness in his writing. *If the Pharisees weren't so blinded by greed and bloated with piety, they would see why Jesus' explanation of why he is equal with God is rational. If they are looking for the Messiah about whom Moses wrote, they should believe Moses' writing and believe in Jesus. Because the Pharisees persist in denying the works of Jesus, none of his explanations or miracles will satisfy their concerns* (John 5:19–47, summarization).

Jesus' time in Jerusalem appears to have been short, or else the Gospels ignore his activities while in Jerusalem. We surmise that not all of Jesus' teachings and miracles are recorded.

The second Sabbath controversy took place on a Sabbath in Galilee. Jesus and the disciples decided to take a shortcut across a ripened field of grain. Some of them were hungry, so they pulled the heads off the stalks, blew away the chaff, and popped the kernels into their mouths. Once again, the ever-stalking Pharisees accused Jesus of breaking the Sabbath, even though the law of Moses allowed eating on the Sabbath and, in emergencies, even entering the Holy Place in the temple and eating the consecrated bread.

Jesus' response to their accusation was simple: "The Sabbath was made for man, not man for the Sabbath. So the Son of Man is Lord even of the Sabbath" (Mark 2:27–28). Blinded by their rage, the Pharisees resolved to

THE POOL OF BETHESDA (John 5:2)

The ruins of the Pool of Bethesda are just inside the Stephen's Gate (Lion's Gate) near the Church of St. Anne. John 5 records that near the Sheep Gate (Neh. 12:39) a pool called "Bethesda" in Hebrew had five porticoes (colonnades). The name in Hebrew had three spellings: Bethesda, Bezetha, or Bethzatha. It is not unusual for a place to have multiple names and/or spellings. This is confirmed since the same spellings survive in various extant manuscripts.

The famous Copper Scroll discovered at Qumran from the first century AD suggests there were two pools at the site. Later pilgrims also refer to two pools, and modern archaeologists have uncovered two pools at the location. The channel leading from one pool to the other may have caused the "moving of the waters" referred to in some modern translations. Archaeologists have found numerous fragments of the "porticoes." The pool may date to the Hellenistic period (332–164 BC) for use by the residents of Jerusalem as their water supply. The location may also be a reservoir called "Beth Hasda" (House of Mercy). The name would justify the belief that the pool had healing properties.

Pools of Bethesda. Of the two large pools here, only the southern one has been partially excavated. A dam separates this pool from the one to the north. In 200 BCE a priest built these pools to provide water for the temple, since large quantities of water were needed for the temple sacrifices. At this location, a street drainage canal was dammed to form the pool. By Herod's time, another pool was added, perhaps for washing animals. Apparently the pool was believed to have some healing properties.

The Church of St. Anne is claimed to be the place of Mary's birth (primarily mentioned in *Protevangelium of James*, a New Testament apocryphal writing from the second century. In AD 614 the Persians destroyed the original "Church of the Lame Man" (built sometime prior to AD 451), and later the Byzantines built a chapel over the ruins. The Crusaders (early twelfth century) built a church in approximately the same place as the current Church of St. Anne. In 1192 the Muslim warlord Saladin converted the church into a Muslim school, and an Arabic inscription on the doorway still remains.

Church of St. Anne and pools of Bethesda

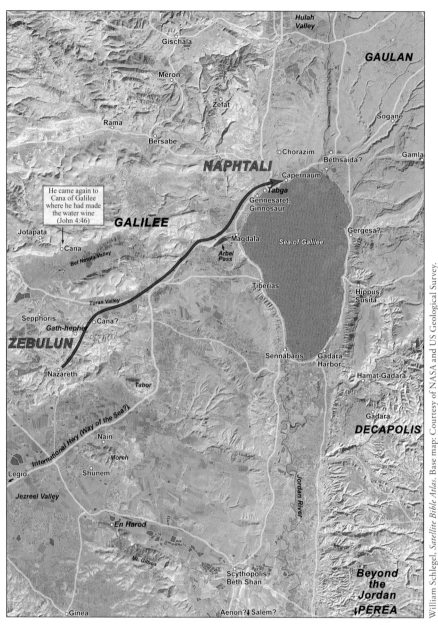

He came again to
Cana of Galilee
where he had made
the water wine
(John 4:46)

Jesus' move from Nazareth to Capernaum and first miracle at Cana.

find a way to take Jesus' life. His purported violation of the sanctity of the
Sabbath provided just such an excuse.[8]

The priests' third accusation against Jesus followed immediately in an
unidentified synagogue, perhaps in the vicinity of Tiberias. "The Pharisees

and the teachers of the law were looking for a reason to accuse Jesus, so they watched him closely to see if he would heal on the Sabbath" (Luke 6:7). The Pharisees charged Jesus with violating the command not to heal on the Sabbath. Jesus refuted their charge by appealing to their own practice, "I ask you, which is lawful on the Sabbath: to do good or to do evil, to save life or to destroy it?" (v. 9) The Pharisees did not like his answer. They "were furious and began to discuss with one another what they might do to Jesus" (v. 11).

The plotters continued to pester Jesus to gather as much information as they could to accuse him to the authorities. Accusing Jesus of violating the Sabbath provided the excuse to consider him in violation of the law of Moses. The Herodians (a political party) joined the Pharisees in their plan to kill Jesus. All Jesus' faithful followers could do at this point was to pray faithfully and expect the Father to protect his Son. Pharisaical opposition was now out in the open.

The Pharisees had laid down the gauntlet: they could allow Jesus to proclaim his power and stand by as people believed his message or destroy him by whatever means possible.

The choice was simple, and a plan that would forever change history was about to be set into motion.

JESUS' EARLY MINISTRY IN GALILEE
(Spring – Fall AD 31)

Cana:
   Came again to Cana (John 4:46)
Capernaum:
   Jesus' new home in Capernaum (Matt. 4:13)
   Jesus calls four disciples (Matt. 4:18–22)
   Demonic healed in synagogue (Mark 1:21–26)
   Peter's mother-in-law healed (Matt. 8:14–17)
   Call of Matthew (Mark 2:13–14)
   Child healed in Capernaum while Jesus in Cana (John 4:46–54)
Nazareth:
   Jesus rejected (Luke 4:16–30)
Jerusalem/Galilee:
   Sabbath controversies (Matt. 12:1–14; John 5)

CHAPTER 5

MESSIANIC DISCOURSE: THE SERMON ON THE MOUNT AND PARABLES BY THE SEA

SPRING AD 31? – FALL AD 31

Matthew 12:15 – 13:53; Mark 3:7 – 4:34; Luke 6:12 – 8:21 (T&G 52 – 64)

WITH A RENEWED AWARENESS that the authorities were seeking his destruction, Jesus withdrew to the Sea of Galilee. However, he could not escape the multitudes that followed him from Judea, Jerusalem, Idumea, Decapolis, Tyre, and Sidon. They heard about his message that the kingdom of God was at hand and that he had performed miracles to authenticate his message.

Those gathering around Jesus wanted desperately to be healed. They forced their way close enough to him to touch his garments. Jesus knew when he was in the presence of unclean spirits. He acknowledged their question when they asked, "Are you the Son of God?" In the past, Jesus had silenced demons who acknowledged he was the Son of God because he did not want the testimony of demons, who are liars and followers of Satan, to confirm his authority (Mark 3:11 – 12).

At first glance, Jesus' response to silence demons may be puzzling. Early in his ministry, he used miracles to "get the word out" and proclaimed his message publicly and confrontationally, using healing to authenticate his message. But Jesus never allowed Satan to testify for him. Later in Jesus' ministry, after the Jewish leaders and many Jews rejected him, he spent more time teaching his disciples privately. In this phase of his ministry, he did not want the crowds following him. They had already demonstrated they wanted a Messiah on their own terms, and it no longer served Jesus' purpose to heal the masses, because miracles no longer gained more followers. What terms would they accept? Jesus turned to the message that cleared the confusion and answered their fundamental question.

SERMON ON THE MOUNT
(Matthew 5:1 – 7:27; Mark 3:13 – 19; Luke 6:12 – 49; T&G 53 – 54h)

Although he may have appeared tireless, Jesus was fully human, and the rigors of preaching, teaching, and mentoring the disciples were exhausting. Jesus attempted to escape the crowds by going up the mountain of Eremos west of Capernaum, just above Sower's Cove. There, resting in the tall grass, he appointed the twelve apostles and sent them out, giving them authority to cast out demons and preach the kingdom of God.

Although exhaustion pulled at his spirit, Jesus' mission called for a night in prayer. The weeks, and even months, prior had taken a toll on him. Only one thing could keep life in eternal perspective — communication with his heavenly Father was the heartbeat of his strength from day to day.[1]

As the disciples drew near the mountain of Eremos, they were surprised to see a scene they did not anticipate: a huge crowd of followers waiting to get a glimpse of Jesus. They seemed eager to hear what he had to say. Of course, some came only for healing, but others heard reports and wanted to hear Jesus' message for themselves. If, as Jesus proclaimed, the kingdom of God was near, what kind of righteousness would make it possible for them to enter

The hill traditionally known as Mount Eremos, between Tabgha and Capernaum, just above the Cove of the Sower, in close proximity to important places in Jesus' ministry

The suggestion of this hill for the location of the Sermon on the Mount is strongly supported. The spacious hillside provides enough room for crowds to gather, as evidenced by the preparation for a hundred thousand Catholics to observe Mass nearby with the pope's visit in March 2000 (it rained and fewer came, but the space was available).

that kingdom? The Pharisees taught of an external righteousness by which God judged. And those same Pharisees followed Jesus, trying to persuade his followers that Jesus was a false prophet who could not be trusted.

And so the people came to hear for themselves.

Jesus moved among them, healing the sick and cleansing others from evil spirits. As he taught, his voice echoed throughout the valley, every word clear and precise. "Blessed are the poor in spirit...." Standing on the side of the Eremos mountain overlooking the beautiful Sea of Galilee with the snowy slopes of Mount Hermon painting a backdrop, Jesus gave a stirring message that moved hearts.

A soft sea breeze fanned the faces of his listeners as they sat on the green hillside. Some nodded in agreement as he presented the Beatitudes. "Blessed are those who hunger and thirst for righteousness, for they will be filled. Blessed are the merciful, for they will be shown mercy" (Matt. 5:6–7). Others thought pensively, *What wonderful concepts.*

Some of his listeners asked, "Who is this man whose words ring true and who speaks with such authority? Surely he must be the Son of God." Yet in the same crowd, detractors whispered their doubt: "Who does he think he is? No one has the right to speak with such authority but God himself."

The message Jesus delivered that day was unlike any the Jews had heard before. In his disciples' presence, he wanted to clarify the true nature of righteousness to the multitudes. The Pharisees taught that righteousness was gained through strict obedience to the letter of the law. Jesus caused a great stir in Galilee with his miracles and his message. John's message also raised serious questions for many Jews concerning the validity of the Pharisees' teaching on "righteousness." Now the crowds were seriously asking the 64,000-shekel question, "What kind of righteousness is necessary for entrance into this kingdom that Jesus talks about?"

Jesus clearly rejected the Pharisees' teaching when he said in a steady voice, "I tell you that unless your righteousness surpasses that of the Pharisees and the teachers of the law, you will certainly not enter the kingdom of heaven" (Matt. 5:20). Their distortion of the law led them to practice hypocrisy.

THE BEATITUDES (Matthew 5:3–12; Luke 6:20–26; T&G 54b)

The "big idea" in Jesus' Sermon on the Mount is that God's concept of holiness exceeds the Pharisees' legalistic interpretation of Moses' law. The sermon begins with the famous "Beatitudes" (blessings) describing the characteristics of a righteous person and the basis for receiving God's blessing. The person who displays these clearly defined characteristics possesses these principles of true righteousness. One enters the kingdom of God through personal repentance and faith, by which he or she receives the righteousness of Christ.

The eight beatitudes do not describe eight different kinds of people (poor in spirit, mournful, meek, etc.) and eight different kinds of rewards (kingdom of heaven, comfort, inheritance of the earth, etc.). Rather, they describe the qualities of one person who will receive one reward—entrance into God's kingdom. Those who receive the kingdom of heaven are those who inherit the earth, are comforted, will see God, and will be called children of God. These people are indeed blessed, though until the kingdom comes they may face great persecution, just as the prophets did.

SALT AND LIGHT TO THE WORLD
(Matthew 5:13–48; Luke 6:27–36; T&G 54c–54e)

Addressing a Jewish audience consisting of his disciples and the curious, Jesus proclaimed that God intended them to be salt and light to the nations. Salt creates a thirst for the righteousness of God, and light attracts others to the message of the gospel (Matt. 5:13–16). Israel had been placed in the center of the nations (Ezek. 5:5) and was in danger of failing their commission.

Pharisees' Interpretation of the Law and Practice Rejected
(Matthew 6:1 – 7:6; Luke 6:37 – 42; T&G 54f – 54g)

Jesus' message was clear: he came to fulfill the law, not to destroy it. His message exposed the Pharisees' ignorance and false application of the law. Point by point, Jesus articulated his message to his listeners.

Jesus repeated the phrase six times: "You have heard that it was said … but I tell you…" He made it clear that he wanted no part of the Pharisees' corrupt doctrines and practices as he stated the true intent of the law. In each case, Jesus' alternative to the law focused on the intent of the heart regarding God's commandment.

Portion of Hebrew scroll from the Pentateuch

D. Brake

Jesus' explanation that the righteousness of the Pharisees was not good enough to qualify someone to enter the kingdom seemed shocking (Matt. 5:21 – 6:18). So, adding fuel to the fire, Jesus contrasted the Pharisees' definition of righteousness with God's demands. For instance, the Pharisees said that someone was guilty of murder if they killed a person. But Jesus explained that someone could break the sixth commandment based on their attitude and thoughts. The Pharisees deemed divorce acceptable if a certificate was given, but Jesus explained that divorce results in adultery. As Jesus taught, he repudiated the Pharisaic version of the law of Moses, making it clear that what God truly demanded in the Mosaic law was much more difficult to fulfill. But the question remained: Who can enter the kingdom of God? Jesus' answer was only those who are like God himself.

Because they misunderstood the law, the Pharisees practiced a false, legalistic religion. Their perversion of acts of righteousness, such as giving alms to the poor, praying out loud in public, and fasting focused on outward reward, rather than on inward righteousness. Jesus saw them for what they were: hypocrites.

MOUNT OF THE BEATITUDES

The traditional site of Jesus' Sermon on the Mount is a small hill just above Tabgha called the Eremos. The hills of this area are dotted with bright green grass, red poppies, and wild cyclamens. From the hillside one can see the lake and the surrounding villages. In the spring, the site offers a breathtaking view in the early morning sunrise above the hills of the Golan Heights. This area overlooks the often glassy Sea of Galilee with the Golan Heights and the Jordan hills in the background. The earliest identification of this mount as the site of Jesus' sermon dates to the pilgrim Egeria in the late fourth century when she identified a cave in the hillside at Tabgha as where the Lord ascended to preach the Beatitudes.[2]

Matthew 5:1 refers to the hill as a mountain, and Luke 6:17–20 speaks of it as a plain (level place). It should be remembered that westerners often see a "mountain" in Israel as a "hill." This "mountain" is not to be compared to the one Moses went up to receive the Law. The mountain referred to as Eremos is a hill overlooking the Sea of Galilee that swoops down to the water. The hill gives way to many suitable level areas where Jesus addressed the crowds. This location was a logical geographical place to deliver the sermon and provided excellent acoustics.

The famous Italian architect Antonio Barluzzi built a Roman Catholic Church on top of the hill with eight sides representing the eight beatitudes. The mosaic floor uses the seven virtues mentioned in the sermon as its motif. The inlaid designs in blue and gold represent the colors of the Sea of Galilee at different times of the day.

Cove of the Sower and Mount of Beatitudes

INSTRUCTIONS FOR THE RIGHTEOUS
(Matthew 7:7 – 8:1; Luke 6:31, 43 – 49; T&G 54h – 54i)

Jesus concluded the Sermon on the Mount by giving people a clear choice: either follow the Pharisees down the broad road to destruction or follow Jesus on the narrow path into the kingdom. The real proof of people's character is not what they claim but what they produce. The wise will take Jesus' words to heart and build their lives on them. Those who ignore Jesus' call to righteousness will be destroyed like the house built on the sand. "But" said Jesus, "the one who hears my words and does not put them into practice is like a man who built a house on the ground without a foundation. The moment the torrent struck that house, it collapsed and its destruction was complete" (Luke 6:49).

The crowds sat, amazed, as Jesus finished speaking. Then slowly a murmur rustled through them as one man spoke, and the message of affirmation rippled through the crowd. For many, Jesus' words provided all the confirmation they hoped and prayed for. "He is teaching as one having authority and not as the teachers of the law," they said (see Matt. 7:29). The message of God's kingdom was presented and now stood before them. But a presentation of the facts themselves was not enough. Jesus continued to aggressively spread his message.

JESUS' GROWING FAME AND INTENSIVE DEBATE
(Matthew 7:28 – 8:13; 11:2 – 30; Luke 7:1 – 50; T&G 55 – 59)

Jesus' famous Sermon on the Mount (Matt. 5:1 – 7:29) laid the foundation for more controversy. As Jesus' opponents dug in their heels, some of his supporters grew weary and confused about his mission.

Meanwhile, John the Baptist had questions (Matt. 11:2–3). John, having preached that the kingdom was near, was expecting Jesus to establish the kingdom soon. It would seem reasonable, then, that John would be released from prison as part of that plan. But since John was still in prison, he wanted to know if the plan was still on. He sent his disciples to ask Jesus, "Are you the one who is to come, or should we expect someone else?" (Matt. 11:3). At first some disciples were disgusted with John, but now they began to sympathize with his confusion.[3] Jesus comforted him by explaining that the evidence of his miracles was sufficient. John should be patient and trust him.

In a few days at home, Jesus healed the demon-possessed man, heard the Pharisees' request for a miracle, and suffered through their rejection of him as their Messiah.

The others understood very well when Jesus said of John, "Among those born of women there has not risen anyone greater than John the Baptist." Of course, he went on to say, "Whoever is least in the kingdom of heaven is greater than he" (Matt. 11:11). Jesus made it clear: John was greater than any prophets who foretold the coming of the Messiah because John introduced the Messiah. And yet the least in God's kingdom is greater than John. The meaning of this message confused some, but those destined for the kingdom knew what he meant and found comfort. Jesus knew his life on earth would be cut short. Above all, he knew he was the Son of God. The time had arrived for him to present himself as Messiah.

Jesus retreated to the seashore. What happened next was the watershed moment of his career. The Jewish leaders accused Jesus of demon possession, preaching under false authority, and breaking the law of Moses.

The Watershed in the Life of Jesus
(Matthew 12:22 – 50; Mark 3:20 – 35; Luke 8:1 – 21; T&G 60 – 63)

Jesus' next miracle changed the direction of his ministry. He healed a demon-possessed man who was both blind and mute. The crowd immediately recognized that this act signified that Jesus was the Son of David, a messianic title. "All the people were astonished and said, 'Could this be the Son of David?'" But the Pharisees accused him of casting out the demons by the power of Beelzebul. "It is only by Beelzebul, the prince of demons, that this fellow drives out demons" (Matt. 12:23 – 24).

Jesus' followers knew that meant trouble. And his words confirmed their worst fears when he spoke sternly, "Anyone who speaks a word against the Son of Man will be forgiven, but anyone who speaks against the Holy Spirit will not be forgiven, either in this age or in the age to come" (Matt. 12:32).

The disciples were shell-shocked. "The Pharisees will never accept his teachings now!" And sure enough, Jesus did not preach, "The kingdom of God is at hand" again. The direction of his message changed from a focus on the multitudes to training the disciples — and soon his death and resurrection.

Jesus sent the twelve disciples out with specific instructions: "Do not go among the Gentiles or enter any town of the Samaritans. Go rather to the lost sheep of Israel" (Matt. 10:5 – 6). Yet at the end of his earthly ministry his challenge was clearly a universal mission: "Therefore go and make disciples of all nations, baptizing them in the name of the Father and of the Son and of the Holy Spirit, and teaching them to obey everything I have commanded you" (Matt. 28:19 – 20).

ORIGINS OF RABBINIC JUDAISM

The destruction of the temple in Jerusalem in AD 70 brought dramatic changes in Judaism. Jewish leaders met at the city of Yavneh in AD 90 to restructure Judaism. Yavneh replaced Jerusalem as the new seat of authority of a reconstituted Sanhedrin. First-century Judaism was built on temple rituals, but the new reality called for a new form of Judaism. Temple rituals were replaced with an emphasis on obedience, and prayer conducted in synagogues developed during the Babylonian exile. The previous oral laws were codified in the Mishnah and became the primary source for sanctioned behavior.

Originally Jewish scholarship was oral. Rabbis expounded and debated the law as expressed in the Hebrew Bible without other written sources. The new realities called for new literature.

The Talmud has two components: the Mishnah (c. AD 200), the first written synopsis of Judaism's oral law, and the Gemara (c. AD 500), a commentary on the Mishnah. The Talmud contains the opinions of rabbis on these topics. The Talmud is the basis for all codes of the reconstructed rabbinic Judaism.

Mishnah does not develop new laws, but is a collection of existing oral laws, traditions, and conventional wisdom. The Gemara is the part of the Talmud that contains rabbinical commentaries and analysis of the Mishnah.

Halakah includes religious practices and beliefs as well as many aspects of day-to-day life. It is considered the "Jewish Law" and contains the collective body of religious laws, including biblical law, traditions, and customs.

Midrash is a method of interpreting biblical stories that goes beyond recounting the moral and religious teachings to include additional material to fill in gaps omitted in the biblical narrative.

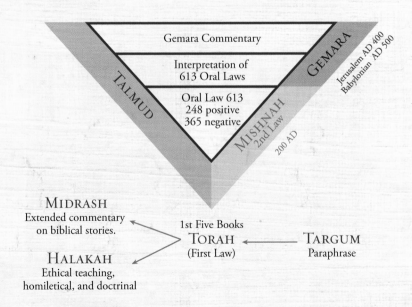

Why did Jesus' message change? Did Jesus change his mind? Or was this his intention all along? The nation of Israel to whom he came rejected him. Yet the rejection did not come as a surprise to God; it was anticipated in the Old Testament (Isa. 53:3–12).

The disciples thought they had heard everything. But while they were standing outside Peter's house, they heard with their own ears the hypocritical scribes and Pharisees ask Jesus for a sign (Matt. 12:38). Their words dripped with falsehood. They had seen signs for days and weeks; how dare they ask again? They were obviously trying to set a trap.

Jesus' response to the Pharisees' request sealed his fate. He responded directly to their request: "A wicked and adulterous generation asks for a sign! But none will be given it except the sign of the prophet Jonah. For as Jonah was three days and three nights in the belly of a huge fish, so the Son of Man will be three days and three nights in the heart of the earth" (Matt. 12:39–40).

A concerned onlooker interrupted Jesus to tell him that his mother and brother wanted to talk to him. Jesus' reply undoubtedly shocked some of his listeners: "Who is my mother, and who are my brothers?" Then he pointed at the disciples and continued, "Here are my mother and my brothers. For whoever does the will of my Father in heaven is my brother and sister and mother" (Matt. 12:48–50).

Jesus' family are those who do his will, whether a nuclear family or obedient followers. He was undoubtedly making a veiled reference to the Jewish leadership's rejection of him — the rejection of his own "tribe" and family.

Mary would certainly have felt hurt by her Son's words. But she also knew Jesus was not an ordinary son and that, above all, he had been sent to earth to do the will of his heavenly Father. This moment was perhaps Mary's watershed moment, as she laid aside her earthly role as mother of Jesus and stepped into her own new role as follower of the Son of God.

THE KINGDOM PARABLES
(Matthew 13:1–53; Mark 4:1–34; Luke 8:4–18; T&G 64a–64k)

The nation's leadership rejected Jesus as their Messiah and King. Jesus now turned to training the disciples and introduced this new direction in a series of parables.

Jesus headed down the mountain to the seaside followed by a great number of people. Just outside Jesus' house in Capernaum on the beautiful shore of Galilee, he began preaching the famous parables detailed in Matthew.

When the crowds overwhelmed the area, Jesus stepped into a boat with the disciples. Anchored off the shore of the Cove of Capernaum, Jesus continued to address the crowds; then later in confidence he revealed the meaning of the parables to his disciples.

The disciples turned to each other as Jesus began to speak. They were surprised by this new way of teaching. Although he had occasionally used parables before, he now was using them as his primary means of teaching.

After listening to his first parable about the sower and the seeds, the disciples questioned his method. "Why are you teaching in parables?"

Jesus' answer was succinct, "The knowledge of the secrets of the kingdom of heaven has been given to you, but not to them" (Matt. 13:11). The leaders of Israel rejected the message of the "kingdom of God" and squandered their opportunity to know more. Jesus offered no further word for them. Teaching in parables disclosed the truth to true disciples but hid it from unbelievers. Jesus didn't bother to separate the crowds that followed him into believers and unbelievers. He simply spoke his message, and his words produced a dividing of thoughts and intents in the souls of his followers.

Because the disciples did not fully understand what Jesus meant by his parables, he invited them into the house where he spent time explaining their meaning. Mary Magdalene always enjoyed learning more about the things of God as the men discussed and laughed together. It seemed her hungry heart could not absorb the truth quickly enough as Jesus talked and clarified his message. Once the disciples understood the basic truth that the parables

Cove of the Sower. Can a person stand at the top of the hill and hear a speaker at water's edge? On a still day when cars are not passing by on the road, the answer is yes. Groups scattered across the hillside have heard the speaker's voice, distinctly and without difficulty in understanding every word. Furthermore, conversations between people separated by distance are also possible in this cove.

taught about the kingdom of God, they were able to use the same principles to interpret Jesus' other parables later.

Jesus spent much of his ministry explaining his work and words to common men and women as well as to the leaders of the nation. He called on both the nation and individuals to respond to the evidence he presented. The Pharisees and leaders accused him of doing his miracles by the power of Satan. When they rejected God's kingdom, Jesus changed his message. From this time forward, the cross, not the throne, became his central message. The message of the kingdom was not abandoned but delayed.

The content of the parables detailing the kingdom of God extend over the period of Israel's rejection of the Messiah to his reception in the future. This time frame includes the rest of Jesus' life and throughout the rest of history until he returns in power and glory to reign on his throne, the throne of David.

Access to the kingdom was taken from Israel. "Therefore I tell you that the kingdom of God will be taken away from you and given to a people who will produce its fruit" (Matt. 21:43). The parables describe the mysteries of the future form of the kingdom in the hands of this "other people." That is why Jesus said, "The knowledge of the secrets of the kingdom of heaven has been given to you, but not to them" (Matt. 13:11). He repeatedly reminded them of this truth when he said, "The kingdom of heaven is like..."

The parables of Matthew 13 are given as specific aspects of the kingdom of the present age. The Old Testament prophets had much to say about the

PARABLES

A parable is a literary device that uses common events or everyday cultural practices to clarify or emphasize a spiritual truth. It can employ a metaphor (John 10:7), similitude (Matt. 13:33), story (Luke 16:1–13), or a proverb (Luke 4:23). The parables of Matthew 13 are used to reveal truth to the disciples and to hide the truth from unbelievers, perhaps as an act of grace to prevent heaping more judgment on them (Matt. 11:21–24).

To understand a parable, the reader must thoroughly understand the history, culture, and customs of the day. It is important to interpret only those details central to the main idea of the parable. Behind every parabolic meaning is a literal truth. Parables require literal interpretation from the known to the unknown. Parables do not grant license to let the reader's imagination seize on every detail for spiritual embellishment, but an opportunity to find the central, literal meaning or application of the parable.

CITIES AROUND THE SEA OF GALILEE

Tiberias

Herod Antipas, son of Herod the Great, founded the city of Tiberias in AD 19.[5] Early coins dated "the year 24" (of Antipas) help date the city. Because the founding builders came

Tiberias from the north

upon an ancient Jewish cemetery in Tiberias, Antipas had trouble populating it with Jews.[6] He even offered free houses, land, and an exemption from taxes for the first few years for anyone who would move into the new city.[7] He finally felt compelled to populate his new capital by force. Antipas named the city after his patron, the emperor Tiberius.

No record exists that suggests Jesus went to Tiberias. Undoubtedly his travels took him very near the city, but Herod's threat is the most likely reason Jesus did not frequent the area (Luke 13:31). The Gospels note that some of Jesus' followers lived in Tiberias (John 6:23), but the Gentile flavor of the city prevented religious Jews from embracing it. Its therapeutic hot springs may explain the attraction for sick people who came to Jesus for healing. Jesus predicted judgment on Korazin, Bethsaida, and Capernaum, and they vanished. He did not pronounce judgment on Tiberias, and it remains a thriving city.

Nof Ginosar

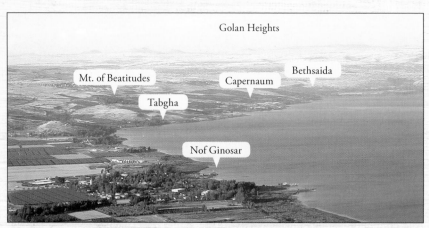

Traveling by boat to Bethsaida, Jesus and his disciples were blown off course and landed instead at the region of Gennesaret.

Nof Ginosar

A drought in Galilee in 1985 brought water levels in the sea to previously unknown levels. It exposed undetected harbors, and in January 1986, men discovered the remains of an ancient boat. Archaeologists carefully preserved the remains and housed them in a museum at Nof Ginosar near Tiberias. Though we cannot say that Jesus or his disciples used this boat, this is the same kind of boat used by fishermen in the first century.

Josephus referred to Magdala as one of the two main administrative centers in the region, along with Tiberias. Magdala was also known as Taricheae (place for salting fish), according to Josephus, which indicates that it was an important fishing center.[8]

Immorality was prevalent in Magdala, and it also became a base for Zealots in the first Jewish revolt. Josephus tells of a great sea battle fought here against the Romans during the revolt. The Jews lost, and the Romans put twelve thousand of the inhabitants of the city to death in the theater of Tiberias. They sent another six thousand to build Nero's canal in Corinth, and an additional thirty thousand were sold into slavery.

This fishing village is never mentioned explicitly in Scripture, but Mary Magdalene "from whom seven demons had come out" lived here (Luke 8:2). Matthew called it Magadan (15:39). The "region of Dalmanutha" (Mark 8:10) appears to be equivalent to the "vicinity of Magadan" (Matt. 15:39). The Aramaic word *dalmynyth* means "of the harbor." It could be said that "Matthew recorded the arrival of Christ in the neighborhood of Magadan (Magdala), whereas Mark, who depended on the preaching of Peter, recorded that Jesus had reached the site of the harbor."[9]

All the settlements along the lake had harbors, even if they were very small. They varied in structure, depending on the town's particular need. However, common to all were facilities such as breakwaters, quays (waterways for parking boats), promenades, administrative buildings, storage facilities, boat repair shops, toll houses, and watchtowers.

First-century boat used on the Sea of Galilee (a.k.a. the "Jesus Boat"). In 1986 a wooden vessel from the first century was discovered near Nof Ginosar on the lake's northwestern shore. Studies have determined it was made of cedar and oak, and from the wood and pottery found in it, it belonged to the first century. It measures 26 by 7 feet, big enough for fifteen men. It has thus been called the "Jesus Boat."

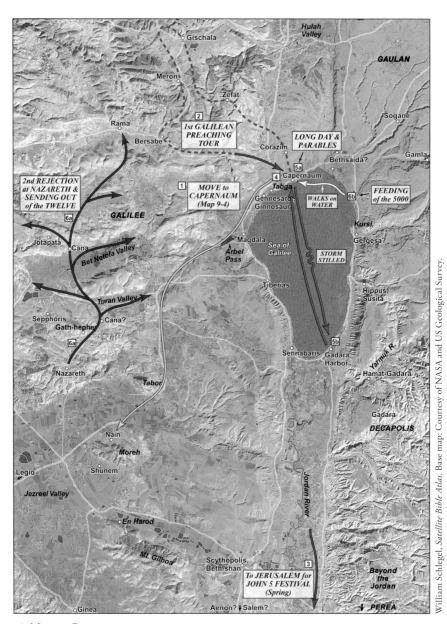

William Schlegel, *Satellite Bible Atlas*. Base map: Courtesy of NASA and US Geological Survey.

1. Move to Capernaum
2. First tour of Galilee — Preaching and performing miracles
3. To Jerusalem for festival — Lame man healed at Pools of Bethesda
4. Sermon on the Mount
5a. Parables by the Sea
5b. Healing of the Gadarene
6a. Second rejection. Twelve sent out
6b. Feeding of the 5,000 and walking on water, then to Capernaum for sermon on the Bread of Life.

fulfillment of the covenant given to Abraham (Gen. 12:1–3; 15:18), to Moses (Deut. 28–30), to David (2 Sam. 7:4–16), and to Jeremiah (31:31–34). The Messiah will return to fulfill his promises to his people. His coming promises redemption and a new kingdom that will be a reign of peace and righteousness (known as the millennial kingdom). In these parables, Jesus is explaining new truths about the kingdom, the same kingdom predicted in the Old Testament and the one Jesus preached.

In the parable of the sower, Jesus reveals that his teaching about the kingdom is going to be largely rejected. Only one of four soils receives the seed and bears fruit (Matt. 13:1–23).

In the parable of the weeds, Jesus reveals that Israel is a mixture of the righteous and wicked, which will be sorted out in the judgment before the kingdom is established (13:24–30, 36–43). In other words, because Jesus' teaching will not be accepted by all, there will be a period of time in which good and evil will flourish before Jesus establishes the kingdom. (The period before the kingdom is not the kingdom.)[4]

The description of the mustard seed doesn't mean that the kingdom will be small and insignificant, for one day it will flourish like a tree and permeate the whole earth (13:31–35).

The parables of the hidden treasure and of the pearl teach that the kingdom is worth any amount of sacrifice, and pursuing its entrance is necessary (13:44–46).

The parable of the net reminds the readers that those who do not enter the kingdom will experience horrible judgment. "The angels will come and separate the wicked from the righteous and throw them into the blazing furnace, where there will be weeping and gnashing of teeth" (13:47–50).

In light of the rejection of the kingdom, there will be a delay in establishing the kingdom that was once near.

Jesus insisted that the disciples needed to understand these new truths about the kingdom, together with the previous revelation given in the Scriptures, as they went forth teaching others. " 'Have you understood all these things?' Jesus asked. 'Yes' they replied" (13:51–52).

JESUS' WORDS AND WORKS IN HIS MINISTRY AROUND CAPERNAUM
AD 31–32

Sea of Galilee:
    Stilled storm (Mark 4:35–41)
    Walked on water (Mark 6:47–52)

Gadara harbor (HaOn):
    Sent demons into swine (Mark 5:1–20)

Bethsaida (or Tabgha?):
    Fed 5,000 (Mark 6:35–44)

Capernaum:
    Called four disciples (Tabgha) (Matt. 4:18–22; Luke 5:1–11)
    Taught in synagogue (Mark 1:21–22)
    Healed demoniac in synagogue (Mark 1:23–26)
    Short circuit to nearby villages (Matt. 4:23–25)
    Healed paralytic (Luke 5:17–26)
    Called Matthew (Levi) (Luke 5:27–28)
    Withdrew from masses (Mark 3:7–12)
    Twelve disciples named (Mark 3:13–19)
    Sermon on the Mount (Matt. 5:1–7:27)
    Healed centurion's servant (Matt. 8:1, 5–13)
    Healed Jairus's daughter (Mark 5:21–24, 35–43)
    Healed two blind men (Matt. 9:27–31)
    Healed demon-possessed man (Matt. 12:22–37)
    Visited by mother and brothers (Matt. 12:46–50)
    Parables by the sea (Matt. 13:1–52)

Nazareth:
    Preached and rejected (Luke 4:16–30)
    Second rejection (Mark 6:1–6)
    Sent Twelve out (Matt. 10:1–42)

Magdala?:
    Feet anointed by sinner (Luke 7:36–50)

Tiberias:
    Recounting of John's death perhaps in Tiberias(?) (Matt. 14:1–12)

Nain:
    Raised widow's son (Luke 7:11–17)
    John sought confirmation of Messiah (Matt. 11:2–19)

MESSIAH FACES INTENSE OPPOSITION: THE CALL TO TRUE FAITH

SUMMER AD 31 – SPRING 32
Matthew 8:18 – 9:38; 13:54 – 18:35; Mark 4:35 – 9:50;
Luke 8:22 – 9:62; John 6:1 – 7:1 (T&G 65 – 93)

TRAINING THE DISCIPLES IN THEIR FAITH
(Matthew 8:18, 23 – 27; Mark 4:35 – 41; Luke 8:22 – 25; T&G 65)

Jesus finished a full day of teaching parables by late afternoon. By the time he reached the beach of the Sea of Galilee,[1] night nearly overtook him and his disciples, but the crowd wanted more. He instructed his apostles-in-training to take him to the other side of the sea. As he climbed into the boat, a number of other boats may have come alongside, so he encouraged the disciples to set sail quickly. Before long the winds

Modern passenger boat on the Sea of Galilee

LC-matpc-07411-t/www.LifeintheHolyLand.com

Small fishing boats with fish on Sea of Galilee

began to blow in a typical fall storm, and those attempting to follow them would have turned back.[2]

A violent storm erupted as Jesus and the disciples headed across the water toward Kursi. The storm tossed the small boat like a leaf in the wind, and the waves washed over the sides, drenching the men and nearly swamping the well-tested vessel. Although many of the disciples were seasoned fishermen and sailors, the raging storm frightened them. Jesus lay calmly enjoying a much needed restful sleep in the back of the boat. The disciples, however, were anything but calm. In their panic, they tried to awaken Jesus by shaking him and shouting his name.

Jesus woke from his slumber and stood in the center of the rocking boat. With a sweep of his hands, he spoke a command into the tumult: "Quiet! Be still" (Mark 4:39). As the words fell from his lips, the wind stilled and the sea returned to glass.

The disciples stared at one another in wonder, trying to process what they had just witnessed. Only Peter spoke, muttering to himself as he shook his head.

The peaceful calm of the Sea of Galilee can quickly become transformed by violent storms. Winds funnel through the east-west aligned Galilee hill country and stir up the waters quickly. Even more violent are the winds that come off the hills of the Golan Heights to the east. Trapped in the basin, the winds can be deadly to fishermen. A storm in March 1992 sent waves 10 feet high crashing into downtown Tiberias, causing significant damage.

"That was impossible. But, of course, Jesus **made** it possible. And we saw it..." Peter's voice trailed away.

Jesus turned to the disciples. "Why are you so afraid? Do you still have no faith?" Their faces revealed the answer to his question. After all they had experienced in the past months, they still struggled with their faith, and the Master's simple question embarrassed them. It also provoked new fear.

Yes, they were called to be disciples of Jesus. And that meant they were called to follow the divine Son of God who ruled creation itself. Who knew where their journey with this Jesus might take them?

The men survived both a hard day and a stormy night. The storm may have blown them off course so that they ended up in a southern harbor rather than the sardine fishing harbor of Kursi.

HEALING OF THE DEMONIACS
(Matthew 8:28 – 34; Mark 5:1 – 20; Luke 8:26 – 39; T&G 66)

Gadara harbor area

As the disciples docked their boat, a naked man in shackles suddenly charged them. His strength proved too much for anyone to subdue him. As the skittish men turned to reboard the boat and clear out, Jesus calmly walked toward the raving maniac. The man ran to Jesus and bowed down at his feet. Onlookers stood spellbound as Jesus asked the man his name. The demoniac responded that his name was Legion because many demons controlled him.

The terrified demons immediately spoke and begged Jesus to leave them alone. By now a few onlookers had gathered, and every eye was glued on Jesus. What would he do? What could he do? Certainly no man had the ability to command the powers of darkness. But everything about this Jesus was different — the

En Gev harbor

way he spoke of God as if he were his own father, the way he defied religious tradition, not to mention the power he displayed through his miracles.

THE LOCATION OF THE SWINE DIVE

Many Bibles include footnotes where Matthew, Mark, and Luke name the place where Jesus sent the demons into a herd of pigs. The oldest manuscripts of Matthew locate the miracle in the region of the Gadarenes, but other manuscripts read Gerasenes or Gergesenes. The earliest texts of Mark and Luke place Jesus in the region of the Gerasenes.[4] Because a significant amount of confusion exists, even among experts in the field, a few words of explanation can help to sort out the matter.

Kursi cliff view to the north, a traditional site of the pig incident

HaOn from above, the area of the ancient harbor of Gadara (Mark 5:1 – 20).[5] The likely location of the pig incident

According to Matthew, the miracle occurred in the region of the city of Gadara, but some scholars have criticized this view because Gadara is six miles southeast of the Sea of Galilee. Scholars who hold this view believe the distance is too far for pigs to run. Yet Matthew does not write that the miracle occurred in the city of Gadara but in the region. Recent archaeological finds show that Gadara controlled territory as far as the shore of the Sea of Galilee. In fact, the largest harbor on the lake belonged to Gadara. Coins from Gadara from the second century depict ships engaging in naval war games, an indication of the importance of the harbor area to the city. There is no reason to doubt that Gadara is an accurate location for the miracle.

Mark and Luke, however, place the miracle in the region of the city of Gerasa. How could a city twenty-five miles further inland be identified as the location where pigs drowned in the lake? The answer is to be found in the audiences for the gospels of Mark and Luke. While Matthew was writing to a more local Jewish audience, Mark and Luke were telling the story of Jesus to people throughout the Roman Empire who had little familiarity with the land of Israel. Gerasa was a major city, well-known throughout the world of that time. Mark and Luke thus chose the name of the famous Gentile city to help their audiences understand. We might compare it with a famous figure today who claims Portland, Oregon, as his place of origin, but to those familiar with the area, he explains that he grew up in the suburb of Tigard.

Visitors today are often taken to a steep slope or shown a Byzantine church at Kursi. This site may have been known as Gergesa in the first century. It is an easy stop for tour groups, but there is no evidence that the miracle occurred here. Later Christians, including the church father Origen, appear to have altered some of the gospel manuscripts to read Gergesa because they thought that the readings of Gadara and Gerasa were mistaken. Fortunately, studies in textual criticism and archaeology allow us to identify the correct location today near present-day HaOn.

Hippos harbor. In Jesus' day, Hippos, a Decapolis city, was Rome's most intrusive footprint on the sea, a constant and visible reminder to the Jews that Rome had the land under its surveillance. Jesus' words "A town built on a hill cannot be hidden" (Matt. 5:14) had an authentic ring as he spoke to the disciples on the other side of the lake. The city certainly illuminated the horizon.[6]

Jesus ordered the demons to leave the man and enter a herd of pigs grazing nearby. Within seconds the pigs sprinted down the nearby slope and plunged into the water, thrashing and gasping for air.

Those who were tending the pigs ran off, and when the people in the village heard what had happened, they came running to find the former demoniac sitting quietly beside Jesus. What they saw and heard frightened them. They insisted Jesus leave immediately;[3] but in his gratitude, the delivered man spread the details of what had happened to everyone he encountered.

The healing of the demoniac probably took place in the region of Gadara. This event helped Jesus demonstrate his authority to the disciples. It also followed the Jewish leaders' rejection of Jesus' divine power in performing miracles. Jesus now turned to training the twelve disciples.

JESUS INTENSIFIES HIS TRAINING OF THE TWELVE: HEALING JAIRUS'S DAUGHTER AND THE WOMAN WITH A BLOOD MALADY
(Matthew 9:18 – 11:1; Mark 5:21 – 6:13; Luke 8:40 – 9:6; T&G 67 – 71a)

The time came for Jesus to cross over the Sea of Galilee and head back home to Capernaum. Not surprisingly, as he arrived on shore, a crowd gathered

FISHING IN THE SEA OF GALILEE

The disciples and Jesus spent a great deal of time in and around the Sea of Galilee. Many of the disciples were experienced fishermen. The Sea of Galilee, known for its wide variety of fish, provided them with a modest living.

Fish in the modern Sea of Galilee:[7]

Musht ("comb"; St. Peter's fish) have a long dorsal fin that looks like a comb (five species).

The barbels carp family (three species) have barbs at the corners of their mouths. When Jesus found the four-drachma coin in a fish's mouth, the fish was most likely a barbel (carp; Matt. 17:24–27).

Sardine fishing centers were located at Magdala and Kursi.

Catfish were the largest fish in the sea.

Net fishing in the Sea of Galilee

Tabgha is a fishermen's paradise. The warm winter waters at the site draw schools of fish to the springs, especially musht (St. Peter's fish). Fishing is especially good in spring and winter. Most of the events in the Gospels relating to fishing probably happened here.

Several types of fishing are done on the Sea of Galilee. Net fishing takes place with a variety of nets.

Seine (dragnet). This is the oldest type of net and one of the most important in the sea. A typical dragnet measures 275 feet long and 300 feet high and needs eight to ten men to handle it (cf. Matt. 13:47–48).

Cast-net circular net. This type of net measured 10 feet in diameter and had bars of lead attached to the edge. A single fisherman used it to catch sardines or large fish, depending on the size of the mesh. It is no longer in use (cf. Mark 1:16–18).

Trammel net. The fishing net used most today is the trammel net. It is a compound net consisting of three layers held together by a single corked head rope and single leaded footrope. Different

St. Peter's fish (musht)

sizes of trammel nets are used to catch catfish or musht (cf. Matt. 4:21–22; Mark 1:19–20; Luke 5:1–7).

Veranda net. This net is used for catching schools of musht.

Fishing net anchors in En Gev fishing museum

When the collectors of the two-drachma temple tax came to Peter in Capernaum and asked, "Doesn't your teacher pay the temple tax?" He replied, "Yes, he does." Jesus then asked Peter, "From whom do the kings of the earth collect duty and taxes — from their own children or from others?" Peter answered, "From others." Jesus then said, "Then the children are exempt," but he told Peter that to avoid offense, he should go to the lake and throw out his line. The first fish he caught would have a four-drachma coin that he could use to pay Jesus' tax as well as Peter's. Just as Jesus said, when Peter drew the fish out, he found a coin in its mouth (Matt. 17:24–27). The musht today is called "St. Peter's fish," but it could not have been the kind of fish Peter caught on this occasion because it is caught in nets, not with lines, and usually feeds on the bottom of the sea.[8]

Dragnet

around him, pressing in to get a glimpse of him, to be healed, and to hear him speak. As Jesus made his way through the crowd, a synagogue official named Jairus approached him. The man had left his daughter on her deathbed and

was distraught. As Jesus followed him through the crowd, a woman who had a serious bleeding disorder approached him. She had spent all of her funds on doctors, but her condition had only worsened. Desperation gripped her.

Believing that by simply touching Jesus' robe she could be healed, the woman reached out in faith. She knew she was violating the law that required an unclean woman to remain at a distance from others. But when she touched Jesus' garment, she was healed. In her simple act of faith, the woman embraced Jesus' authority as the Son of God.

The fringe (Hebrew *tzitzit*) was required to be on the four corners of the garment of every male in accordance with God's instructions (Num. 15:3; Deut. 22:12). Each fringe was personally crafted and symbolized the wearer's status (Matt. 23:5). The presence of *tzitzit* may be the reason the woman in Matt. 9:21 reached out to touch Jesus' garment.

While this was happening, word came that Jairus's daughter had died. From all appearances, Jesus was too late. The crowd pleaded with Jairus to do the sensible thing and not waste Jesus' time. But Jesus comforted Jairus with the words, "Don't be afraid; just believe, and she will be healed" (Luke 8:50), and made his way to Jairus's house.

When Jesus arrived at the house, he announced that the girl was just sleeping. The people knew she was dead, but the Messiah stirred life into her again through his powerful word and she arose, alive again.

As Jesus left Capernaum and headed toward Nazareth, he encountered two blind men who were crying out, "Have mercy on us, Son of David!" (Matt. 9:27–34). They obviously heard Jesus' messianic claims and wanted him to heal them—which he did. Jesus then made an unusual request: "See that no one knows about this." He proclaimed earlier that he would give no more signs other than the sign of Jonah, which would be his own resurrection from the dead. However, the blind men could not contain themselves, and they spread the news everywhere.

The synagogue at Capernaum: The dating of the synagogue is problematic, but it is clearly later than the first century. Excavations (the foundation under the current synagogue) have revealed a synagogue from the time of Jesus with walls made of worked stone four feet thick. In Capernaum Jesus healed the servant of the Roman centurion who was credited with building the synagogue (Luke 7:3).

Finally, Jesus arrived at his hometown of Nazareth where he began teaching in the synagogue (Matt. 13:54).[9] The people who knew him best used his humble origins as a reason to reject him, and this resulted in Jesus limiting the miracles he performed there because of their lack of faith. But rejection was not the only bad news Jesus faced; he was soon to learn the fate of his cousin John the Baptist.

THE DEATH OF A GREAT MAN — JOHN THE BAPTIST
(Matthew 14:3 – 12; Mark 6:17 – 29; T&G 71b)

John's fame had increased among the people. His actions reminded some people of Elijah. News of his death shocked people who had been exposed to his ministry — especially the disciples. Herod's fear and guilt in ordering John's execution was obvious in his words, "John, whom I beheaded, has been raised from the dead!" (Mark 6:16).

Even Jesus, who knew that John's eternal home was with the heavenly Father, grieved deeply and withdrew alone in a boat to a lonely place (Matt. 14:13).

John's death revealed insight into Jesus' soul and Jesus' love for his friend. John's life had been extraordinary and his deeds benevolent.

John's beheading took place at Machaerus, where Herod Antipas had imprisoned John for more than a year for his public condemnation of Herod's adulterous marriage to Herodias. Herod had built the highly fortified opulent palace of Machaerus overlooking the Dead Sea, and it is believed that Herod lured John to the palace under false pretenses and then imprisoned him there, closely guarded in a dungeon because of Herodias's hatred for him.

For a time, Herodias was unable to convince Herod to kill John because Herod feared John's holy character. However, at Herod's lavish birthday party, Herodias presented her daughter Salome as an exotic dancer who made a startling request. The guests were undoubtedly flushed with wine and raging hormones as Salome entranced the audience with her lewd dancing. Herod and his high-society guests were pleased, and he found himself caught in the snare of the wily Herodias. He promised to give the girl anything she asked, up to half of his kingdom. Salome, prompted by her mother, asked for John's head on a platter.

Herod, who was likely in a half-drunken stupor, realized he had been tricked. Reluctantly, he sent the executioner to fulfill the promise made to the wicked Herodias. Shortly afterward Herod journeyed to Rome seeking the title of king. Not only did he fail in being named king, but he was banished to Lugdumin in Gaul. Salome married her uncle Philip, tetrarch of Trachonitis and Batanea but soon became a widow and disappeared in history.[10]

The palace/fortress at Machaerus located at the top of a defensible hill. In the foreground is a spur that connects Machaerus to a hill to its south. An aqueduct system was built over this spur to bring water to cisterns along the side of the hill.

THE JOURNEY AROUND THE SEA
(Matthew 14:13 – 18:35; Mark 6:31 – 9:50; Luke 9:10 – 50; T&G 72b – 92)

The heartache Jesus experienced with the news of John's death did not dissuade him from continuing his ministry. In the spring of AD 32, just one year prior to Jesus' death, his work shifted from a predominately public ministry proclaiming the coming kingdom to an increasingly but not exclusively private ministry emphasizing his person and work as King. He would soon ask the disciples for their personal decision regarding his identity.

Jesus' first two years of constant conflict, confronting the masses, and training the disciples had taken its toll. Exhausted and in need of rest, Jesus and the Twelve retreated in a boat to a lonely place for much-needed relaxation. But this period of respite did not last long. People gathering on the shore saw them leave in a boat, and when Jesus and the disciples sailed toward the other side (to Bethsaida), the people ran along the shore to arrive before Jesus did (Mark 6:33; Luke 9:10). With his arrival, Jesus' intense ministry of about three months in the vicinity of the sea began.

FEEDING THE FIVE THOUSAND
(Matthew 14:15 – 21; Mark 6:35 – 44; Luke 9:12 – 17; T&G 72c)

The crowds that followed Jesus were enormous by first-century standards. Men and women came from villages miles distant to hear the Teacher's words. Perhaps Jairus's young daughter whom Jesus healed (Mark 5:21 – 43) ran the entire way to hear the one responsible for her full recovery. The news of Jesus' visit spread quickly, and she wanted to see him firsthand to both thank him and listen to his message.[11] That day she sat in awe as Jesus expounded the wonders of the kingdom message.

As evening approached after this particularly long day of teaching, the disciples busied themselves with meeting the physical needs of the people. They were in a remote place with no way to obtain food for thousands of people. Nevertheless, Jesus surprised them by ordering them to give the people something to eat. When they told him that all they could scrounge up was five loaves of bread and two fish (perhaps sardines or musht),[12] Jesus surprised them by miraculously multiplying it, producing enough food to feed five thousand men (adding women and children, perhaps more than ten thousand people in all), with twelve full baskets of fragments left over.[13]

Our speculation continues. When Jesus called for his followers to bring their lunches in order to feed everyone, Jairus's daughter was bewildered. *How can Jesus possibly feed us all with these few loaves and fishes?* she wondered.

The feeding of the five thousand most likely took place on the plain of Bethsaida. Mark 6:32 says the feeding took place at a "solitary place," and verse 39 says that the people sat down on "the green grass." After this, however, Jesus made his disciples go over "to Bethsaida." About five square miles (eight square kilometers) in area, the plain of Bethsaida is very spacious and is crisscrossed by streams, aqueducts, and irrigation canals. There are many flat areas on which it would be possible to seat large numbers of people.

The answer came as she patiently waited for the baskets to be passed to her. Bartholomew, one of Jesus' followers, offered the basket to a woman nearby. She watched as he reached down and pulled out the final loaf. But as he reached again for the man next to her, another loaf appeared, along with a fish — and then another and yet another. The bread and fish seemed to grow out of the baskets.

The crowds cheered and danced in celebration of the one they gladly wanted to accept as King. Jesus had reached the pinnacle of his popularity — even though popularity was never his goal. And the atmosphere of exuberance would be short-lived.

PETER'S WALK OF FAITH
(Matthew 14:24 – 33; Mark 6:47 – 52; John 6:16 – 21; T&G 74)

Following the feeding of the five thousand, Jesus told the disciples to cross over to the other side of the sea from Bethsaida to Gennesaret. He would come later. If he sent them off in the evening (about 6:00 – 9:00 p.m.; Mark 6:47) and rejoined them during the "fourth watch" (3:00 – 6:00 a.m.) in the

TABGHA (TABGA)

Jews inhabited the western side of the lake, whereas Gentiles lived primarily on the eastern side. Jesus spent most of his teaching time on the western shores of the Sea of Galilee among the Jews. Many of the events in the Gospels that are associated with fish took place at Heptapegon (modern Tabgha).[14]

LC-matpc-05555/www.LifeintheHolyLand.com

According to tradition, it was also where Jesus met with his disciples after the resurrection (John 21:1–25).

Tabgha lies just a short distance southwest of Capernaum, a small fishing village named after seven ancient hot springs that once functioned as a power source for a number of flour mills. The warm waters from the springs made for good fishing, especially for the winter fish called musht (St. Peter's fish).

The church built at Tabgha by the Franciscans in 1935 celebrates the feeding of the five thousand.[15] Some scholars support an alternate location as the place of this miracle. However, visitors are drawn to the large mosaic in the Tabgha church that depicts a basket with five loaves and a fish on each side of the basket.

Location of the traditional feeding of the five thousand at Tabgha

The church is called the Church of the Multiplication of Loaves and Fishes and is a typical Byzantine basilica with a central nave separated from aisles on each side by large colonnades. The large atrium at the entrance of the church was reserved for nonbaptized believers. Once they were initiated by baptism, they could enter the nave.

Fish and loaves mosaic at Tabgha. A commemorative Byzantine mosaic depicting a bread basket flanked by two fish representing the feeding of the five thousand is on the floor of the church. The fish appear to be of the musht family (tilapia, or St. Peter's fish), the fish most prominent in Tabgha. However, the artist apparently was unacquainted with the fish in the lake, as none have two dorsal fins.

Bethsaida from the east

morning (Mark 6:48), he was away from them for between nine and twelve hours. During this time, the disciples fought against a tumultuous storm on the Sea of Galilee.

Judas, who was not a seasoned fisherman,[16] would likely have been the first to complain about the surging storm. "Where is Jesus when we need him? Is he just going to sleep through this and let us drown? I thought he cared about us."

As the disciples fought against the raging waves, Simon spotted Jesus walking on the surface of the water.

Terrified, the disciples exclaimed, "It's a ghost!" As the figure drew near, Jesus spoke to them and identified himself. Although he told the men not to be afraid, his words of comfort did not immediately console everyone.

Bold Peter asked Jesus to tell him to come to him on the water, and when Jesus did, Peter stepped over the side of the boat into the stormy sea. The water was cold as it thrashed about his ankles, but his feet gripped the surface of the waves as though he were on solid ground. He fixed his eyes on Jesus and walked forward, trying to ignore the lashing of the water and the rolling waves that surrounded him. A clap of thunder split the clouds, and he glanced up as panic flooded his heart.

What am I doing? I must have been out of my mind, he thought, glancing down. The water was black and churning beneath his feet. In that instant, he felt his body begin to sink into the cold water. Terror tore through him. He was about to drown.

The grip of a strong hand on his arm pulled Peter's eyes away from the black water, and he looked up. Jesus stood before him, his hands extended.

"You of little faith; why did you doubt?" Jesus asked (Matt. 14:31).

Moments later the two were in the boat with the other disciples. Impetuous Peter was the only one of the twelve who had possessed enough faith to step out of the boat to meet his Master. Although his bravery faltered, as he began to sink, he knew that his rescue was secure in the hands of his Savior. From this time on, Peter assumed the role of leader of the disciples.

THE BREAD OF LIFE (John 6:22 – 59; T&G 76a)

Home again in Capernaum safe and sound, the disciples were ready for Jesus' next lesson. With the feeding of the five thousand fresh in their minds, Jesus identified himself as the "bread of life." He had already offered himself to the woman at the well as "living water" that permanently quenches thirst. One who eats the bread of life and drinks living water will never hunger or thirst.

But why did Jesus chose this time to speak about himself as the Bread of Life? Jesus was the Master Teacher and understood the importance of object lessons and timing. On the previous day, Jesus' miracle had paralleled Moses' feeding the Israelites with manna in the wilderness. The response of the people was predictable: someone this great should be their king and provide food for them every day.

The following day, the crowds found Jesus in the synagogue at Capernaum. Jesus knew what they were thinking, and he redirected their thinking by challenging their desire for physical food. He could feed them bread again today, but they would be hungry again tomorrow. What they really needed was a meal to satisfy their spiritual hunger. But the crowd didn't like this message, so they grumbled against him (just as the Israelites had grumbled against Moses in the wilderness). To accept Jesus for more than just physical bread required more commitment than they were willing to give. They wanted free food without any spiritual demands. The outcome was predictable—many left him.

The discourse on the Bread of Life had an amazing effect on those who heard it. Many of his disciples[17] who heard it said, "This is a hard teaching. Who can accept it?" (John 6:60). Peter, the new leader of the Twelve, boldly declared, "Lord, to whom shall we go? You have the words of eternal life" (6:68). The inquiring disciples became convinced disciples, but their commitment didn't quiet the opposition and hostility that continued toward Jesus and his message.

The spring flowers were blooming and the smell of freshly planted fields reinforced that this was the Promised Land. The newness of life from nature's cycle promised hope. But beneath the beauty, trouble was brewing. Would the Jews accept Jesus or reject him? Controversy hung like a thundercloud over the land, and a storm was about to break over the nation of Israel (Matt. 15:1–20).

MINISTRY IN TYRE AND SIDON
(Matthew 15:21–28; Mark 7:24–30; T&G 78)

Jesus' ministry focused directly on Israel. He instructed his disciples, "Do not go among the Gentiles or enter any town of the Samaritans. Go rather to the lost sheep of Israel" (Matt. 10:5–6). Then how do Gentiles fit into God's program, "Go and make disciples of all nations" (Matt. 28:19)?

Jesus' presented himself as the Messiah to Israel. The Gentiles did not yet have the Old Testament and were unprepared for the Messiah.[18] God's plan throughout the Old Testament included Israel as the carrier of his message and blessings to the nations. Jesus continued the same pattern. The Jewish leaders (Matt. 12) and Jewish masses (John 6) had recently rejected him. His ministry in Tyre and Sidon was a new phase of ministry in which he no longer tried to convince the nation of his identity. In order to get time alone with his disciples, he needed to withdraw to private places, including the region of Tyre and Sidon. Unfortunately, the news of his trip leaked out. A Gentile woman came to Jesus pleading for a miracle, and Jesus' resistance to her request provided her with an opportunity to demonstrate her faith in him. Unlike so many who were offended at Jesus' words, this humble woman believed and persisted in her request. Jesus honored her faith by healing her daughter.

JESUS GOES TO THE DECAPOLIS
(Matthew 15:29 – 17:20; Mark 7:31 – 9:29; Luke 9:18 – 43; T&G 79a – 87)

From Tyre and Sidon, Jesus continued his ministry in Gentile territory. Opposition from Jewish leaders gave Jesus the opportunity to continue his ministry on the east side of the Sea of Galilee in the Decapolis.

The feeding of the four thousand is a distinct miracle from the feeding of the five thousand. Matthew 16:9 – 10 mentions them together, "Do you still not understand? Don't you remember the five loaves for the five thousand, and how many basketfuls you gathered? Or the seven loaves for the four thousand, and how many basketfuls you gathered?" This miracle included Gentiles, while the feeding of the five thousand was primarily among the Jews.

Tel Hadar, two miles north of Kursi, which is located on the northeast side of the Sea of Galilee near the Wadi Samakh, is the traditional site for this miracle.[19] The waters at Kursi are known for their abundance of sardines, or "small fish" (Mark 8:7). Seven small baskets were collected after the multitudes were fed. These are distinguished from the large

Mosaic on the floor at Kursi depicting a pannier[21] (small basket) commemorating the feeding of the four thousand. Most likely the fish were sardines.[22] These baskets are distinguished from the larger baskets associated with the feeding of the five thousand.

D. Brake

Wadi Samakh from the west

baskets referred to in the feeding of the five thousand. The mosaic floors of the ruins of a Byzantine church depict these small baskets and commemorate the miracle.[20]

Jesus and the disciples left the Decapolis and arrived on the western shore of the Sea of Galilee, arriving in the region of Magadan (or Magdala, district of Dalmanutha). Once again, he encountered venomous attacks by the Pharisees and Sadducees. This time they were accusing him of teaching against the purity prescribed in the law. Having just come from feeding the five thousand and four thousand, Jesus took the opportunity to use the example of the leaven of the bread to confound the teachings of those opposing him. They understood perfectly that he was not talking about bread but about their teaching (Matt. 16:12). Time arrived for a midterm exam: how were the disciples progressing in their lessons? The test was about to be graded.

Kursi Byzantine church with mosaic floor depicting the feeding of the four thousand.

Magdala from the north

PETER'S CONFESSION
(Matthew 16:13 – 20; Mark 8:27 – 30; Luke 9:18 – 21; T&G 82)

From Magdala, Jesus and his disciples returned to their home in Capernaum. After a brief rest, they departed to seek solitude in the territory of Herod Philip. Unlike his brothers Archelaus and Antipas, Philip was not as suspicious of Jesus.

While in transit to Caesarea Philippi, Jesus took time to pray with the disciples. The opportunity came for him to ask the big question regarding his identity: "Who do people say I am?" Jesus asked them (Mark 8:27; cf. Matt. 16:13; Luke 9:18). He offered himself as King, but the leadership of Israel rejected him. How would those closest to Jesus respond to the same question? They listened to gossip and accusations as Jesus taught. Among themselves they listed possibilities: "Some say John the Baptist; others say Elijah; and still others, one of the prophets" (Mark 8:28; cf. Matt. 16:14; Luke 9:19).

Now the question was personal. For months Jesus had been training his disciples regarding faith and the kingdom of God. It was time for their midterm exam.

"But what about you? Who do you say I am?" (Mark 8:29; cf. Matt. 16:15; Luke 9:20).

Peter pounced on the question. "You are the Messiah, the Son of the living God" (Matt. 16:16).[23] But did Jesus view Peter's response as an answer for all the disciples? Even Judas? Or was he hoping to hear words that reflected the heart of each one of his disciples? Evidently Peter answered for all the disciples.

Jesus rewarded Peter's act of faith by giving him the keys to the kingdom, the building of the church (in Matthew's gospel only). The church Jesus is referring to is the one that began on the day of Pentecost (Acts 2) after his resurrection and ascension into heaven. Entrance into the church comes when individual believers are baptized by the Holy Spirit so as to form one body (1 Cor. 12:13).

Much has been written about what Jesus meant when he referred to Peter as the rock on which the church is built. Peter had just made a monumental declaration that Jesus is the Son of God. There seems to be a play on the word Peter (*petros*) (a small stone) and the foundation stone (a large rock) on which the church is to be built. The church will supply the leadership of the earthly administration and covenant aspect of God's work on earth until Jesus comes again. Darrell Bock puts it this way:

> The image pictures Jesus starting a new building, a new work. The gates of Hades — the authority of death and the underworld — will not prevail against it (cf. Isa. 38:10). In the community formed around this confession, there is victory provided by accepting the revelation of God. In fact, this community will have the "keys" of the kingdom of heaven (cf. Isa. 22:22; John 20:23; contrast Luke 11:52). Entrance into the rule of God and into the life and victory it contains is bound up in the authority of the message coming from this new community. They will have the right "to bind and loose." Jesus is describing a community engaged in a struggle against other forces residing below, but the note throughout is of eventual victory. Jesus' remarks surely led to the later church imagery of the apostles as the foundation of the church (Eph. 2:20; Rev. 21:14).[24]

The New Testament church has the responsibility for the safe-keeping of its members. Judgments made by the proper authorities among the leadership of the church are met with approval in heaven. Those who believe in Christ have eternal life.

JESUS PREDICTS HIS REJECTION, CRUCIFIXION, AND RESURRECTION
(Matthew 16:21 – 26; Mark 8:31 – 37; Luke 9:22 – 25; T&G 83)

Immediately after the disciples' declaration that Jesus is the Messiah, the Son of God, Matthew recorded Jesus' first overt statement regarding his death and resurrection. "From that time on Jesus began to explain to his disciples that he must go to Jerusalem and suffer many things at the hands of the elders, the chief priests and the teachers of the law, and that he must be killed and on the third day be raised to life" (Matt. 16:21).

Peter, with misguided zeal, rebuked the Lord for his statement. Jesus responded with his famous reprimand, "Get behind me, Satan!" (Matt.

Mount Hermon from the south

16:23). Peter was so certain of Jesus' messianic intentions that he couldn't accept anything less than his coronation. However, Peter's statement mirrored Satan's temptation that Jesus' kingdom could be inaugurated without the cross (Matt. 4:8–9).

Jesus promised suffering to those desiring to be his followers. "Whoever wants to be my disciple must deny themselves and take up their cross and follow me. For whoever wants to save their life will lose it, but whoever loses their life for me will find it" (Matt. 16:24–25). This statement marks another milestone in Jesus' teaching. Suffering and opposition were part of Jesus' life, and they would also be the shared experience of his followers.

THE TRANSFIGURATION OF JESUS NEAR CAESAREA PHILIPPI
(Matthew 17:1–13; Mark 9:2–13; Luke 9:28–36; T&G 85–86)

Six days after Jesus startled his disciples by saying, "Truly I tell you, some who are standing here will not taste death before they see the Son of Man coming in his kingdom" (Matt. 16:28), he chose Peter, James, and John and took them to the slopes of snow-capped Mount Hermon (Mark 9:2). There, in a private moment, Jesus was transformed. The three chosen disciples saw with their own eyes Jesus radiant with the glory of his Father. This appearance was a revelation of Jesus' divinity and a foreshadowing of how he will appear when he returns to earth at the end of this age.

Jesus' blinding brilliance and the appearance of Moses and Elijah caused Peter to embrace what his heart told him was true: "Lord, it is good for us to be here. If you wish, I will put up three shelters—one for you, one for Moses and one for Elijah" (Matt. 17:4).

In that moment, everything within Peter aligned with one polarizing truth: he was in the presence of the Son of God. His heart leaped with a desire to worship and to lead the other disciples to that same place of adoration. His mind flew to the familiar, the Jewish Feast of Tabernacles (shelters) memorializing Israel's exodus from Egypt and prefiguring Christ's deliverance in death and resurrection — the very message Jesus wished to convey.

Knowing that the men did not fully understand what they witnessed, Jesus instructed the disciples not to tell anyone what they experienced. They were unaware of what would be involved in Jesus' pending death, burial, and resurrection, and speaking of things they were just beginning to understand could easily cause great confusion.

GALILEE MISSION COMPLETE[25]
(Matthew 17:9 – 18:14, 8:19 – 22;[26] Mark 9:11 – 50; Luke 9:36 – 50; T&G 86 – 93)

From Caesarea Philippi, Jesus and the disciples journeyed south on the east side of the Sea of Galilee. Jesus' teaching of the Twelve included the healing of a boy with a demon and declaring his own coming death and resurrection for the second time (Mark 9:30 – 32).

Caesarea Philippi arch. Augustus Caesar gave the city once known as Panias to Herod the Great, who in turn built a marble temple to Augustus. After Herod Philip inherited it, he renamed the city Caesarea Philippi in honor of Caesar and himself and to distinguish it from the Caesarea on the Mediterranean Sea. Panias (today Banias) was named after the Greek god Pan who was worshiped there. No record exists of Jesus entering the city, but the great confession and the transfiguration both occurred in the vicinity of the city (Matt. 16:13), which was then known as Caesarea Philippi. The city flourished during the Byzantine, Arab, Crusader, and Mamluk periods but lost its importance during the Ottoman era.

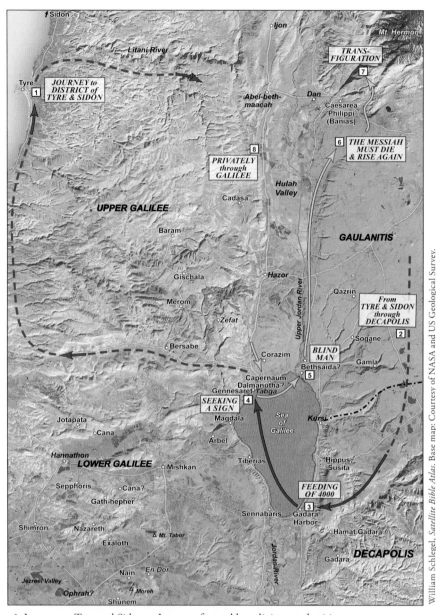

1. Journey to Tyre and Sidon—Jesus confronted by religious authorities
2. From Tyre and Sidon to Decapolis—Gentiles heard and glorified the God of Israel
3. Feeding of 4,000 (Tradition places this event at Tel Hadar; some today prefer HaOn.)
4. Leaders sought a sign
5. Blind man healed and exhorted not to publicize it
6. First message the Messiah must die and rise again
7. Transfiguration
8. Private (secret) ministry throughout Galilee

William Schlegel, *Satellite Bible Atlas*. Base map: Courtesy of NASA and US Geological Survey.

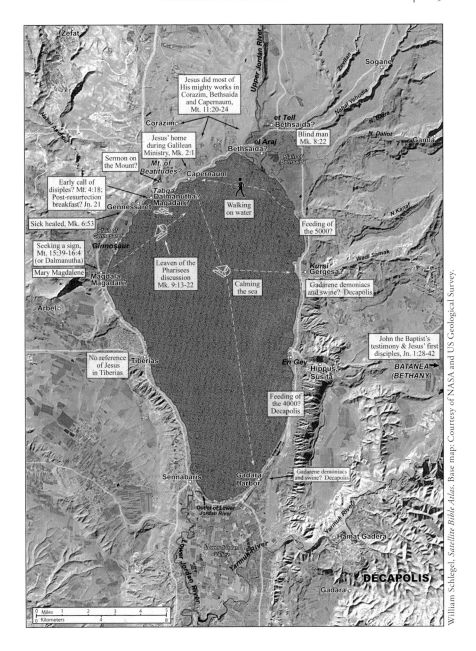

Zefat

Sogane

Jesus did most of
His mighty works in
Corazim, Bethsaida
and Capernaum,
Mt. 11:20-24

Corazim○

et Tell
○ Bethsaida?

Blind man
Mk. 8:22

N. Daliot

Gamla

Jesus' home
during Galilean
Ministry, Mk. 2:1

Sermon on
the Mount?

Mt. of
Beatitudes? △

el Araj
Bethsaida?

Plain of
Bethsaida

Capernaum

Early call of
disiples? Mt. 4:18;
Post-resurrection
breakfast? Jn. 21

Tabga
Dalmanutha?
Magadan?

Gennesaret

Walking
on water

Sick healed, Mk. 6:53

Plain of
Gennesaret

Feeding of
the 5000?

N. Kanaf

Seeking a sign,
Mt. 15:39-16:4
(or Dalmanutha)

Ginnosaur

Wadi Samak

Mary Magdalene

Magdala
Magadan?

Leaven of the
Pharisees
discussion
Mk. 9:13-22

Kursi
Gergesa?

Calming
the sea

Gadarene demoniacs
and swine? Decapolis

Arbel○

John the Baptist's
testimony & Jesus' first
disciples, Jn. 1:28-42

No reference
of Jesus
in Tiberias

Tiberias

En Gev

Hippus
Susita

BATANEA→
(BETHANY)

Feeding of
the 4000?
Decapolis

Sennabaris

Gadara
Harbor

Gadarene demoniacs
and swine? Decapolis

Outlet of Lower
Jordan River

Lower Jordan
Valley

Lower Jordan River

Yarmuk River

Hamat Gadera

DECAPOLIS

Gadara○

Miles 0 1 2 3 4 5
Kilometers 0 4 8

William Schlegel, *Satellite Bible Atlas*. Base map: Courtesy of NASA and US Geological Survey.

Jesus' Words and Works in Galilee and Surrounding Area
Spring AD 31 – Spring 32

Tyre and Sidon:
  Healed Gentile woman (Matt. 15:21–28)
Decapolis:
  Healed many (Matt. 15:29–31)
  4,000 fed at Tel Hadar (Kursi) or HaOn (Gadara harbor) (Matt. 15:32–38)
  Healing Gerasene demoniac(s) at Gerasa (Kursi or HaOn) (Mark 5:1–20)
Caesarea Philippi:
  Peter's confession (Matt. 16:13–20)
  First teaching on death and resurrection (Matt. 16:21–28)
  Transfiguration (Matt. 17:1–8)
Sea of Galilee:
  Calming of the sea (Mark 4:35–41)
  Jesus walked on water (Mark 6:47–52)
Capernaum:
  Jairus's daughter healed (Mark 5:21–43)
  Discourse on Bread of Life (John 6:22–59)
  Rivalry over greatness in kingdom (Mark 9:33–37)
Nazareth:
  Final visit (Mark 6:1–6)
Bethsaida:
  Feeding of the 5,000 (Tabgha?) (Mark 6:35–44)
  Healing of the blind man (Mark 8:22–26)

CHAPTER 7

MESSIAH UNCOVERS DEVOTION: FAITH FOUND AND FAITH SPURNED

FALL AD 32 – WINTER AD 33?

Matthew 8:19 – 22; Luke 9:51 – 13:21; John 7:2 – 10:42 (T&G 94 – 112)

FROM THE FEAST OF TABERNACLES TO DEDICATION/ HANUKKAH

Enduring the storm on the Sea of Galilee and seeing Jesus walk on the water strongly affected the disciples. They continued to wrestle with the implications of Jesus' identity, asking themselves deep questions. "Who is Jesus? We saw his miracles, heard his message, and confessed our belief in him. We believe he is the Messiah. But what does he mean when he says he must go to Jerusalem and die? What does this mean for our future? And certainly he knows that we would fight for him and never let the priests take him."

But the disciples didn't ponder their questions for long, for Jesus soon called them to travel with him to Jerusalem by way of Samaria.[1]

Up to this point, Jesus' ministry centered in Galilee with Capernaum as his headquarters. That all changed as he began to focus on Samaria and Perea. His message focused on his words and sayings rather than his works. He had no central headquarters for this extensive period of ministry. Luke is the primary recorder of this portion of Jesus' ministry, during which Jesus

THE SAMARITAN PASSOVER

The Samaritans today live in two separate communities. Half live in Holon near Tel Aviv and carry out their lives among Israelis. The other half live on Mount Gerizim among the Arab communities; they speak Arabic and have generally good relations with the Arabs. But they also desire good relations with the Israelis and are often caught in the middle of the conflict. It doesn't appear that Samaritans have participated in the activities of intifadas against Israel. When the Samaritans host their annual Passover sacrifice, many Israelis come to see the service, and they are welcomed warmly. The Samaritans are today such a small, struggling community that it's difficult to see them as an enemy.

The Samaritans were not allowed to participate in the rebuilding of the temple. They opposed the rebuilding of Jerusalem's city wall (Ezra 4:1–5; Neh. 4:1–9). Josephus wrote that a Samaritan temple was built on Mount Gerizim with the permission of Alexander the Great.[3] The temple is called Zeus Xenios ("the Hospitable"; NRSV: "Zeus-the-Friend-of-Strangers") in 2 Maccabees 6:2. It was modeled after the temple in Jerusalem and later was destroyed by John Hyrcanus (129/128 BC).

The chief difference between the Jewish and Samaritan Passover is location, and this goes back more than two thousand years to when the Jewish temple was still standing in Jerusalem but the Samaritans were sacrificing at the temple on Mount Gerizim (destroyed by John Hyrcanus in 129 BC). That location issue may seem superficial to us with a Christian mind-set, but it is enormous for the ancient and traditional peoples.

Today the Samaritans sacrifice lambs even though they don't have a temple. The Jews don't have a temple either, and that prevents them from sacrificing. The Samaritan prayers sound very Arabic, a result of living side by side with Muslims for hundreds of years. The basics of the Samaritan service are the same as what the Jews used to do: a sacrifice in late afternoon, removing of entrails, roasting of the animal, and a late night family meal. Today the Jewish people spend the evening (not having a sacrifice to carry out) in a lengthy seder

The Samaritan high priest was a direct descendant of Aaron. The last one died without an heir in AD 1624. Today the appointed religious head is known as ha-Kohen (the priest) and is of Levitic descent.

(program) around the dining table with all kinds of rituals and symbols. One very important difference is this: the Samaritans follow what is written in the five books of Moses, but they don't hold to any of the other books of the Old Testament or any of the Jewish rabbinic writings that play such a huge role in the daily practice of the Jewish people.

The Passover was and is a central part of the Jewish calendar. The New Testament records that Jesus attended each Passover during his ministry. He was part of the noisy crowds and a spectator to the bloodletting of the sacrificial animals. He saw, heard, and smelled the same sights, sounds, and stenches as participants in the Samaritan Passover experience today. No other event so effectively transports the modern person back to the ceremonies of biblical days, because the Passover sacrifices are offered today by the Samaritans in the same manner they have been presented since before the time of Christ.

Samaritan Passover lambs: The Passover sacrifice is a family affair. The children are at the ceremony playing with the sheep beforehand. In the Old Testament the Lord commanded the Israelites to bring the lamb into the household on the tenth day of the month, four days before the sacrifice. The family would get "acquainted" with the lamb in the course of those days, and the children would be especially impacted when the father put the knife to the lamb's throat. You can imagine the cries of the children as their new pet was killed.

Samaritan men, who are the heads of their households, take their place with their family's lamb at the sacrificial trough. Their families gather around; guests maneuver to get a good vantage point to watch the bloody festivities. To the Samaritan or the ancient Israelite, the Mosaic statement "The life of a creature is in the blood" (Lev. 17:11) was a profound truth regarding the price for the payment for sin.

Christians today who worship in the sterile environment of church sanctuaries

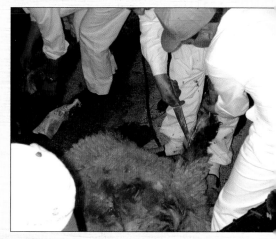

Samaritan Passover sacrifice

often lack a deep understanding of the gravity of sin and its invasiveness in the life of its victims. The judgment for sin is death, and God allowed the substitution of an animal's death until he provided the "bloody" substitute of his very own Son.

challenged the crowds to believe, prepared the disciples for his destiny, and confronted the Jewish leaders.

REJECTED IN SAMARIA
(John 7:2 – 9; Luke 9:51 – 56, Jerusalem Narrative;² T&G 94 – 95)

Jesus found himself rejected once again — this time by the Samaritans. They were offended by Jesus' preference to worship in Jerusalem rather than at Mount Gerizim, and they rejected him. James and John wanted to call down a consuming fire from heaven to put the Samaritans in their place, but Jesus rebuked them, then moved on with his disciples to another village.

Imagine the embarrassment that washed over James and John as they realized they had spoken in haste — how much they still had to learn.

JESUS GOES TO JERUSALEM FOR THE FEAST OF TABERNACLES/BOOTHS
(John 7:11 – 10:21; Luke 10:1 – 13:21; T&G 96a – 110)

Jesus now prepared for his last few months of ministry prior to his work on the cross. The Feast of Tabernacles provided an opportunity for him to offer more instruction to his followers.[4] It was a time when all faithful Jews gathered, but it also provided an opportunity for Jewish leaders to locate him. For three months (from Feast of Tabernacles to Dedication)[5] Jesus taught in Jerusalem and Judea. He withdrew from Judea early in his ministry, but now as time was running out, he made another attempt to preach his message to the unbelieving. The time had come for him to set his sights on Jerusalem and Judea. His trip would take him through the hated Samaritan territory.

The disciples couldn't help but notice yet another shift in Jesus' approach to his ministry. He was now preaching without as many accompanying miracles. However, his message continued to challenge the nation's leaders to accept him as Messiah.

As the disciples walked toward Jerusalem, perhaps they wondered how its citizens would respond to Jesus' message. If his previous visits were any indication, they had no reason to be hopeful. But they were about to find out.

As Jesus and the Twelve approached the city, a man stopped them. He was obviously seeking Jesus and addressed him immediately.

"Teacher, I will follow you wherever you go," he declared.

Jesus warned the man of the hardships to be faced by those who chose to follow him.

The man's face fell. Hardship? This was not the life he dreamed of with a miracle-worker and great teacher.

Then Jesus rebuked the man's lack of commitment: "No one who puts a hand to the plow and looks back is fit for service in the kingdom of God" (Luke 9:62). Jesus' words crushed his superficial interest, and he disappeared into the crowd.

Jesus and his entourage soon arrived in the city, where they learned that Jewish leaders were plotting to capture him. The disciples also reported that many of the people were grumbling about his presence in the city and debating among themselves whether he was truly a good man or was leading people astray. The controversy never seemed to change.

"Here we go again," the disciples muttered among themselves. "The same reaction we got about the Sabbath when we were in Galilee."

Wherever Jesus went, controversy followed—contention that always centered on his divine authority as the Messiah (John 7:25–31). The disciples were never surprised when people believed, but they were also learning not to be surprised by rejection. They came to expect the authorities' continued attempts to seize Jesus in spite of their continued failures.

The last day of the feast was highlighted by a special celebration. The faithful left their booths at daybreak and formed a musical procession that began at the temple and was led by a priest bearing a golden pitcher. They dressed in festive clothes and marched toward their final destination singing Psalm 118:25–26. When they arrived at the Pool of Siloam, they filled the golden pitcher with its water. The procession then returned to the temple, where they poured water into the silver basin near the altar. As they made the journey, they proclaimed the words of Scripture, "With joy you will draw water from the wells of salvation" (Isa. 12:3). But this time, Jesus completed the message with a declaration above the noise of the crowd: "Let anyone who is thirsty come to me and drink" (John 7:37).

Jesus' offer mirrored his message to the Samaritan woman at the well. His message was clear: "Anyone who believes in me will have eternal life." His messianic claim sharply divided the multitudes. The Pharisees once again rejected Jesus by stating that no Pharisee ever believed in him. Then they claimed no prophet ever came out of Galilee. They were wrong on both accounts: Nicodemus was a Pharisee, and the prophets Jonah, Nahum, and Hosea all came from Galilee.

Jesus' ministry was continuing to stir intense conflict and create division between those who would accept him and those who would reject him as Messiah. Yet the lessons continued for the disciples.

THE WOMAN CAUGHT IN ADULTERY
(John 7:53 – 8:11;[9] T&G 97)

While Jesus was delivering his morning sermon on the temple grounds, the Pharisees brought a woman caught in adultery to him for condemnation. They didn't necessarily want Jesus to punish the woman; their ploy was an attempt to trap Jesus into breaking the Sabbath. In front of the crowd gathered at the temple, they humiliated the woman in a pretentious attempt to force Jesus to choose between siding with them and breaking the law. However, Jesus reminded them that judgment belongs to God. Because unholy, flawed people are incapable of righteous judgment, Jesus directed, "Let any one of you who is without sin be the first to throw a stone at her" (John 8:7). Faced with the weight of their personal guilt and enraged at Jesus, the Pharisees turned away from the woman one by one. Once again they were foiled in their attempt to discredit him.

REFERENCES TO JESUS OUTSIDE THE NEW TESTAMENT

Ancient noncanonical Christian-related literature abounds with references and details about Jesus' life. While they are not considered canonical, they are considered sympathetic writings and therefore cannot be totally discarded. Secular sources are sparser and sometimes hostile, but they give evidence of Jesus' life and activities and of his later followers. The Roman author Suetonius, who in AD 120 compiled biographies of some of Rome's emperors in his *Life of Claudius*, wrote, "He expelled the Jews from Rome, on account of the riots in which they were constantly indulging, at the instigation of Chrestus [Christ]."[6]

The Roman historian Tacitus, in *Annals*, AD 115–17, mentions the origins of Christianity when he writes, "They [Christians] got their name from Christ, who was executed by Pontius Pilate in the reign of Tiberius. That checked the pernicious superstition for a short time, but it broke out afresh—not only in Judaea, where the plague first arose, but in Rome itself."[7]

The historian Flavius Josephus, writing in the first century in his *Antiquities of the Jews*, penned the earliest extrabiblical words acknowledging Jesus.

> Now there was about this time Jesus, a wise man ... for he was a doer of wonderful works, a teacher of such as receive the truth with pleasure. He drew over to him both many of the Jews and many of the Gentiles.... And when Pilate, at the suggestion of the principal men among us, had condemned him to the cross, those that loved him at the first did not forsake him.... And the tribe of Christians, so named from him, are not extinct at this day.[8]

JESUS, THE OBJECT OF FAITH (John 8:21 – 59; T&G 99a – 99b)

The unbelieving Pharisees could not grasp Jesus' message. They interpreted his prediction of his death and resurrection as foretelling his planned suicide. He continued to state that he spoke for the Father and that the evidence rested in his coming resurrection. Furthermore, he asserted that salvation came by believing in him. Yet again, while religious officials rejected him, many seekers from among the poor, the common, and the disdained among the Jews believed in him.

Predictably, the Jews fell back on the fact that they were Abraham's offspring and, as such, had always been free. "We are Abraham's offspring and have never been slaves of anyone. How can you say that we shall be set free?" (John 8:33). Jesus made it clear that his reference to freedom had nothing to do with physical slavery. Rather, everyone who commits sin is a slave to sin. Freedom and forgiveness do not come from natural birth; true freedom comes from the forgiveness of sin by faith in the everlasting God, not from natural birth through Abraham. In response to Jesus' message of salvation, the Pharisees attempted to stone Jesus, but he escaped.

The disciples were listening and watching the Master at work—sometimes cheering and sometimes worried and afraid. In spite of the fact that they expected Jesus to be arrested at any moment, they continued to follow him with a growing sense of wonder and awe.

"We have chosen the right man to place our faith in," they reasoned among themselves. Some, perhaps, were overwhelmed by gratitude. Others were likely wrestling with thoughts of pride and power.

LESSONS OF SERVICE AND PRAYER
(Luke 10:1 – 11:13; T&G 102a – 5)

Sometime later Jesus chose seventy-two more disciples[10] from other parts of Judea and sent them out two by two ahead of him to every city he planned to enter, with the power to heal to confirm their authority. They preached Jesus' same familiar message: the kingdom of God is near you. Like John the Baptist, they prepared the way for the Messiah.

These disciples joyfully returned from their mission, reporting that even the demons submitted to them in Jesus' name. "Lord, even the demons submit to us in your name" (Luke 10:17). Jesus reminded them that the true reason for joy was not in the fact that demons submitted to them but that their names were recorded in heaven. They were privileged, for many prophets and kings had wished to see the things they saw.

Ascent of Adummim. Remains of Roman road from Jericho to Jerusalem

From their first mission journey, the disciples learned that ministry extends beyond preaching. For ministry to be effective, the message must be translated into action. The Good Samaritan provides an excellent example. The story of the good Samaritan is a familiar story told to children in Sunday school, acted out in school plays, and included in all stories when discussing Jesus' teachings. It is a simple story with a profound lesson.

A pompous lawyer arose and posed what he perceived was a penetrating test: "What must I do to inherit eternal life?" (Luke 10:25). Jesus' answer astonished the inquisitor: " 'Love the Lord your God with all your heart and with all your soul and with all your strength and with all your mind'; and, 'Love your neighbor as yourself' " (v. 27). The loquacious attorney, knowing he could not do all Jesus demanded, posed the avoidance question, "And who is my neighbor?" (v. 29).

Jesus told the dramatic story. A traveler making his way from Jerusalem to Jericho embarked on a journey wrought with hazards. The road extends from 2,475 feet above sea level to 825 feet below sea level. The traveler could encounter miserable weather conditions, rough to impassable roads, and perilous encounters with thieves; and indeed, he fell into the merciless hands of highway thugs who stripped him of his clothing, beat him, and left him half dead.

A pious priest saw the half-conscious traveler, but unwilling to endanger himself, he avoided the stranded, helpless victim. Soon after a Levite happened along and ignored him as well. But a certain Samaritan, often consid-

Good Samaritan inn on road to Jericho

ered an adversary of the Jews, stopped, gave comfort, bandaged his wounds, and took him to an inn and paid for his convalescence. The answer to the lawyer's inquiry is simple: a "neighbor" is one who shows mercy and helps another.

As he traveled through Judea, Jesus came to the small village of Bethany, where a woman named Martha opened her home to him. Martha and her sister, Mary, were about to learn an important lesson. Busy bee Martha complained to Jesus that Mary wasn't helping with the meal preparations. But Jesus mildly rebuked her, saying, "Martha, Martha, you are worried and upset about many things, but few things are needed—or indeed only one. Mary has chosen what is better, and it will not be taken away from her" (Luke 10:41). Jesus taught them that true fellowship is not just meeting physical needs but spending time together. Mary and Martha perhaps best exemplify the balance needed in serving and "soaking in" the presence of others.

Jericho from the south (early twentieth century)

While he was in Bethany, Jesus provided an example of prayer for his kingdom followers. In what we call the Lord's Prayer today, the message of the coming kingdom is prominent, as believers are given a pattern for repentance and supplication in coming persistently before a Father who lovingly and freely gives.

KINGDOM REJECTED IN JUDEA (Luke 11:14 – 36; T&G 106)

Jesus once again cast out a demon, this time in Judea; and he was once again accused of doing so through the power of Satan. The disciples, however, responded in awe as they witnessed Jesus' authority over the powers of darkness. They were reminded of similar events in Galilee when Jesus cast out a demon and the Pharisees challenged Jesus (Matt. 12). Others in the crowd tested him by demanding a sign from heaven. But Jesus' typical practice was to refute only arguments that challenged his person or authority. For example, when he was accused of performing a miracle by the power of Beelzebub, as happened in Galilee, Jesus said, "A wicked and adulterous generation asks for a sign! But none will be given it except the sign of the prophet Jonah" (Matt. 12:39).

These events established the future of the kingdom for Galilee and Judea, as both the leadership and the masses rejected Jesus as the Messiah. Jesus, however, continued to train and instruct his disciples. They were about to get another glimpse of the nature of the Pharisees.

WARNINGS TO SCRIBES AND PHARISEES
(Luke 11:37 – 54; T&G 107)

Andrew, one of Jesus' disciples, was bewildered when a Pharisee invited Jesus to his home for lunch. Andrew must have questioned the man's motives: *What is this Pharisee up to? Is he planning to deceive the Master and turn him over to the authorities?* His questions were soon answered when the Pharisee observed that Jesus did not ceremonially wash before the meal and used the occasion to criticize him.

Jesus responded by reprimanding the Pharisee about the impure motives of religious hypocrites. He then pronounced a series of "woes" upon spiritual leaders. The Pharisee was insulted, and the disciples were horrified. Certainly Jesus knew the Pharisees were looking for an opportunity to trap him into breaking the law. And the Rabbi's disciples were certainly in jeopardy as well.

Sure enough, Andrew's fears were confirmed. As Jesus left the house, the scribes' and Pharisees' questions became hostile. Each day their treacherous motives grew. It seemed only a matter of time before they would make a move to play their hand.

FEAST OF SUCCOTH (TABERNACLES)

Succoth commemorates the time the Hebrews lived in the wilderness prior to entering the Promised Land. The word *Succoth* means "booths" and refers to the command to live in temporary dwellings during this holiday.

The Festival of Succoth begins five days after Yom Kippur, from the 15th to the 21st day of the Hebrew month of Tishri (September or October). It is preceded by the "High Holy Days" of the New Year and Yom Kippur, all a part of the fall holiday season.

Like Passover, Succoth celebrates both historical and agricultural events. The holiday commemorates the forty-year period during which the children of Israel wandered in the desert, living in temporary shelters. Succoth is also a harvest festival and is sometimes referred to as the Festival of Ingathering. The holiday lasts seven days. No work is permitted on the first day of the holiday but is permitted on the remaining days.

Putting palms on *succah* roof at Feast of Tabernacles (Succoth).

In modern Israel, the celebration features living in temporary shelters commemorating the ancient Israelites dwelling in the wilderness. The commandment "to dwell" in a *succah* can be fulfilled by simply eating all of one's meals in the *succah*, but if the weather permits, participants are encouraged to spend their nights there as well.

The Feast of Succoth at Neot Kedumim. The Lord instructed Moses to tell the Israelites, "'On the first day you are to take branches from luxuriant trees—from palms, willows and other leafy trees—and rejoice before the LORD your God for seven days. Celebrate this as a festival to the LORD for seven days each year. This is to be a lasting ordinance for the generations to come; celebrate it in the seventh month. Live in temporary shelters for seven days: All native-born Israelites are to live in such shelters so your descendants will know that I had the Israelites live in temporary shelters when I brought them out of Egypt. I am the LORD your God'" (Lev. 23:40–43).

Faithfulness, Reward, and Judgment
(Luke 12:1 – 13:21; T&G 108a – 10)

The term *disciple* is used to refer not only to the twelve disciples chosen by Jesus but also to those who were convinced of Jesus' message. Jesus warned against the leaven of the Pharisees: their hypocrisy, greed, and wealth. True wealth belongs to those who are rich toward God.

Jesus exhorted his disciples—all his followers, past and present—to be ready with their lamps burning as they wait for the final coming of their Master. "Be dressed ready for service and keep your lamps burning, like servants waiting for their master to return from a wedding banquet, so that when he comes and knocks they can immediately open the door for him" (Luke 1:35 – 36). His return is imminent, but the timing is unknown.

The disciples had just witnessed the rejection of both the King and his kingdom, and now they were receiving instruction in light of the kingdom's rejection. God's promises were not abandoned; they will be fulfilled later. "It will be good for those servants whose master finds them ready, even if he comes in the middle of the night or toward daybreak" (Luke 12:38). Peter, concerned about his future and remembering Jesus had taken them aside earlier and given them private instructions, spoke up and asked, "Lord, are you telling this parable to us, or to everyone?" (12:41).

Jesus answered Peter indirectly. His exhortation was for the faithful. Jesus then warned that when the Master returns there will be an accounting of the faithful and the faithless. "From everyone who has been given much, much will be demanded; and from the one who has been entrusted with much, much more will be asked" (Luke 12:48).

Teaching at the Feast of Dedication/Lights
(Hanukkah) (John 10:22 – 42; T&G 111 – 12)

For three months following the Feast of Tabernacles, Jesus taught primarily in Judea. Jesus came to Jerusalem to celebrate the Feast of Dedication. The authorities knew Jesus would be at the feast.

While at the feast, Jesus healed a blind man. The healing became an important event. The Pharisees went to great lengths to deflect the intended results of the miracle. The disciples asked, "Rabbi, who sinned, this man or his parents, that he was born blind?" (John 9:1). Jesus responded to the disciples that the blindness was not a result of the man's sin nor his parents' sin. Some accepted Jesus' miracle as from God, and others did not. The Pharisees quickly concluded, "This man is not from God" (9:16). The healing became an event to teach the validity of Jesus' claims as Messiah. Jesus took the opportunity to claim that he is the "light of the world" (John 9:5).

The blind man became an object lesson for all those in attendance. Although the Pharisees warned that anyone who confessed Jesus as Messiah would be excommunicated from the synagogue, many believed Jesus, for how could a sinner perform such a miracle? The blind man—now with perfect sight—confessed, "Whether he is a sinner or not, I don't know. One thing I do know. I was blind but now I see!" (John 9:25).

The Pharisees claimed to have all the knowledge they needed; Jesus could offer them no additional wisdom. Confirming his object lesson, Jesus pronounced them spiritually blind. They had made their choice.

Jesus heaped further condemnation on the Pharisees with the allegory of the Good Shepherd. No doubt Jesus alluded to the role of the shepherd in Ezekiel 34. The Good Shepherd is the God of Israel, and the Pharisees didn't know him. His sheep hear his voice and follow him.[11] Those who do not recognize his voice are strangers. Jesus' presence will always stir controversy and a call to faith: some will believe and some will reject—so we all must count the cost.

The Hanukkah menorah has nine branches, unlike the seven-branched candelabrum that functioned in the tabernacle and temple. One branch holds the *shamash* candle used to light the other eight candles over the course of the eight-day holiday (signifying the one-day supply of oil for the temple menorah that lasted for eight days during the Maccabean period).

FEAST OF DEDICATION (HANUKKAH)

Hanukkah recalls the miracle during the time of the Maccabees (164 BCE) when the one-day supply of oil for the temple menorah lasted for eight days. It is a joyous festival in memory of the purification of the temple by Judas Maccabaeus. Hanukkah is celebrated over an eight-night-and-day span, beginning on the 25th day of Kislev according to the Hebrew calendar, and occurs sometime between late November and late December in the Gregorian calendar.

THE FEAST OF TRUMPETS (ROSH HASHANAH)
(Leviticus 23:23 – 25; Numbers 10:9 – 10; 29:1; Nehemiah 8:1 – 12)

The Bible says less about the Feast of Trumpets than any of the other feasts. The holy day celebration began on the first day of the seventh month (Tishri or September – October) with a simple blast of the trumpet. The call signaled a call to action or gathering of an assembly, such as the calling of troops to war or the ceremonial welcoming of a king.

While this feast is not specifically mentioned in the Gospels, an important prophetic event described as a trumpet blast announcing the return of Christ does occur in Matthew 24:31.

The modern celebration of the Feast of Trumpets is accompanied by several blasts of a shofar (trumpet made of a ram's horn). This is a solemn time anticipating the holiest day in the Jewish faith — the Day of Atonement (Yom Kippur). The ten days beginning with Rosh Hashanah and extending through Yom Kippur are called the Days of Awe. This is a time of repentance and the pondering of one's sins before God. According to Jewish tradition, during this time God decides who will live and who will die that coming year. God sits in judgment; before him are three great books. The first book lists the names of those who are good; the second lists the names of those who are bad; the third book lists the names of those who are neither good nor bad. Prayers during this time are made to persuade God to move their names to the first book.

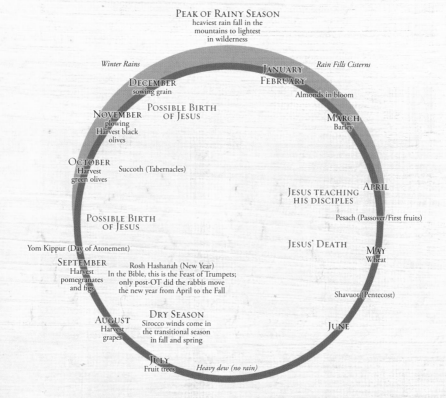

AGRICULTURAL CALENDAR
CYCLE OF FEASTS, AND HARVESTS

PEAK OF RAINY SEASON
heaviest rain fall in the
mountains to lightest
in wilderness

Winter Rains

JANUARY
FEBRUARY

Rain Fills Cisterns

DECEMBER
sowing grain

Almonds in bloom

POSSIBLE BIRTH
OF JESUS

NOVEMBER
plowing
Harvest black
olives

MARCH
Barley

OCTOBER
Harvest
green olives

Succoth (Tabernacles)

APRIL
JESUS TEACHING
HIS DISCIPLES

POSSIBLE BIRTH
OF JESUS

Pesach (Passover/First fruits)

Yom Kippur (Day of Atonement)

JESUS' DEATH

SEPTEMBER
Harvest
pomegranates
and figs

Rosh Hashanah (New Year)
In the Bible, this is the Feast of Trumpets;
only post-OT did the rabbis move
the new year from April to the Fall

MAY
Wheat

Shavuot (Pentecost)

AUGUST
Harvest
grapes

DRY SEASON
Sirocco winds come in
the transitional season
in fall and spring

JUNE

JULY
Fruit trees

Heavy dew (no rain)

CHAPTER 8

MESSIAH'S DEMANDS: COUNTING THE COST

FALL AD 32 – SPRING 33

Matthew 19:1 – 20:34; Mark 10:1 – 52; Luke 13:22 – 19:28;
John 10:40 – 11:54 (T&G 112 – 27)

FROM THE FEAST OF DEDICATION TO PASSOVER

The Pharisees' hatred toward Jesus and his message grew so intense that they attempted to stone him at the Feast of Dedication. Galilee had rejected him. Then Judea closed its doors. Jesus determined that the time had come to cross the Jordan and retreat to Perea.[1] The move would not only be an opportunity for Perea to repent, but a chance for Jesus to prepare the disciples for what would happen to him next.

The disciples followed Jesus nearly everywhere he went, sometimes in the background and sometimes near the center of attention. They probably often wondered, *Where will we eat and spend the night tonight? Winter has come, and it's growing cold and rainy.* At times they muttered among themselves, but Jesus redirected their self-absorption into action as he prodded them to move on.

The disciples struggled with the pull of doubt as they watched Jesus. Of course they believed he was the Messiah. How could they not? They had witnessed his miracles, sat under his teaching, and been with him in the storm on the Sea of Galilee. But his message left them puzzled. Why did he insist that he must go to Jerusalem to die?

Surely there was another way, they reasoned. He escaped his enemies' continued attempts to stone and kill him. To choose to die made no sense. If he claimed to be the Son of God, why give up now?

Jesus was aware of their concerns, and he used the time in Perea to prepare them for his inevitable meeting with destiny as he became the sacrifice for human sin.

NARROW IS THE WAY
(Luke 13:22 – 30; John 10:40 – 42; T&G 112 – 13a)

According to John 10:42, "many" people believed in Jesus, yet others rejected him. In the midst of the continuing controversy regarding Jesus' identity, someone approached him and asked, "Lord, are only a few people going to be saved?" (Luke 13:23). The person's question indicated uncertainty about his or her salvation.

Jesus reminded the person that seekers face two choices: "Enter through the narrow gate. For wide is the gate and broad is the road that leads to destruction, and many enter it. But small is the gate and narrow the road that leads to life, and only a few find it" (Matt. 7:13 – 14). He encouraged the man to enter the narrow gate, because once it closes, people will no longer be permitted to enter. Jesus will say, "I never knew you. Away from me, you evildoers" (Matt. 7:23). Jesus will deny that he ever knew those outside the door. Those inside will take their place at the feast in the kingdom of God, but those outside will be cast into a place of weeping and gnashing of teeth.

A SABBATH AT THE TABLE OF A PHARISEE
(Luke 13:31 – 14:24; T&G 113b – 14)

Herod Antipas ruled Perea and Galilee, where Jesus previously encountered opposition from him. Although the Pharisees warned Jesus that Herod Antipas sought to kill him,[2] they didn't want to protect Jesus from Herod; they wanted to force him back into Judea where he would fall under their jurisdiction. But Jesus reminded them he would return to Judea and Jerusalem, where he would die by divine appointment—not by royal decree. He mourned Jerusalem for killing the prophets and stoning those sent to her. The "Holy City" he loved had become far from holy.

Once again the Pharisees charged Jesus with violating the Sabbath. A Pharisee invited Jesus to his home with the intention of catching him breaking the law. Jesus healed a man and sent him on his way. Knowing their malicious intent, Jesus asked a question in the presence of the Pharisees: "Is it lawful to heal on the Sabbath or not?" (Luke 14:3).

The question was met with silence.

Jesus followed the question with another. "If one of you has a child or an ox that falls into a well on the Sabbath day, will you not immediately pull it out?"

Again his question was answered with silence. The Pharisees knew Sabbath prohibitions did not include preserving life on the Sabbath. Jesus' question once again demonstrated not only his knowledge of the law but his sinless nature.

The Pharisee had offered Jesus a personal invitation to come to his home, but the other guests were close friends, and they began to clamor for seats of honor at the table. Jesus used the opportunity to teach a lesson about humility and sharing with the less privileged. Then he went on to teach a parable about a great banquet that revealed that those who were invited into the kingdom, Abraham's descendants, would not enter the kingdom. Those who were invited to the banquet but declined the invitation made the same excuses the Jews made to Jesus when they rejected him as the one God sent to establish the kingdom.

THE COST OF TRUE DISCIPLESHIP (Luke 14:25 – 35; T&G 115)

Jesus continued to attract great multitudes. Perhaps out of impatience, he warned them that anyone wanting to be his disciple must be willing to lay aside material possessions and follow him. Those who make a genuine commitment have considered the cost.[3] In response to Jesus' challenge, some in the crowd slinked away while others deepened their resolve.

PARABLES FOR PHARISEES
(Matthew 19:1 – 20:28; Luke 15:1 – 18:30; John 11:54; T&G 116 – 24b)

The scribes and Pharisees continued to complain about Jesus' compassion for the "unsavory" in society (Luke 15:2). So he presented several parables to explain why he sought out sinners. The parables of the lost sheep, the lost coin, and the prodigal son demonstrate that the person who loses something valuable experiences joy when he or she recovers the lost treasure. Jesus' application is obvious: he rejoices over a single person who repents, just as the father in the parable of the prodigal son rejoices: "But we had to celebrate and be glad, because this brother of yours was dead and is alive again; he was lost and is found" (Luke 15:32).

SALVATION IS FREE; DISCIPLESHIP COSTS EVERYTHING

The 4:00 a.m. wake-up call to begin a trek into the southern Ethiopian lowland for a large church conference was tough but exciting. This was our first assignment as missionaries with Serving In Mission (SIM), and with only a few days in the country, this would be something to "write home about." Still unenthusiastic about local food, I asked my wife, Carol, to prepare a pan of cinnamon rolls for the trip. The thought of soft dough laced with cinnamon and sugar would make the trip more pleasant, I reasoned.

The cool, foggy mountain air was refreshing as we began our trip by Land Rover. After a bouncing two-hour journey, we arrived at a village and were served a breakfast of popcorn and a strange-looking pancake with ground hot red pepper as an accompanying dip. I wanted to save my rolls until later, so I enjoyed the popcorn.

Another hour passed before our next mode of transportation arrived—mules. Ethiopian saddles were wooden frames draped with feather pillows cinched loosely over the animal's back. After a few minutes, the feathers settle and the rider rests on the animal's backbone and wooden saddle. After a few hours of crossing the hot, dry desert, I was exhausted.

Sometime in the late evening, we arrived at the host church, who had waited until we arrived before they butchered and cooked the chicken. By the time the evening meal was ready, midnight had passed. The chicken stew laced with unfamiliar spices was tasty, but I was so tired I ate very little. I retired on a cowhide bed for the night, dreaming of the wonderful breakfast I would have the next morning.

The next three days were filled with unusual food, fatigue from preaching with two interpreters, lack of sleep, and the great burden of knowing my children were miles away in boarding school.

Things certainly were not playing out the way I had envisioned. Suddenly I found myself asking a question I had never expected: "What am I doing here?"

I thoroughly enjoyed my studies for service at Moody Bible Institute, Cedarville University, and Dallas Theological Seminary. Initially I had followed Jesus' call without hesitation. Now my commitment was faltering.

In total despair, I walked down to a lake to spend time alone with God. I sat for hours, questioning God and complaining about my situation. I quarreled with myself about how I could save face and still go back to America. I was ashamed of my lack of trust, and I didn't know what to do.

The moments ticked by as I tearfully pleaded with God, and in those moments, a quiet realization settled into my soul. Discipleship meant surrender, and I had surrendered my life to God's will. I had answered a call to Ethiopia. My sense of desperation was simply a response to my circumstances. I renewed my dedication to God's call and declared I would not leave Ethiopia until he directed me to do so.

In that moment, the calm and peace that I had longed for descended over my soul. In the years that have passed since that day, challenges have come, but the question of my commitment was settled and has remained firm for more than forty years.

Salvation is free, but discipleship costs everything.

Through the parable of the unjust steward, Jesus taught the larger implications of wealth management. Handling small matters determines how a person reacts to larger issues. Stewardship establishes our commitment to the master, and no one can serve two masters. The Pharisees, on the other hand, valued things that God viewed as worthless, and they foolishly believed that wealth was a sign of God's blessing. Jesus spoke directly to the sneering Pharisees: "You are the ones who justify yourselves in the eyes of others, but God knows your hearts. What people value highly is detestable in God's sight" (Luke 16:15).

Jesus taught yet another parable about honoring the law. A rich man lived in the lap of luxury, while Lazarus lived in deep poverty, dependent on the garbage that fell from the rich man's table. In death, the rich man was tormented in Hades, while Lazarus dwelt in luxury in the breast of Abraham. The rich man pleaded for the opportunity to return to his family to warn them of the truth, but his cries fell on deaf ears. Jesus addressed the issue: "If they [relatives] do not listen to Moses and the Prophets, they will not be convinced even if someone rises from the dead" (Luke 16:31).

Jesus continued to focus on instructing his disciples. His warning was stern: "Things that cause people to sin are bound to come, but woe to anyone through whom they come" (Luke 17:1). He exhorted them not to offend others, to forgive, and to nourish faith. Then he made an astonishing promise: "If you have faith as small as a mustard seed, you can say to this mulberry tree, 'Be uprooted and planted in the sea,' and it will obey you" (Luke 17:6). Jesus knew his persistence would have far-reaching results in his present ministry, as well as in the future growth of the church. The kingdom was at stake, and not a moment spent instructing his disciples would be wasted.

THE JEWS REACT TO THE RAISING OF LAZARUS
(John 11:1 – 54; T&G 118a – 19)[4]

Bethany lies about two miles east of Jerusalem in Judea. While most of the events prior to Jesus' famous triumphal entry occurred in Perea, across the Jordan, the raising of Lazarus took place in Bethany.

Jesus' relationship to the family of Martha and Mary is well recognized: "Jesus loved Martha and her sister and Lazarus" (John 11:5). His fondness for the family appears to have prompted his next moves. He received word that Lazarus, the brother of Mary and Martha fell ill. To the disciples' surprise, Jesus did not respond immediately. In order to make his point, he merely stated that "this sickness will not end in death" (John 11:4). Two days later, Jesus

Bethany: home of Mary, Martha, and Lazarus

determined to go back to Judea. His decision met with the disciples' warning that the Jews sought to stone him. Thomas (Didymus) bravely announced that they should go and die with him. At least Thomas seemed to sense the gravity of the situation (John 11:16).

When they arrived at the home of Martha and Mary, they found Lazarus dead. Since John notes Lazarus had been dead four days, he may have

Bethany from the north in the late 1800s

already been dead when Jesus received word that he was ill.[5] Again he claimed the moment as an opportunity to teach his disciples and those present, making a bold claim: "I am the resurrection and the life. The one who believes in me will live, even though they die" (John 11:26). While his listeners did not completely understand Jesus' words, Martha responded with an amazing confession of faith: "Yes, Lord, I believe that you are the Messiah, the Son of God, who is to come into the world" (John 11:27). We can only imagine why Jesus was moved as he approached Lazarus's tomb. "When Jesus saw her [Mary] weeping, and the Jews who had come along with her also weeping, he was

Inside the traditional tomb of Lazarus

deeply moved in spirit and troubled" (John 11:33). Perhaps his heart was torn as he witnessed his friends' grief. Perhaps he gained a glimpse of his future death and his Father's grief. Or perhaps he was reflecting on Lazarus's loss as he was called back to earth from paradise. Scripture does not reveal the reason.

But in the moments that followed, Jesus reached beyond the grave and commanded, "Lazarus, come out!" (John 11:43). And in obedience to his Savior, Lazarus walked out of his tomb. Perhaps not surprisingly, the event brought a mixed response: "Many of the Jews who had come to visit Mary, and had seen what Jesus did, believed in him" (v. 45).

But Pharisees who had heard of the event reported it to the chief priests. A council convened to determine a response. Behind closed doors, religious powers called a meeting of the Sanhedrin and argued among themselves how to handle the threat of a self-proclaimed king who could raise the dead. Surely the Romans would see Jesus as a threat and crush the "Jesus revolt" and Judaism along with it.

"If we let him go on like this," they argued, "everyone will believe in him, and then the Romans will come and take away both our temple and our nation" (John 11:48). Caiaphas offered a prophetic statement: "You do not realize that it is better for you that one man die for the people than that the whole nation perish" (v. 50). In other words, Jesus was to be offered as

Traditional tomb of Lazarus

a sacrifice at the hands of the Romans in order to secure Judaism and the authority of the priesthood. How ironic that Jesus would die as one man — but for the sins of the world. The council's decision sealed Jesus' fate: he must die. After this the religious leaders plotted to kill him.

The Pharisees asked Jesus when the kingdom of God would come. Jesus replied (Luke 17:21) and yet the sad reality was that the one God sent to establish his kingdom on earth was speaking directly to them, but they refused to believe it. From this moment on, Jesus made no further mention of the offer of the kingdom of God.

The long day came to an end, and Jesus and the disciples returned to the home of Mary and Martha for refreshment. The early spring winds were chilly, but the courtyard fire warmed the night air. We can imagine that James, John, and Peter sought a quiet corner to deliberate the significance of Jesus' power over death in raising Lazarus.

"Where is all of this taking us?" Peter asked as he glanced at his friends. "Is Thomas right? Are we going to Jerusalem to die with Jesus? Would the Master let this happen — to him, to all of us? From the time he chose us to follow him, we have seen him perform extraordinary miracles and speak words that have come from God himself. Surely he has not finished his work."

Peter paused as John nodded and extended his hands toward the warmth of the fire. "Peter, we watched as you walked on water at his command, and you spoke for all of us in Caesarea Philippi when you confessed Jesus to be the Messiah, the Son of the living God. We are committed to help establish his kingdom. Yet we have watched Jewish leaders in Galilee and Judea reject his work and even declare that Jesus performs miracles by the power of Satan. This could not be how Jesus' plan was supposed to unfold." He pulled his hands back into the folds of his robe.

Peter waited as James tossed his comments into the discussion. "When Jesus began his ministry, he declared that the kingdom was near. We rejoiced to know that Jesus was the promised coming King and longed for that to happen. Would he raise an army of believers to overthrow Rome, or would he do it by the power of his command? But now he speaks of his death, and his words seem contradictory."

Peter stood as the questions tumbled from him. "But why now? After teaching us for nearly three years—why would he be talking about giving up and walking into Jerusalem to die? He said he was our King, that he came to bring God's kingdom. Does he expect us to die with him when nothing makes sense? How can any of this possibly be a plan?"

The words fell into the silence of the cold night air. Unspoken questions still stirred in the minds of the disciples. It would be a long night with little sleep.

The disciples' concerns were legitimate. Jesus' message was clear: he was the coming Messiah who was offering the kingdom to Israel. While many believed and accepted him, Israel's leaders rejected him. The crowds that ate their fill wanted Jesus as king, but on their own terms. They wanted a king who provided free food, but they were unwilling to submit to God. Jesus called them to seek his kingdom first, but they sought blessing without obedience and prosperity without submission.

ON TO JERUSALEM (Matthew 19:1 – 20:34; Mark 10:1 – 52; Luke 17:22 – 19:28; T&G 120b – 27b)

After Jesus raised Lazarus in Bethany of Judea, he and the disciples began their final journey to Jerusalem.[6] Knowing his time was limited and that the disciples still wrestled with many questions, Jesus continued his instruction, explaining the necessity of his death, and charging the disciples to look for his glorious return. He also taught them about divorce, prayer, faith, and how to gain entrance into the kingdom of God. For the third time, he predicted his death and resurrection—but they did not understand these things (Luke 18:34).[7]

As the Perean ministry ended and Jesus and the disciples approached

Jerusalem, he clarified their misconceptions about the kingdom. The Pharisees asked Jesus when the kingdom of God would come, and Jesus replied, "The coming of the kingdom of God is not something that can be observed, nor will people say, 'Here it is,' or 'There it is,' because the kingdom of God is in your midst" (Luke 17:20–21).[8]

The meaning and purpose of the kingdom of God as preached by John the Baptist and offered by Jesus has been defined differently among scholars. To some it is synonymous with the eternal state of heaven and has no connection to the present earthly realm. To others it is a simple nonmaterial, spiritual realm in which God rules over the hearts of people.

Scripture provides a broad understanding of the kingdom. On the one hand, it is eternal and temporal, and on the other, it has a definite historical beginning and ending. It is administered by God, and yet it has a local administration through representatives.

God rules eternity as one with absolute authority. The biblical concept of "kingdom" includes several concepts: the right to rule, a king, and a realm in which ruling authority is exercised.

The central drama of biblical history incorporates God's rule. This theme is traced from Genesis to Revelation and seeks to answer the question, "Who has the authority to be obeyed?" This question is fundamental to the battle between God and Satan as played out in human history.

God's kingdom program developed through a series of covenants God made with the nation Israel: the Abrahamic covenant promised Israel's continuing existence and a land (Gen. 15:18–21); the Davidic covenant promised that David's house and kingdom would be established forever (2 Sam. 7:13); and the new covenant promised forgiveness of sin (Jer. 31:31–34). These eternal, unconditional, and irrevocable covenants determined the ultimate significance of God's kingdom on earth.

Jesus came to fulfill the old covenant (law of Moses, Ex. 24:6–8) and inaugurate the new covenant (spoken at the Last Supper, Matt. 26:28), which brought the forgiveness of sin by means of payment through an eternal sacrifice. The blood of bulls and goats of the old covenant was temporary. The blood of Christ permanently sealed the new covenant. He also came to offer himself as King and to sit on the Davidic throne.

From the covenant promises of the Old Testament, first-century Jews were looking for a kingdom that would give them personal freedom and material blessing. They sought relief from excessive taxation, foreign laws, and the brutality of oppression. Yet, like the Old Testament prophets, Jesus taught that the kingdom would come only to people who were obedient to the covenant.[9]

The inscrutability for Israel had been: Why does God use unbelieving nations to have mastery over his chosen people? Many thought Israel should be ruling nations like Adam was to rule the animal kingdom. Yet Rome, like previous illegitimate nations, controlled God's people at the time of Jesus. The Jews wanted the benefits of a political kingdom but without obedience to God.

While the covenants promised a kingdom here on earth, the prophets described the glories of that kingdom that extended beyond a mere political, earthly kingdom. Through David's line, the Messiah would bring peace, righteousness, and prosperity to the nation. He would come as a Savior to redeem fallen humankind and as a Sovereign to reign on the earth. Jesus, David's greater Son, was the King who would fulfill God's promise as he sat on the Davidic throne and ruled his people.

John the Baptist brought the Old Testament message to life as he proclaimed, "Repent, for the kingdom of heaven is at hand." Jesus furthered the message, preaching the kingdom of heaven (God), its values and demands. But the kingdom would not come if Israel refused to submit in obedience to Jesus, the heir to the Davidic throne, and his teaching. The demands of kingdom principles were too harsh for the leaders and threatened their political status.

From their knowledge of the Old Testament, the Jews were expecting a Messiah. Their mistake was the nature of the Messiah's kingdom. Jesus of Nazareth plunged the nation into a great debate: Was he the promised Messiah? Or was he a blasphemous imposter doing Satan's bidding? Jesus supported his claims with both his words of authority and the miracles he performed. The people were given a choice. Some believed and some rejected him.

After the nation's leaders officially rejected him, Jesus turned his message to judgment on that generation in Israel[10] and promised that the kingdom would be given to others.[11] Their rejection did not nullify the covenant promises concerning the earthly Davidic kingdom; they will be fulfilled in the future. The expected kingdom program that Jesus taught began with high hopes at the beginning of his ministry and ended with judgment and deferment.[12]

Jesus' teaching ministry on earth lasted about three and a half years. His final days of ministry shifted from the countryside, with a few visits to cities, to the holy city of Jerusalem. To get a clear picture of Jesus' last days, an understanding of the city of Jerusalem is essential. Let's take a closer look in the next chapter.

William Schlegel, *Satellite Bible Atlas*. Base map: Courtesy of NASA and US Geological Survey.

1. Feast of Tabernacles—Man born blind sent to Pool of Siloam
2. Jesus rejected in Samaria
3. Feast of Hanukkah: "I and the Father are one."
4. Ministry in Perea—parable of the rich man and Lazarus
5. Bethany—Lazarus raised
6. Seclusion in Ephraim
7. Ten Lepers healed (Samaria?)
8. Final journey to Jerusalem (dotted lines indicate uncertainty): childlike faith required for entrance into the kingdom
9. Blind Bartimaeus healed and Zacchaeus's life changed

JESUS' WORDS AND WORKS IN JUDEA, PEREA AND SAMARIA
Spring AD 31 – Spring 32

Jesus retired on the other side of the Jordan (John 10:40–42)

Bethany/Ephraim:
    Lazarus raised (John 11:38–44)
    Sanhedrin plotted to kill Jesus (John 11:45–57)

Jerusalem:
    Leaders attempted to arrest Jesus (John 7:32–52)
    Woman taken in adultery (John 7:53–8:11)
    Leaders attempted to stone Jesus (John 8:31–59)
    Man born blind healed (John 9:1–34)
    Discourse on Good Shepherd (John 10:1–18)
    Jesus stoned for affirming his claims as the Christ (John 10:22–39)

Judea:
    Seventy-two sent forth (Luke 10:1–16)
    Seventy-two returned (Luke 10:17–24)
    Parable of the good Samaritan (Luke 10:25–37)
    Lesson on prayer (Luke 11:1–13)
    Blind and demon-possessed man healed; Pharisees blasphemed Jesus
        (Luke 11:14–53)
    Feast at Pharisee's home (Luke 11:37–54)
    Parable of the rich fool (Luke 12:13–21)
    Parable of the barren fig tree (Luke 13:1–9)
    Infirm woman healed on the Sabbath (Luke 13:10–17)
    Parables of the mustard seed and leaven (Luke 13:18–21)
    Blind man examined by the Pharisees (John 9:1–34)

Perea (Region across the Jordan?) (John 10:40):
    Jesus dined with Pharisee (Luke 14:1–24)
    Parable of the great supper (Luke 14:15–24)
    Qualities of good disciples (Luke 14:25–35)
    "Lost" parables (Luke 15:1–32)
    Parable of the unjust steward (Luke 16:1–13)
    Parable of the rich man and Lazarus (Luke 16:19–31)
    Discourse of stumbling (Luke 17:1–10)
    Example of childlike faith (Mark 10:13–16)
    Rich young ruler (Matt. 19:16–30)
    Parable of the laborers (Matt. 20:1–16)

Jesus told disciples of pending death (Mark 10:32–34)
James and John's ambition (Matt. 20:20–28)
Samaria:
Ten lepers healed (Luke 17:11–19)
Lesson on the coming kingdom (Luke 17:20–37)
Jericho:
Blind Bartimaeus healed (Mark 10:46–52)
Zacchaeus (Luke 19:1–10)
Parable of the minas (talents) (Luke 19:11–27)

CHAPTER 9

MESSIAH'S HOLY CITY: FOREVER YOUNG, FOREVER OLD

JERUSALEM FOREVER YOUNG

We have followed Jesus from his birth in Bethlehem to his early life in Nazareth. We have shadowed his movements as he proclaimed his message, and we have wondered at his compassion and miracles while he was in Judea, Galilee, and Samaria. But it is in Jerusalem, the Holy City that we will follow his footsteps through the ancient streets as he completes his earthly mission. An understanding of the Holy City and a visit to the places that so profoundly shaped the gospel will deeply enhance our understanding of God's Word.

My bucket list always included investigating ancient sites where Jesus walked. So it was no surprise that my first visit to the Holy City in 1977 held me in the grip of anticipation. The stress and anxiety of our Ethiopian experience faded into the past as I looked forward to a country wide open to visits to ancient Old and New Testament archaeological tels (remains of civilizations on small hills) and sites. Many areas closed today because of Arab-Israeli tensions were then open and accessible to the public.

While I was president of the Institute of Holy Land Studies (Jerusalem University College), some of the students and I decided to visit, on one of their free days, sites in the "occupied zones"[1] of Samaria, Jericho, Hebron, and Beersheba. Jerusalem, the city of "peace," and its people exuded a quiet calm, although all men and military women wore guns slung over their shoulders or pistols on their belts. Military service was mandatory, with only

Orthodox Jewish males receiving exemption. Happily, only minor conflicts surfaced during the short time we roamed the antiquities.

When I returned to the Holy City in 1984 to serve the institute as a visiting professor, times had changed. Tensions between the Jews and Arabs had escalated. One day I stood atop the institute's main building on Mount Zion, looking over the Hinnom Valley, as an Arab bus loaded with commuters suddenly exploded. The street below erupted into chaos. Passengers cascaded out of the bus, and casualties were lined along the streets.

I was in shock and could barely comprehend the scene I was witnessing in a street I so often frequented. Ambulances responded quickly, with paramedics rushing to load victims into their vehicles. Police and the bomb squad located the weapon responsible for the explosion, a man-portable recoilless rocket, but they found no perpetrator.

The lingering memories of Israel from 1977 and 1984 made my appointment in 1990 as president of the Institute of Holy Land Studies in Jerusalem an exciting challenge. My anticipation grew as I waited the final three months for my departure to the Holy City. Our belongings packed and our

Today the Old City of Jerusalem is divided into four quarters. The Muslim and Christian Quarters get their names from the major holy places in their respective quarters.

ANNEXATION OF EAST JERUSALEM

By the late 1980s, terrorist activity was occurring regularly. Cars were torched, bombs were left on the streets in unattended packages in west Jerusalem, and personal attacks became all too common. Arabs were accused of most terrorist activities. The bus bombing incident marked a heightened period of tension. However, radical Jews, not Arabs, claimed responsibility for this act of terrorism. The Jewish community condemned the violence.

In 1980 Arabs constituted 27 percent of the total population of Jerusalem. The Israeli government under Likud leader Menachem Begin formally annexed more than five hundred acres of Arab-owned land just outside Jerusalem.[3] While the Arab homes on the land were allowed to stay, the unoccupied land became Jewish settlements. The communities on the eastern slope of French Hill and Neve Yaakov had been developed, even though they were in so-called "occupied territories" annexed during the 1967 Six-Day War. Jerusalem mayor Teddy Kollek objected in vain because of the obvious effect such a move would have on Jewish-Arab relations.[4]

affairs in order, we "set sail." Little did we know the exciting adventure that awaited us as we said our good-byes to friends and family. All too soon the dangers of the Palestinian Liberation Organization (PLO) terrorists surfaced. And as if things couldn't get any worse, we were about to be confronted with an even greater threat in the Intifada.[2]

Control of Jerusalem, the Holy City, is clearly the focal issue of the modern-day Jewish-Muslim conflict. Politics, war, and controversy are the legacies of the city founded by Israel's greatest king, David, son of Jesse, and the purported place of the ascension of Islam's greatest prophet, Muhammad.

An understanding of the modern conflict will help twenty-first-century Christians understand the deep-seated political and religious turmoil in Jesus' day and perhaps speak to the need for biblical expectations for the future coming of the Messiah.

A visit to modern Jerusalem

An abandoned Syrian tank rests near the 1967 Syrian-Israel border, reminding passers by of the recent conflict

Israeli soldiers patrolling the Old City

reminds the twenty-first-century believer of the turmoil Jesus faced in the first century. In Jesus' day it was the tension between religious Jews and an oppressive Roman rule. Today the conflict includes religious friction and an ongoing political battle for survival threatened by radical Muslims.

Students at the Institute of Holy Land Studies loved to go into the Old City to bargain with Arab shopkeepers to purchase Palestinian goods, art, or

Women with assault weapons in modern Ben Yehuda Street

crafts. As tensions began to build in the early 1990s, the shops would close for whole days at a time. Rumor had it that some Islamic religious groups forced Arab shops to go on strike by closing their businesses. Students complained that the strike did not help the cause but simply punished Arab shopkeepers. The question of the day around the institute became, "Is the Old City on strike today?"

In August 1988, Hamas published its founding charter. Hamas began as a militant branch of the Muslim Brotherhood called the Islamic Resistance Movement. Its popular name, an acronym, HAMAS (*Ḥarakat al-Muqāwamah al- 'Islāmiyyah* means "Islamic Resistance Movement"), was the Arabic word for "zeal." Their charter called for a permanent jihad against Israel until every part of Palestine was liberated. Appealing to their followers as an alternative to the PLO, they called for the Muslim world to join them in a "holy war" to liberate Palestine and destroy Israel. The charter concluded with the famous saying of the prophet Muhammad, "The day will come when Muslims will fight the Jews and kill them, to the degree that the Jew will hide behind rocks and trees which will call out to the Muslim and tell him, 'Servant of Allah, a Jew is hiding behind me, Come and kill him!'"[6]

The latest threats to peace are the war in Syria, the nuclear threat in Iran, and prevalent worldwide anti-Jewish sentiment. It seems that every few months a new destabilizing event erupts in the Middle East.

THE INTIFADA: THE WORLD'S NIGHTMARE

On December 9, 1987, a Palestinian uprising known as the Intifada,[5] began as a violent challenge to the Israeli occupation. No longer did isolated, unorganized terrorist activity dominate the Jewish/Arab conflict. The popular uprising grew among the common people who had grown tired of Jewish control and soon took on a life of its own.

Burning cars belonging to Jews became a nightly occurrence. Palestinian youths roamed the streets hurling stones. Nightly stabbings, purse snatchings, and attacks on neighborhood houses accelerated. In many ways, this uprising gained more momentum than the tactics of the Palestinian Liberation Organization. The world looked on with sympathy as Palestinians witnessed their youths killed and injured on a regular basis. Those in the West found it difficult to support Israel when news analysts and observers continually charged Israel with mistreating Palestinian youths. The Arabs took advantage of world opinion to pressure Israel into concessions.

Many Christians looking at the situation in Israel today throw up their hands and say, "Why can't Jews and Arabs just get along?" Modern-day circumstances provide insight into the Holy City in Jesus' day. The pressure Jesus and the Jews faced in the first century is similar to the Jewish predicament today. Yes, the people have changed, but hatred for Israel's presence in the land still plagues the Jews. Yet Israel's resolve is unwavering, as stated in Prime Minister Yitzhak Rabin's 1995 quote: "Undivided Jerusalem is the heart of the Jewish people and the capital of the State of Israel. Undivided Jerusalem is ours."[7]

THE HOLY CITY: FOREVER OLD

Israel's claim to Jerusalem is well documented in Scripture. David founded the city of Jerusalem in the tenth century BC for the purpose of building a temple in which God could dwell. Jerusalem was a small Jebusite village (less than eleven acres and with no more than a few thousand inhabitants) perched on the top of a ridge between the Hinnom and Kidron Valleys. The Gihon Spring, located just outside the city wall, provided the much-needed water supply for its inhabitants. David recognized Jerusalem as a natural fortress in a

City of David from the east; Old City walls in background

strategic location in the middle of the kingdom over which he had just been crowned (2 Sam. 5:4–5). David purchased an area just north of the Jebusite city from Araunah, a Jebusite who used the bedrock for a threshing floor (2 Sam. 24:18–25). King David insisted on paying for the property and the oxen working the press at the hefty price of fifty shekels of silver. There David built an altar for the Lord and offered burnt and fellowship offerings. On this very spot, David's son Solomon built the temple.

Solomon extended the City of David to include the areas David took from the Jebusites and purchased from Araunah, built the supporting terraces, and filled the gaps in the wall from the original city northward. This enclosed area is identified as the Ophel.[8] Solomon built the temple to the Lord on the site of David's altar. The borders of the city remained until the divided monarchy in the eighth century, when the city expanded to include the western hill.

LC-matpc-12310–10/www.LifeintheHolyLand.com

Gihon Spring, "Virgin's Spring"

From Solomon's accession in 971 BC to Hezekiah about 715 BC, the city expanded beyond the City of David, the Ophel, and the Temple Mount to include the western hill. Although little is known of the size of Jerusalem during the time of the divided kingdom, several clues help determine the basic area of the city's walls. Second Chronicles 26:9 refers to the possible expansion of the city during Uzziah's reign in the mid-eighth century: "Uzziah built towers in Jerusalem at the Corner Gate, at the Valley Gate and at the angle of the wall, and he fortified them." While no direct evidence exists for the location of these walls, it is believed the area began to be developed during this period. Evidence does exist for Hezekiah's reign a few years later.

The divided kingdom represents a dark stain on Israel's history. The death of Solomon brought a period of self-destruction. During the divided monarchy, the two tiny kingdoms became mere pawns in international politics and power struggles. God's promise of blessing came only in response to kings who exercised faith in the God of their fathers. During the eighth century, the cruel and determined Assyria ultimately destroyed the northern kingdom. When they carried off the northern kingdom, those ten tribes never reassembled as a people again. They became known as "the lost tribes of Israel."

Hezekiah's tunnel with Warren's Shaft base

Hezekiah, king of the southern kingdom (Judah), was determined to save Jerusalem and his temple. He agreed to pay Sennacherib a ransom, going so far as to strip all the silver and gold from the temple to make the payment. Of course, Sennacherib didn't keep the agreement and laid siege anyway. God answered Hezekiah's prayer for divine deliverance. The miraculous respite was only temporary. Even Assyria's success was temporary.[9] Scripture records the divine intervention: "That night the angel of the LORD went out and put to death a hundred and eighty-five thousand in the Assyrian camp. When the people got up the next morning—there were all the dead bodies! So Sennacherib king of Assyria broke camp and withdrew. He returned to Nineveh and stayed there" (2 Kings 19:35–36).

The invasion and destruction of the northern kingdom and the siege of Judah terrified Jerusalem's inhabitants. Many took refuge within the city walls. This influx of refugees motivated Hezekiah to expand the actual city walls.

Archaeologist Nahman Avigad discovered an ancient wall known as the "broad wall" while excavating the Jewish Quarter shortly after Israel won the Six-Day War in 1967. According to Avigad, the wall was built on a system of dry riverbeds in the city,[10] and a small section of the wall was uncovered. The foundations of buildings were destroyed in order to construct the massive fortified wall. The prophet Isaiah, in describing Hezekiah's preparation for the Assyrian invasion, penned these words: "You saw that the City of David were broken through in many places; you stored up water in the Lower Pool. You counted the buildings in Jerusalem and tore down houses to strengthen the wall" (Isa. 22:9–10). The unmistakable reference is to Hezekiah's broad wall and the tunnel he built to bring water into the city during the siege.

Avigad, who directed the excavations of the Jewish Quarter, described his view of the extent of the city of Jerusalem in Hezekiah's reign:

> Our archaeological finds in the Jewish Quarter clearly show that this area was settled in the period of the first temple, from the eighth century BCE on. Together with the finds from other minor excavations, in the Citadel, in the Armenian Garden, and on Mt. Zion, our evidence indicates that Israelite houses were spread over the entire plateau of the Western Hill. To date, with the exception of a few isolated shreds, no pottery from before the 8th century BCE has been found here.[11]

LIVING ON HISTORIC WALLS

The view from my wife Carol and my Jerusalem apartment was breathtaking. Olive trees, grapevines, and flowers provided splashes of color in our backyard. To the southeast stretched the seemingly endless hilly Judean wilderness. To the southwest the Hinnom Valley carved its way just outside the walls of the Old City and snaked along until it intersected the Kidron Valley. The campus of the Institute of Holy Land Studies stood high on Mount Zion just outside the medieval walls of the Old City. It was an idyllic setting and atmosphere in which to study the Bible in its geographical context. Shortly after we moved into the apartment and I assumed the responsibilities of president of the Institute, we discovered that my office and our apartment were set atop the actual city wall of Hezekiah's time. A magnificent view in this historical paradise reinforced my love for living in Jerusalem.

Donald Brake's office atop Hezekiah's wall

Donald Brake's apartment at Institute of Holy Land Studies.

Bedrock remains of Hezekiah's wall in the right corner with reused Herodian stones in the right forefront.

Sketch by Louise Bass

Sketch by Louise Bass, former Wycliffe Bible translator and illustrator: Jerusalem University College (former Bishop Gobat School)

The biblical accounts of this "City of God" are the primary sources of our knowledge of the glories of the city and the temple. But like so many great things in life, sin soon overpowered the kings of Judah, and their lack of obedience brought an end to the kingdom and their beloved Jerusalem. The Babylonians stormed the city in 586 BC, and King Nebuchadnezzar's army set the city ablaze. The city had seen street battles as various kings of Judah fought for the throne, but no one was prepared for the devastation the Babylonians rained down on the city.

> Nebuzaradan commander of the imperial guard, an official of the king of Babylon, came to Jerusalem. He set fire to the temple of the LORD, the royal palace and all the houses of Jerusalem. Every important building he burned down. The whole Babylonian army ... broke down the walls around Jerusalem. Nebuzaradan ... carried into exile the people who remained in the city.... The Babylonians broke up the bronze pillars, the movable stands and the bronze Sea that were at the temple of the LORD and they carried the bronze to Babylon. They also took away the pots, shovels, wick trimmers, dishes and all the bronze articles used in the temple service. (2 Kings 25:8–11, 13–14)

Nebuchadnezzar left Jerusalem devastated in 586 BC. He carried off the upper classes into captivity. The poorest classes of people were left to tend the vineyards and farm the crops. Judah and Jerusalem lay in waste. The First Temple period came to an ignominious close.

After the destruction of the first temple, the city of Jerusalem was once again reduced to the size of the City of David and the Temple Mount. The walls around the western hill, while in ruins, continued to define Jerusalem, but very few inhabitants lived inside. Nehemiah suggests that while the city lay in ruins, the walls did provide some sort of protection for its citizens during the years of captivity.[12]

This all changed when Persia conquered Babylon and King Cyrus decreed that the Jews return to Judah in 536 BC. He sent them back with the treasures of the temple confiscated by the Babylonians seventy years before (Ezra 1:9–11). The Babylonian captivity ended.

Zerubbabel led the return from the Babylonian captivity. The Jerusalem he found differed significantly from the beauty and splendor of the Solomonic temple and the city that had known glory under the kings of the pre-exilic period. The city, while still occupied, showed little progress in rebuilding. Although little is known of the condition of the Temple Mount, Jeremiah, in describing the events of Gedaliah's assassination in the aftermath of the fall and destruction of Jerusalem, suggested that ruins of the foundation of the temple may have stood. He wrote, "The day after Gedaliah's assassination, before anyone knew about it, eighty men who had shaven off their beards, torn their clothes and cut themselves came from Shechem, Shiloh and Samaria, bringing grain offerings and incense with them to the house of the LORD" (Jer. 41:4–5).

Ezra described the returnees as going immediately to the "house of the LORD" to give freewill offerings to assist in financing the rebuilding of the "house of God on its site" (Ezra 2:68). Apparently some of the original temple structure still stood.

Old City west wall from the south (built by the Ottoman leader Suliman the Magnificent in sixteenth century)

While little is known about Zerubbabel's temple, it certainly differed from Solomon's. King Cyrus's decree describes the temple (538 BC) to be rebuilt with varying dimensions: "Let the temple be rebuilt as a place to present sacrifices, and let its foundations be laid. It is to be sixty cubits [ninety feet] high and sixty cubits [ninety feet] wide, with three courses of large stones and one of timbers" (Ezra 6:3–4). In contrast, Solomon's temple is described as "sixty cubits [ninety feet] long, twenty [thirty feet] wide and thirty [forty-five feet] high" (1 Kings 6:2).

Places of significance on the Temple Mount

Modern Day Boundaries

The return under Zerubbabel revised the spiritual and political life of the once defeated people of Judah. Twenty-two years after their return, the temple stood as a monument worthy of God, and Zerubbabel dedicated it with full pomp and circumstance in 516 BC. The Holy City once again became the capital of Judah, the center of Jewish life. Even so, the city itself remained in ruins. Ezra, a teacher well versed in the law of Moses, returned in 458 BC with a host of determined Jews. A period of reformation prepared for the rebuilding of Jerusalem's walls.

Under God's authority, with Artaxerxes's permission and Nehemiah's leadership, the rebuilding of Jerusalem's walls began in 444 BC. Following Nehemiah's detailed description of the condition of the walls after his famous nocturnal reconnaissance mission, Nehemiah penned these often-quoted words:

> I went to Jerusalem, and after staying there three days I set out during the night with a few others. I had not told anyone what my God had put in my heart to do for Jerusalem. There were no mounts with me except the one I was riding on. By night I went out through the Valley Gate toward the Jackal Well and the Dung Gate, examining the walls of Jerusalem, which had been broken down, and its gates, which had been destroyed by fire. Then I moved on toward the Fountain Gate and the King's Pool, but there was not enough room for my mount to get through; so I went up the valley by night, examining the wall. Finally, I turned back and reentered through the Valley Gate. (Neh. 2:11–15)

The size of the city of Jerusalem as described by Nehemiah is somewhat smaller than the size of the city prior to the captivity of 586 BCE. The size roughly mirrored the size of the City of David plus the Temple Mount. In spite of opposition, Nehemiah and his followers completed the restoration of the walls in fifty-two days (Neh. 6:15). The newly refurbished walls of the city gave it a new status among its neighbors.

At the time of the outbreak of the Hasmonean revolt (167 BC), Jerusalem's size equaled that of the city in Nehemiah's day. Dan Bahat, former official archaeologist for the city of Jerusalem described the expansion of the city

Identities of modern sites in the Old City (Jaffa Gate from the southwest)

during the Hasmonean period: "The beginning of Jerusalem's expansion to the west on the eve of the Hasmonean period was one of the most important milestones in its development. Apparently the first temple period walls (such as the Broad Wall) were still visible above the ground and served as the boundary for the renewed expansion of the city."[13]

Bahat suggested the expansion began in the second century BC after the victory of Antiochus III over the forces of the Seleucids about 200 BC. The penetration of Hellenistic culture into Jerusalem and especially in the Upper City promoted the development of an attractive urban center. The Hasmoneans built atop the first temple period walls, what Josephus termed the "Old Wall."[14] These walls incorporated the walls around Mount Zion. First Maccabees 10:11 describes this effort: "And Jonathan dwelt in Jerusalem and began to build and renew the city. And he commanded them that did the work to build the walls and the mount Sion round about square stones for defense." Josephus mentions a city council building, a gymnasium with a large courtyard, and the large Hasmonean Palace overlooking the Temple Mount.[15]

THE "FOOTPRINTS" OF JESUS IN FIRST-CENTURY JERUSALEM

Jesus' final few days in Jerusalem occupies a major portion of the gospel accounts. The places he visited are central to his work on earth.

The Mount of Olives

The Mount of Olives overlooks the Valley of Jehoshaphat. Its steep elevation prevented Jerusalem from growing to the east. Its elevation peaked at 2,691 feet above sea level or 250 feet above the Temple Mount. Across the Kidron Valley, the Dome of the Rock with the Al-Aqsa Mosque is the central feature of the Temple Mount. Below is the City of David, the Gihon Spring, and the Pool of Siloam (where Solomon was anointed, 1 Kings 1–2), Mount of Offense (NIV: "Hill of Corruption," 2 Kings 23:13), where Solomon worshiped false gods (modern Arab area of Silwan).

Israel's enemies always attacked Jerusalem from the north because the Hinnom and Kidron Valleys protect the city from the east, south, and west. The Golden Gate aligns with a direct view from the Mount of Olives, where all three religions believe the Messiah will enter Jerusalem. A Jewish fable says a bridge of paper and iron will span the Kidron Valley. All humanity will cross the bridge to face God. Those choosing the iron bridge will perish, and those crossing on the paper bridge will show trust in God and be saved.

Church of Pater Noster and Chapel of Ascension or Eleona (Olive Grove)
Latin for "Our Father," the Church of Pater Noster is maintained by the
Catholic Carmelite cloistered sisters. As with many modern sites, Constantine
built the first church in the fourth century at the request of his mother, Queen
Helena. She also was responsible
for building the Church of the
Nativity and Church of the Holy
Sepulcher. The Pater Noster commemorates the ascension of Jesus.
After its destruction in AD 614
by the Persians, the Crusaders
rebuilt it (associating it with the
Lord's Prayer) in the twelfth century, only to see Saladin destroy
it again in 1187. More than a
hundred plaques bear the Lord's
Prayer in as many languages. The
princess of de la Tour d'Auvergne
commissioned Charles Clermont-
Ganneau to search out Constantine's church and restore a church

Pater Noster ancient cave of Eleona commemorating Jesus' ascension

on its site. The current church was built in 1875 on the foundations of Constantine's church.

This is the traditional rock located in Gethsemane where Jesus' sweat was like great drops of
blood on the night before his crucifixion (Luke 22:44). The church is built over this rock.

Cave of Gethsemane where Byzantine tradition places the disciples while Jesus prayed in agony.

Cave (Grotto) of Gethsemane

The Cave of Gethsemane served as a place for pressing olives. Some suggest that because this cave would not have been in use during Passover (which is in the springtime), Jesus and the disciples may have used this cave for meeting and sleeping.

Pool of Siloam

The water from the Gihon Spring is diverted to Siloam by means of Hezekiah's tunnel. By the first century, Jerusalem's inhabitants and visitors came to the Pool of Siloam to draw water and the existence of Hezekiah's tunnel may have been forgotten. Today the spring of Gihon is lower than the Kidron Valley because of the centuries of debris that have washed into it.

In David's day, the spring lay outside the city walls. In the Canaanite period, sinking a shaft (known today as Warren's Shaft) from inside the city and then tunneling to the spring solved the problem. The citizens of Jerusalem covered the entry to the spring so enemies besieging the city could not cut off the city from the water. During the invasion of Sennacherib, Hezekiah (701 BC) dug a huge tunnel to get the water diverted to inside the walls (2 Kings 20:20; 2 Chron. 32:2–4, 30; Isa. 22:11).

From the City of David, a shaft allowed inhabitants to get water. Some scholars have concluded that this accounts for 2 Samuel 5:8, where David says, "Anyone who conquers the Jebusites will have to use the water shaft to reach those 'lame and blind' who are David's enemies." The water shaft allowed them to gain entrance to the tunnel. Modern scholars date the tunnel to the time of the Canaanite inhabitants before David.[16]

The gospel of John records the healing of the blind man at the Pool of Siloam (9:7). The spring furnished needed water for temple activities.

Pool of Siloam from the south. Scholars have long believed that this was the area of an ancient pool, but without excavations they have not understood its date, size, or other important details until now. The steps lead from street level to the pool. Pottery and coins indicate that this pool was in use in the first century. Archaeologists believe this is the pool where the blind man washed the mud off of his eyes and received his sight (John 9:1–12).

Modern view of traditional Siloam Pool

The original Pool of Siloam was the reservoir for the water brought into the City of David. It was presumably destroyed in 586 BC when Babylonian king Nebuchadnezzar destroyed the city. The pool of Jesus' time, which was used for ceremonial cleansing, was built early in the first century BC and was destroyed by the Roman general Titus in AD 70.

Gethsemane

Kidron Valley

Dung Gate

Gihon Spring

Central (Tyropean) Valley

Pool of Siloam

St. Peter in Gallicantu

Oskar Schindler's tomb

Temple Mount and City of David from the southwest

In the summer of 2004, workers repairing a sewage pipe in the City of David revealed some large stone steps. Archaeologists Eli Shukron and Ronny Reich discovered that this series of steps led down into the adjacent garden where the pool is located—and water still runs. Steps lead into the stone-lined pool from all sides. The pool is about 225 feet long and lies about 200 yards from the location of the traditional Pool of Siloam. Scholars believe this is the biblical Pool of Siloam of Jesus' day rather than the pool traditionally thought to be the Pool of Siloam.

Western (Wailing) Wall

It is a miracle that any Herodian limestone blocks remain today. The Romans were able to destroy much of Jerusalem when they cut down trees within a twelve-mile radius that included the Mount of Olives and burned them against the massive city walls and Temple Mount. The limestone blocks used in building the city walls burst open when intensely heated. The phenomenon accounts for the utter destruction of the city.

Four portions of the retaining wall of the Temple Mount are preserved. The Western Wall is the place where Jews worship because it is one of the closest to the former location of the Holy of Holies of the temple. The Dome of the Rock on the Temple Mount is the third holiest place in the world to Muslims.[17]

Men praying at the Western (Wailing) Wall

The Western Wall became important in the post-Crusader period because of its location inside the city, adjacent to the Jewish Quarter. Authorities in the Ottoman period (sixteenth century) helped to restore the wall and recognized it as a Jewish holy site.

During the war for independence, the wall fell into the hands of the Jordanians, who originally gave visitation rights to Jews but later rescinded those rights. During excavations after the 1967 war, two more courses of the wall were uncovered and original Herodian stones exposed.

During the Six-Day War in 1967, Israel recaptured the Old City. Rather than force the Arabs from the Temple Mount, Israel relinquished the administration to the Muslim religious authority. The Temple Mount remains a major source of tension between Muslims and Jews.

Temple Mount from the south

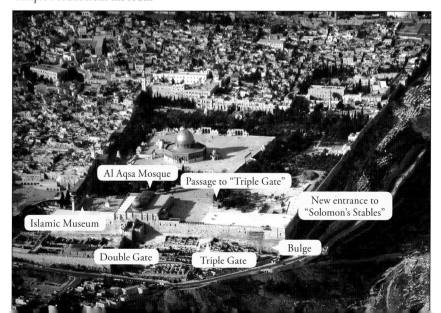

The Double Gate is largely obscured by a Crusader building, the Madrassat el-Khatuniyeh (Religious School of the Lady). Half of the easternmost gate is visible. The protruding arched lintel is from the Umayyad period. Above this is a massive stone with a large margin; this is the original lintel of the Herodian gate.

Triple Gate. The Triple Gate is not original, but the passageways leading from it to the Temple Mount platform are largely original. The triple-arched gate was reconstructed in the Umayyad period. Some believe that this gate was a triple-arched gate in Herod's time; others believe it was originally a double gate.

In front of the Western Gate (Double Gate) is a wide staircase. Some of the thirty original steps remain, and others have been reconstructed. The upper part of the staircase is rock-cut. This is the grandest of all the approaches to the Temple Mount.

Southern Temple Mount Excavations

The main entrances into the Temple Mount, known as the Hulda Gates, although blocked today, can be seen in plain view. Jesus most certainly entered the temple area up the stairs and through the Hulda Gates.[18]

The majority of the population entered the southern area of the Temple Mount through the gate on the east (Triple Gate) and exited through the gate on the west (Double Gate). A person in mourning would enter the (exit) gate, and people seeing him going the wrong direction knew of his mourning and would ask the nature of his problem.

Hulda in Hebrew means "rat," and the entrance from lower ground to higher as one enters the Temple Mount is reminiscent of the way a rat emerges from its burrow. These tunnels now run under the Al-Aqsa Mosque and are decorated with flowers and designs but no human images.

The Triple Gate was built on the foundations of the east Hulda Gate. Not much of the Western Gate remains. After the gates were destroyed by Muslims, the inhabitants did not rebuild the gate in its original form.

Some of the houses below the walls of the southern area are from the Byzantine period, but most of the prominent structures are of the Umayyad palaces, built using Herodian stones that had been pushed down from the Temple Mount by the Romans. Wall structures and debris covered the foot of the wall. The owners built their houses over the debris.

Remains of Robinson's Arch protruding from Western Wall

Robinson's Arch

While touring the Western Wall in 1838, Edward Robinson spotted some large stones protruding out of the Western Wall at the southern end. Earlier historians believed Herod used this bridge to enter the

First-century street beneath Robinson's Arch; debris in foreground

temple area from the west. Josephus noted a royal portico with royal offices in the area. Some questioned why such a large bridge would have been built for so few people. In 1867 Charles Wilson found another arch on the Western Wall. Josephus mentions only one arch. When Warren dug some twenty years later, he found what he believed were the piers of a massive bridge that was 100 meters long and 15.2 meters wide. This bridge traverses the Tyropoeon Valley.[19]

When Benjamin Mazar began his excavations after the 1967 war, despite the objections of fellow archaeologists, he exposed large portions of the area next to the Temple Mount. Hoping to find piers, their discoveries changed

Shops under Robinson's Arch

the view of Robinson's Arch. They uncovered huge piers 15.2 meters long by 3.6 meters wide with shops built right into the piers. Scholars believed this structure formed part of a bazaar belonging to the Temple Mount area.

The piers supported the opposite end of the arch and were found 13 meters from the Western Wall. This row of dentils had been used in a secondary wall built by Muslims at the beginning of the eighth century.

Dirt was piled up in a mound as a form to lay the massive blocks of stone like a giant mold. The archaeologists continued to dig west, hoping to find more evidence of a bridge, but none was found. They turned their efforts south of the piers and to their surprise found more shops. These shops actually supported the arch. What soon became obvious was that the structure was an elaborately conceived staircase for reaching the southern area of the esplanade (royal portico) from the Tyropoeon Valley street. Josephus confirmed this finding: "The last gate [Robinson's Arch] led to the other part of the city, from which it was separated by many steps going down to the ravine and from here up again to the hill [Upper City]."[20]

In the classical world, public buildings housed banks, stock exchanges, and courts of justice. These buildings formed a basilica or portico built near every commercial center. Courthouses and commercial centers flourished on the Temple Mount. The arch enabled merchants and customers to go from the shops below the Temple Mount to the larger commercial enterprises on the Mount.

Many Jews regarded commercialism so close to the temple as outrageous. This corresponds with Jesus' reaction to the money changers (Matt. 21:12–13).

When battling to destroy Jerusalem in AD 70, Titus perhaps encountered the Jewish Zealots led by Simon Bar Giora, who took a stand on the Temple Mount. To improve their defensive position, Bar Giora's fighters destroyed the overpass to impede access of the Romans to the Temple Mount.

The Temple Mount survived, but for Christians, Jews, and Muslims it has become a place of both refuge and conflict.

CHAPTER 10

MESSIAH'S TEMPLE: THE SOUL OF JERUSALEM

THE CHILLING MUSLIM CRY *"Allahu Akbar, Allahu Akbar"* signaled the reality of my worst fears. Based on warnings of trouble on the Temple Mount (Muslims call it Haram al-Sharif), we reinforced our lockdown of the students at the Institute of Holy Land Studies in Jerusalem (Jerusalem University College) on Mount Zion. I had heard rumors for three days that an Israeli group called the Temple Faithful were going to attempt to lay the cornerstone to the "third temple." Their persistence in trying to take control of this holy site of Muslims, Christians, and Jews always resulted in physical confrontation.[1] But in spite of our lockdown, some of our students couldn't resist becoming eye-witnesses to history that day and ran to the Temple Mount to "check it out."

This was Monday, October 8, 1990, the fifth day of the Feast of Succoth (Tabernacles), which is celebrated at the end of the long, parched summer, when water is in short supply. During this sacred feast, an estimated twenty thousand men and descendants of the priestly family gathered at the Western Wall to say Levitical prayers over worshipers. Afterward the ceremony proceeded south a few hundred yards to the Pool of Siloam to invoke God to send rain.

Just as the Jewish prayers concluded, the Temple Faithful came into the plaza singing religious and nationalistic songs and waving Israeli flags. The group, considered to be extremist by most Jews, had rolled a three-ton stone into the plaza with the intention of forcing it onto the Muslim sacred site. The police had been warned, however, and quickly moved to force the group toward their destination at Siloam Spring. But as they were leaving, voices were heard over the loudspeakers from the Al-Aqsa Mosque, taunting and shouting religious slogans. Hearing the commotion below on the plaza, several thousand Muslims on the Mount began shouting, "The Jews are coming, arm yourselves."

Hearing those words, the men and boys rushed to the edge of the Temple Mount, armed themselves with stones and rubble, and began to hurl their ballistics down on the Jewish worshipers below. They also attacked a number of armed Israeli soldiers near the entrance to the Mount. The soldiers, in self-defense, retaliated with a canister of tear gas.

LC-matpc—04245-t/www.LifeintheHolyLand.com

Early twentieth-century view of traditional Pool of Siloam

In reaction to hundreds of rushing, screaming Muslims, Israeli soldiers fired rubber bullets. But the Muslims fought back, forcing the badly out-numbered soldiers to retreat. Fueled by the promise of imminent victory, Palestinians overran the military, took aim, and carried out their wrath on the Jews in the plaza. The scene was a nightmare. Women screamed, men ran to protect their children, and the wounded begged for aid. Debris piled up on the plaza as the onslaught continued. While the sight was frightening, it was also a reminder that God was in control of his beloved but troubled city.

Our students couldn't believe what they were witnessing. Amid the wails and screaming, a voice over the mosque loudspeakers pleaded with the Israeli soldiers to stop the shooting. Jewish worshipers ran from the Western Wall through the plaza, terrified and screaming in agony. Some bore wounds from rocks hurled by Muslims from atop the Temple Mount. One student recalled a panicked woman running hysterically, accusing the Muslims of attacking the faithful Jews praying at the wall.

The shooting finally stopped, but not before eighteen Arabs died and hundreds more were injured. The immediate aftermath of the conflict heightened the Jewish-Muslim tensions. Rumors of Jewish gunmen firing

Temple Mount, Jerusalem

into the Al-Aqsa Mosque swept through the Arab community. Three Jews were stabbed to death in the Old City, a Jewish taxi driver was shot through the head, and an eighteen-year-old female Jewish soldier was stabbed to death in West Jerusalem while she was crossing the street. Several Muslims were arrested shortly after the attacks.[2]

On October 8, 1990, a new and deadlier conflict began. No longer a battle for territory or personal human rights, this war was implemented for the essence of Jerusalem, "the sacred sanctuary." This war was not just a Palestinian/Israeli conflict but a much deeper and more hotly debated Jewish-Muslim holy war popularly called jihad. [3]

Model of Herod's temple, now at the Israel Museum

The Temple Mount was the scene of many of Jesus' activities during Passion Week. His famous outburst of righteous anger spilled over into the marketplace. He attacked the money changers and overturned the tables of crooked merchants, shouting, "It is writ-

Muslim Dome of the Rock built over the location of the Jewish temple

ten ... 'My house will be called a house of prayer,' but you are making it 'a den of robbers'" (Matt. 21:13). He debated the religious leaders and finally in sorrow spoke the notable words, "Jerusalem, Jerusalem, you who kill the prophets and stone those who sent you, how often I have longed to gather your children together, as a hen gathers her chicks under her wings, and you were not willing. Look, your house is left to you desolate" (Matt. 23:37–38).

While very little information is available regarding the construction of the Temple Mount, Josephus describes it as being significantly altered during the Hasmonean period. The slope south of the Temple Mount was filled in so the platform could be extended. A distinct seam can be seen on the southern end of the eastern wall today, representing the Herodian extension. The Temple Mount was situated on a mount that had been leveled off, its crest a plateau covering an area of 500 by 500 cubits (820 by 820 feet).[4]

Western Wall and Wilson's Arch from below

The visible seam in the wall on the eastern side of Temple Mount reveals where Herod expanded the sacred platform.

The Temple Mount, temple, Robinson's Arch, and Wilson's Bridge are visible on a model of Jerusalem now on display at the Israel Museum.

Josephus vividly portrays Aristobulus's destruction of a bridge that led from the Upper City to the Temple Mount.[5] Today the remains of the arch of this bridge can be seen hanging from the Western Wall and is known as Wilson's Arch. The Temple Mount continued to be the "soul" of the Holy City during the deeply nationalistic Hasmonean dynasty.

Solomon's temple, when rebuilt by Zerubbabel became a symbol of rebellion. The enemies of the Jews accused them of rebelling against the Persian Empire (Ezra 4–5). The endurance of the temple through time paled in comparison to the magnificent structure built under the Herodian dynasty and the Roman governors. Its beauty and expansion became one of the most dramatic sources of literature and politics in human history. While few people can name the "seven wonders of the world," most know of the splendors of Jerusalem and the temple at the time of Jesus.

Written sources such as Josephus, as well as archaeological discoveries, have painted a well-defined canvas of the Holy City and the temple from the time of Jesus (commonly referred to as the "Second Temple Period"). Herod the Great embellished and fortified Jerusalem beyond what any ruler had done before or since. His desire to expand its economic base, pad his own wealth, and immortalize himself motivated him to tirelessly make Jerusalem a world-class city. His zeal was expressed in architectural style and magnitude. He built palaces, fortified the city, extended the Temple Mount, and renovated the temple.[6]

Dan Bahat described the southern and eastern borders of the city walls and their relationship to the temple during the Second Temple Period:

MORNING MEDITATION AND MEMORIES

The morning air was cool in the empty, quiet streets as an occasional blast from a minaret called Muslims to prayer. I was dressed in full running gear for my physical exercise and a time of daily meditation and prayer. I started at the southwestern corner of the Old City to begin my jog around the city. I often ran up the hill to the Jaffa Gate and on to the northwestern corner and then down the hill to the Damascus Gate. It took about thirty minutes to circle the Old City. For many years, I studied the events of the Old and New Testament that had taken place in the city of Jerusalem. It seemed strange now that in just thirty minutes I could encompass the area that had been the focus of my passion. Not until the nineteenth century did Jerusalem again reach the dimensions of the Second Temple Period. And today the city extends far beyond the confines of the city of biblical times.

The remains of the wall traced in 1894–97 by Bliss and Dickie along the southern crest of Mount Zion are evidence that the wall ran from the area where today the Protestant cemetery is situated, in the direction of ancient Siloam Pool. At this point, the wall traversed the dam at the outlet of the pool, then ran to the east and north along the eastern slopes of the City of David's hill, passed by the Ophel and linked up with the Temple Mount wall.[7]

Once Herod secured his power base as ruler, he began a rigorous building campaign. His plan was executed in such a grandiose magnitude that his buildings stand in history as his greatest accomplishments. His greatest achievement may have been the building of his opulent palace in Jerusalem. But his legacy still stands in his monumental work of building the Jewish temple, a work he began in the eighteenth year of his reign (20/19 BC).[8]

According to Josephus, construction on the temple precincts continued for more than eighty years until Albinus (AD 62–64) laid off eighteen thousand workers.[9] The Temple Mount reached its zenith during this period and is identical to the size and shape of the Mount today. Shops surrounded the Temple Mount, and a large bridge was constructed to carry traffic from the Upper City to the Temple Mount. The ruins of a major staircase (Robinson's Arch) can be seen today protruding from the southern section of the Western Wall. To the south, large steps with multiple gates led worshipers into the temple area. These steps, too, can be seen today.

The glories of Israel and the splendors of Herod's greatest accomplishment came to a sudden end when Titus, the Roman general, and his legions razed

Steps leading up to the Temple Mount from the south

the city and destroyed the temple in AD 70. Israel and the Promised Land lay in the hands of the Gentiles for nearly nineteen centuries.

THE SITE OF THE TEMPLE

There is some controversy today as to the location of Herod's temple in relation to the Dome of the Rock. Is the Dome of the Rock directly over the site of the biblical temple? Or is it, as some suggest, located to the north-west of the Dome of the Rock?

Dome of the Tablets on the Temple Mount. Some suggest this was the actual location of the Holy of Holies in biblical times.

With the Muslims in control of the Temple Mount (Haram esh-Sharif), archaeological studies on the Dome of the Rock and sites considered to be the exact location of the temple have become difficult. Since 1968 the excavations, although limited, have provided

THE GOLDEN GATE (EASTERN GATE)

James Fleming, a student at the American Institute of Holy Land Studies (Jerusalem University College) in the late 1960s, relates a dramatic story of an amazing find he stumbled upon in 1969 while investigating the eastern wall of the Temple Mount. Fleming was making his way along the eastern wall near the Golden Gate where a large Muslim cemetery lay. The heavy rain the night before left the ground soggy. As he walked along the wall in front of the Golden Gate, the ground beneath his feet gave way and he dropped eight feet into a deep hole. He came face-to-face with a cache of bones. To his surprise, he saw five large wedge-shaped stones forming a massive arch. He interpreted the arch as part of the ancient Eastern Gate. In anticipation of sharing his finds, he returned the following day with his archaeology professor, Moshe Kochavi, only to find that the local Muslims had already cemented over the newly discovered area to prevent further violation of the Muslim tombs.[10]

This newly found gate was several feet below the current Golden Gate. This may confirm the idea that the walls of the New Testament period were low enough that the sanctuary could be viewed easily from the Mount of Olives during sacrifices. As the Talmud states, "All the walls that were there on the Temple Mount were high, with the exception of the eastern wall, so that the Priest who burned the red heifer stood on top of the Mount of Olives and was able to see directly into the entrance of the sanctuary when the blood was tossed."[11]

Golden Gate and Dome of the Tablets from the Mount of Olives

further data to assist in locating the possible site of the temple and Holy of Holies.

Scholars have varying opinions about the placement of the Holy of Holies on the Temple Mount. Some would place the Holy of Holies over the Kubbat as-Sakhra rock (the top of the major rock formation in the Dome of the Rock). Other scholars believe the rock is where the altar of burnt offerings was located or on the site where today the Dome of Tablets resides.[12]

A REUNION WITH A PURPOSE

I returned to the Institute of Holy Land Studies in the spring of 1998 to celebrate the school's fortieth anniversary. This was a delightful time of reunion, fellowship, and an opportunity to look to the school's future. The president at the time, Sidney DeWaal, planned a special trip to the Temple Mount for the honored guests. I had never been below the Temple Mount to see what is commonly referred to as Solomon's stables. Not surprisingly, the area had been turned into a mosque. The large room supported by ancient columns had an excellent view of the inside of the southern wall and the gates that were used at one time for temple worshipers to enter the temple area.

A popular view set forth by Asher Kaufman theorizes that the stone beneath the Dome of the Tablets is the bedrock for the foundation stone for the Holy of Holies. This would place the temple's Holy of Holies just outside the modern Dome of the Rock. This theory has been attractive to some Christians because it would allow construction of a new temple without dismantling the Dome of the Rock. This theory is improbable, however, because the stone beneath the Dome of Tablets appears to be a Herodian paving stone rather than the bedrock of Araunah's threshing floor.

Leen Ritmeyer believes that he has identified the pre-Herodian Temple Mount by locating the four corners of a square 500-cubit platform. His first clue to this discovery was his observation that the staircase at the northwest corner of the raised platform (near the Qubbat el-Khadr) is the only staircase that is parallel to the eastern wall near the Eastern Gate (often referred to as the Golden Gate). The platform size was increased after 141 BCE in the Hasmonean period.

The Holy of Holies in the temple sat directly over the Kubbat as-Sakhra (Arabic for "Holy Rock"), the rock mass inside the modern Dome of the Rock. The

A view of the exposed bedrock inside the Dome of the Rock. Some scholars believe that this was the foundation for the temple's Holy of Holies.

Leen Ritmeyer argues that this "step" is actually the top of an earlier wall. He identifies this wall with the western wall of the pre-Herodian Temple Mount. With this location marking his starting point, he claims to have located all four corners of the 500-cubit square Temple Mount from the time of Hezekiah.[13]

rock, which has flat surfaces, measures 43 by 56 feet and is larger than the Holy of Holies (34 feet 6 inches by 34 feet 6 inches). This means that one of the walls of the Holy of Holies was built on the rock. A rectangular indentation can be found in the middle of Leen Ritmeyer's superimposed drawings on a photograph of the Holy Rock. Its measurements were nearly the same as the ark of the covenant (1.5 by 2.5 cubits). Ritmeyer's conclusion was that this indentation marked the spot of the ark.[14]

The view that explains all the evidence is the preferred conclusion: the Dome of the Rock was built directly on the site the Jewish temple once occupied.

Over time, the city limits of Jerusalem have expanded and contracted. From the tiny City of David perched atop the ridge separating the Central and Kidron Valleys to the city of Paul's day (Herod Agrippa's third wall), the city stretched north beyond the walls that are still seen today. Modern-day Jerusalem incorporates the Old City, Jewish West Jerusalem, and Arab East Jerusalem. The constant factor in the ever-changing configuration of Jerusalem has always been the Temple Mount. No period of history has excluded

Modern locations near the Temple Mount

DOME OF THE ROCK

In AD 638 Muslim invaders captured Jerusalem. Construction of the Dome of the Rock began in AD 688, and Abd el-Malik ibn Marwan completed it in 691. The Dome of the Rock was

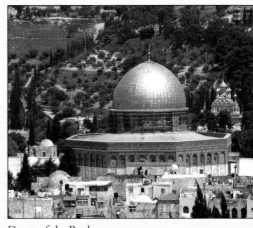

built over a large stone allegedly marked with an impression of Muhammad's footprint. In the story of Muhammad's "Night Journey," Muhammad was transported at night to Al-Aqsa ("the furthest place"). As he ascended a ladder to heaven to talk with Allah and the prophets, he left his footprint behind. Since Muslims believe that they superseded their two predecessor religions (Christianity and Judaism), they desired to build the Dome to specifications that would exceed the imperfections of the structure on the mount of their forerunners.[15]

Dome of the Rock

The mosque's claim to occupy the Jewish sacred location meant Muslims and their faith had supplanted the Jewish religion. The mosque's superior interior decoration demonstrated it was better than the Christians' Church of the Holy Sepulcher. The inscription from the Qur'an on the Dome of the Rock attests to Islam's assertion of superiority over the Christian faith:

> O People of the Book! Commit no excesses in your religion: Nor say of God aught but the truth. Christ Jesus the son of Mary was (no more than) an apostle of God, and His Word, which He bestowed on Mary, and a spirit proceeding from Him: so believe in God and His apostles. Say not "Trinity": desist: it will be better for you: for God is one God: Glory be to Him: (far exalted is He) above having a son. To Him belong all things in the heavens and on earth. And enough is God as a Disposer of affairs.[16]

In 1955, an extensive program of renovation of the Dome of the Rock began by the Jordanian government. The work included replacement of large numbers of tiles dating back to the reign of Suleiman the Magnificent (1494–1566) that had become destroyed by severe weather. In the early 1960s, the lead dome was replaced with an aluminum bronze alloy. The restoration was completed in August 1964.

Using funds from Saudi Arabia, King Hussein replaced the copper dome in the 1990s with one plated of pure gold because the existing one was rusting. "In 1994 a new gold-plated exterior dome, weighing a total of 80 kilograms [180 lbs.], was installed at a cost of $15,000,000. The plating is not more than .0023 mm thick, and the sheen of the gold was slightly muted during the plating so that the dome would not blind anyone gazing upon it."[17]

Solomon's stables under the south end of the Temple Mount

the Temple Mount from the confines of Jerusalem. To control Jerusalem is to control the Temple Mount, the soul of the Holy City.

Following the 1967 war, Israel annexed East Jerusalem, including the Temple Mount. Yet as part of their pledge to maintain the religious "status quo," the Muslim religious authority (Waqf) was granted full control of the Temple Mount. Officially, Israeli building codes apply to the Haram. However, in practice, they have not been enforced because of the extreme religious sensitivities. This carries over into archaeological work, for even though Israel claims authority over excavations, the government usually turns a blind eye to illegal and unethical excavations on the Temple Mount out of fear of exacerbating tensions. Israeli archaeologists fume at the destruction of antiquities to little avail.

Israel's future is secured in the pages of Scripture. But its day-to-day destiny is perhaps best seen in the headlines of the daily newspaper, in the minute-by-minute blogs of the nation's citizens, and in the whirlwind of today's social media.

CHAPTER 11

MESSIAH ON A DONKEY: "O JERUSALEM, JERUSALEM"

PASSOVER WEEK AD 33

Matthew 21:1 — 26:35; Mark 11:1 — 14:31; Luke 19:29 — 22:37; John 11:55 — 18:1 (T&G 128 — 51)

FROM TRIUMPH TO ARREST

The Triumphal Entry

(Matthew 21:1 — 17; Mark 11:1 — 11; Luke 19:29 — 44; T&G 128a — b)

The bright Judean sun pierced the sky, illuminating the stately Herodian temple and its many courtyards. News had spread—from the small village of Bethany to Bethphage—that the one called "the Messiah" was about to enter Jerusalem.

For generations prophets had spoken of this day. The psalmist had sung about it. Now the Messiah would fulfill it. No greater day in history was anticipated than the Messiah's long-awaited triumphal entry. But after three years of intense mentoring and training, the disciples would still fail to grasp the enormity and significance of these seven days in Jesus' life and ministry.

Six days before Passover, Jesus returned to the small village of Bethany, where the resurrected Lazarus and his family lived. The warm and loving home of Martha, Mary, and Lazarus became Jesus' home away from home for the annual Passover. Mary and Martha had spent days cleaning the house and purchasing supplies for the approaching visit of their friend Jesus and his disciples. They would be staying for several days. Lazarus, who was filled with gratitude for Jesus' miracle of raising him from the dead, was determined to make this Passover as pleasant as possible. Neighbors couldn't help but talk about the increased activity around Martha and Mary's home.

But the crowded city also meant danger for Jesus. Wherever he went, crowds followed. Religious leaders were plotting to arrest the "false prophet," who was now a marked man. And he was headed for Bethphage on the eastern side of the Mount of Olives.

As Jesus and his men reached Bethphage, just east of Jerusalem, he motioned for John and Peter to step forward to complete an errand.[1] Knowing they were selected to complete a special task, they dashed forward, fighting their way through the crowd. The other disciples couldn't help but notice that Jesus selected these two men. After all, they talked several times among themselves about whom Jesus favored most among the Twelve.

Jesus gave them his instructions. "Go to the village ahead of you, and at once you will find a donkey tied there, with her colt by her. Untie them and bring them to me" (Matt. 21:2). But the request seemed odd.[2] After

Aerial view of the Jerusalem area from the southeast

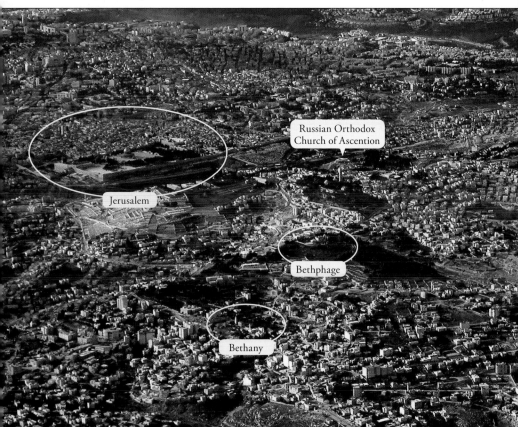

all, shouldn't the King of Israel enter Jerusalem in a more dignified and regal way than on the back of a donkey? What would the high priests and temple guards think if they saw a king bouncing and jerking along the city streets on the back of a common work animal? John and Peter shook their heads as they imagined the sneers.

Bethany from Carriage Road

But we can imagine that one of the other disciples' challenging words broke into their thoughts and questions above the noise of the crowd: "Don't you remember the prophecy of our prophet Zechariah, 'Rejoice greatly, Daughter Zion! Shout, Daughter Jerusalem! See, your king comes to you, righteous and victorious, lowly and riding on a donkey, on a colt, the foal of a donkey'" (Zech. 9:9)? The disciples didn't answer immediately. They simply remained silent and pondered the prophecy in light of the day's events.

The faithful collected palm branches for the occasion. Imagine that a young follower named Ruth was stripping

Bethphage

branches from the nearby trees. The occasion held special significance for her people. She recalled her grandmother's stories about the days when the Hasmoneans ruled their beloved Israel and the people prospered. Praise God, the Messiah would soon overthrow the hated Romans, and once again God's chosen would rule Judea.

Modern celebration of Jesus' triumphal entry

Jesus mounted the back of the donkey and began his final journey into his beloved Jerusalem. The short trip led over the Mount of Olives and down the Kidron Valley to the entrance of the city, where he entered, perhaps through a gate near the pool of Siloam, up the steps near the site of the modern St. Peter in Gallicantu Church, and into Jerusalem proper.

"The palm branch symbolized this glorious period." Ruth remembered her grandmother's words as she began to swing the branches gently back and forth with the rhythm of the morning breeze.

Jesus' triumphal entry is celebrated in the Christian world on Palm Sunday.[3] This official event presented Jesus as the Messiah. Jesus' entry into Jerusalem set up a final confrontation with the Jewish leaders of Israel. The time had come for them to choose: Jesus or corrupt Judaism!

The word spread quickly that Jesus—the one who had raised Lazarus from the dead—had arrived. The crowds jostled and swelled to get a glimpse of the miracle worker from Galilee. Even the Jewish authorities were awaiting his visit—some in genuine wonder, others with the hope of extinguishing this voice forever. The disciples scanned the enthusiastic crowd. There was nothing to indicate that within a few hours the Pharisees, who were incensed that Jesus had raised Lazarus from the dead, would have a warrant issued for Jesus' arrest.[4]

Jerusalem residents greeted pilgrims to the Holy City during Passover by singing Psalm 118: "Give thanks to the LORD, for he is good; his love endures forever" (v. 1). Their exuberance revealed an event beyond the welcoming of a pilgrim to a festival. The King riding on a donkey fulfilled ancient prophecy (Zech. 9:9), and their greeting, "Hosanna! Blessed is he who comes in the name of the Lord! Blessed is the coming kingdom of our father David!" (Mark 11:9–10), indicated that they recognized it as a messianic act.

The moment was intense. Joy, happiness, and promise dominated the atmosphere. Yet in only a few days the crowd turned on Jesus. When they were given a choice to release Jesus or the criminal Barabbas, they vehemently called for Barabbas's freedom. Why? Had the crowd been infiltrated by syco-phants of the Jewish authorities?

The answer is much simpler. The crowds embraced Jesus when he fed five thousand near Bethsaida. They desired him to become a political king, to destroy Rome, and to set up a permanent "food bank." They desired the physical blessings promised by the prophets without submitting to Jesus' demands for righteousness. When Jesus refused to establish a kingdom for unrepentant Israel, the crowds turned on him in anger.

Beginning of Passion Week
Some scholars believe the triumphal entry marked the fulfillment of a portion of Daniel's prophecy of seventy weeks when he wrote, "Know and understand this: From the time the word goes out to restore and rebuild Jerusalem until

JEWISH SECTS: PHARISEES, SADDUCEES, ESSENES, AND ZEALOTS

The Pharisees' roots can be traced to the Hasidim of the second century BC. They believed in strictly following the Jewish law, and their authority came from the Torah and oral tradition. The Pharisees significantly influenced the synagogues of Judea and Galilee.

The Sadducees trace their origins from the Hasmonean period (166–63 BC). The name appears to have derived from the high priest Zadok of David's time.[6] They drew members from the ruling priestly and aristocratic classes of the land, controlling the temple worship in Jerusalem and sitting as members of the powerful ruling council of the Sanhedrin. They denied the authority of the oral tradition and followed the Scriptures only. Their denial of resurrec-tion prompted them to question Jesus about the resurrection (Luke 20:27–40). The Roman destruction of Jerusalem and the temple in AD 70 brought an end to the Sadducean group.

The Essenes, along with the Pharisees, originated among the Hasidim but gradually separated sometime later.[7] They developed from reform movements that arose during the Maccabean revolt in the second century BC. They were overzealous regarding the strict practice of purity laws, practicing asceticism and refusing to worship in the Jerusalem temple. The Essenes are best known for their community near the Dead Sea, where Bedouins found the famous Dead Sea Scrolls that reveal a great deal about the Essenes' faith and practice. A significant Essene community also lived in the southern area of Jerusalem.

The Zealots were radical rebels who sought to overthrow the Romans. They came to the forefront during the Jewish revolt in AD 66–73. They held to strict Jewish traditions and rejected Greek culture and language. The fall of Masada in AD 73 brought them to an abrupt end.

the Anointed One, the ruler, comes, there will be seven 'sevens,' and sixty-two 'sevens.' It will be rebuilt with streets and a trench, but in times of trouble. After the sixty-two 'sevens,' the Anointed One will be put to death and will have nothing" (Dan. 9:25–26). Jesus, the Anointed One, was cut off on the day of his messianic presentation on the day of the triumphal entry.[5] We at least know this event signaled the last week of Jesus' life, known as Passion Week.

The rest of Passion Week is filled with events that consume more space in the gospel accounts than any of the other events recorded. The basis of Christianity rests firmly on the outcomes of these momentous events. The intrigue, the plots, the mysteries, and the suspense fill the pages of Scripture like a well-written novel. This chapter of the real story, however, ends in the payment of sin and the reconciliation of sinners to a just and holy God. While the plot continues to be played out in the twenty-first century, the last episode has already been scripted for a final scene at the end of the age.

Monday: Messianic Actions
(Matthew 21:12–19; Mark 11:12–18; John 12:20–50; T&G 129a–130b)

The morning after Jesus' triumphal entry, he was on his way into the city. Perhaps not wanting to overburden Mary and Martha, he searched along the route for food for his breakfast. He spotted a fig tree; however, the tree had no fruit—only leaves. Jesus cursed the tree.

Jesus' action did not suggest an angry reaction to missing his breakfast. The fig tree was a well-known symbol of Israel—a nation that did not bear fruit would be judged—along with the symbol of Judaism, the temple.[8] Israel's leaders showed outward signs of true faith, but they did not produce the fruits of righteousness. Jesus' immediate lesson to the disciples encouraged them in faith.

Jesus entered the temple area and once again overturned the money changers' tables and scattered the would-be sacrifices.[9] The Jewish priests who observed the act of this rebel claiming to be Israel's Messiah were beside themselves with anger. One may have been heard to fire a response, "Who does this charlatan think he is?" Outraged, they agreed among themselves that this man must be stopped. But this was not the time—too many people were hanging on his words (Luke 19:48).

Faithful Jews from all over Israel were flocking to Jerusalem for the Feast of Passover. Even some Greeks, who may have been among the four thousand Jesus fed a few months prior, came to Philip (John 12:20; from Bethsaida of Galilee) seeking Jesus. Many people wanted him to establish the kingdom of God he had been promising. And then there was the matter of the free food. Some of Jesus' followers began to dream of a time they would receive a version of "manna" from heaven. But Jesus used his demonstration in the temple to warn of coming judgment and the necessity of the resurrection. His actions also intentionally heightened the animosity of the Jewish leaders so that they would not wait to arrest him until after the Passover (as they had planned). Thus Jesus forced their hand to crucify him on the Passover, in fulfillment of God's timing.

Jesus' entry into Jerusalem and anger at the money changers disturbed the rulers. Nevertheless, many, including some of the rulers, believed in him but would not confess it because they loved the approval of their peers rather than God and did not want to be put out of the synagogue (John 12:42–43).

Figs on branch of a fig tree.

A withered fig tree. A healthy tree can grow to nearly twenty feet in height and its large leaves provide pleasant shade. Minute wasps cultivate these trees, and the fig is produced before the leaves emerge. The flower of the tree is never seen, as its many tiny flowers are housed within the fruit bud. Two crops are produced each year. The first crop is eaten fresh, while the second crop is dried for winter.

Tuesday: Day of Conflict (Last Public Ministry)
(Matthew 21:19 – 26:16; Mark 11:19 – 14:11; Luke 21:37 – 22:6; T&G 131 – 42)

Jesus arrived late Monday evening at Mary and Martha's home in Bethany. The disciples had many questions about what happened that day, but they hesitated to approach him. The day dragged on, and the disciples continued to be perplexed about their Messiah. With the evening spent and supper digesting, they all retired for the night.

Archaeological ruins of the proposed house of Mary and Martha

LC-matpc–00960-t/www.LifeintheHolyLand.com

Tuesday began early. The roosters sounded the alarm of a new day beneath a brilliant sky. The disciples were energized to take on another day with the Messiah.

As they passed the same road as the day before, Peter observed the withered fig tree, perhaps hoping it would demonstrate he was paying attention the day before. Always ready to stir the disciples' thinking, Jesus responded with a lesson on faith. "Truly I tell you, if you have faith and do not doubt, not only can you do what was done to the fig tree, but also you can say to this mountain, 'Go, throw yourself into the sea,' and it will be done. If you believe, you will receive whatever you ask for in prayer" (Matt. 21:21–22).

It wasn't long before Jesus encountered three groups whom he would confront in verbal sparring: chief priests, scribes, and elders.[10] They were gathered in the majestic setting of the temple, surrounded by the beauty of its gold and the Hulda Gates, with the whitewashed tombs on the Mount of Olives in view and the Hinnom and Kidron Valleys falling away below. As they listened to Jesus speak, they immediately questioned his words. They wanted to know by whose authority he spoke and acted.

Jesus, surprisingly, refused to answer their question until they answered his regarding the source of John the Baptist's authority. Using three parables, he taught them that true sonship depends on obedience, not on profession. Because the nation of Israel would reject the Messiah, the kingdom would be given to others. Those who tried to enter God's kingdom any way but God's way would be cast into outer darkness where there would be weeping and gnashing of teeth. "Many are invited, but few are chosen" (Matt. 22:14), Jesus told them.

The Sadducees took their turn questioning Jesus. Their questions concerned the resurrection, which they did not endorse. A lawyer, representing the Pharisees, asked about the greatest of the commandments: "Of all the commandments, which is the most important?" (Mark 12:28). Jesus answered, "The most important one ... is this: 'Hear, O Israel: The Lord our God, the Lord is one. Love the Lord your God with all your heart and with all your soul and with all your mind and with all your strength.' The second is this: 'Love your neighbor as yourself.' There is no commandment greater than these" (vv. 29–31). When the lawyer affirmed Jesus' answer by saying, "You are right in saying that God is one and there is no other but him. To love him with all your heart, with all your understanding and with all your strength, and to love your neighbor as yourself is more important than all burnt offerings and sacrifices" (vv. 32–33), Jesus told him, "You are not far from the kingdom of God" (v. 34). "And from then on no one dared ask him any more questions" (v. 35).

Just when the disciples thought Jesus was finished, Jesus took the opportunity to go on the offensive by addressing the Pharisees who had gathered to finally seal his fate. The heat of the discussions likely made the disciples squirm.

Why is Jesus being so antagonistic? Certainly he is falling into their trap, they worried. But Jesus continued to attack his archrivals. His scathing rebuke of the Pharisees centered around seven "woes" (Matt. 23:13–39).[11] Evidently Jesus recognized the Pharisees as legitimate authorities who sat on the seat of Moses. They often taught the true meaning of the law and spoke with scriptural authority, but they also often refused to obey the spirit of the law they

East Jerusalem and Mount of Olives aerial from the south

taught. In those instances, they were hypocrites and nullified the meaning of the law. The seven "woes" spell out their hypocrisy.

Jesus' judgments on the Pharisees encompassed seven areas:[12] (1) they shut the door of the kingdom of heaven in people's faces; (2) they misdirected their zeal; (3) they interpreted Scripture incorrectly; (4) their tithing was misguided and they were blind guides; (5) their cleansing was external, but their sin was internal; (6) their hypocrisy could be compared with whitewashed tombs; and (7) their witness was deceptive.

Jesus concluded the "woes" with a lament over Jerusalem. His indictment of the Pharisees' external view of holiness contrasts sharply with his observation of a widow who quietly gave all the money she had to God in a temple offering.

The Pharisees burned in anger as they listened to a Galilean rabbi instruct them in the true meaning of Scripture. "How dare he speak to us this way?" they whispered among themselves.

The disappearing sun announced the close of the day as Jesus led the disciples toward their temporary living quarters in Bethany. As they left the temple area, the disciples grew silent. Jesus spoke to them about his death and confronted the Pharisees in the harshest terms. What did it mean for them and for the future of their beloved country? How could Jesus speak of his death and coming kingdom and truly be the Messiah?

Anyone looking at the temple would agree that it was beautiful. One of the disciples, however, made a point of reminding his Teacher of just how massive the stones and how magnificent the buildings of the temple were (Mark 13:1) — as if Jesus needed a reminder. The observation may seem oddly timed and even a bit presumptuous. Perhaps he was attempting to lift the spirits of the group or redirect the conversation. But his comment couldn't have been a more appropriate lead-in to Jesus' finals words, "Do you see all these great buildings? . . . Not one stone here will be left on another; every one will be thrown down" (Mark 13:2), as he walked away from the temple.

Herod built the Temple Mount out of beautiful limestone blocks, some measuring forty feet long, eighteen feet wide, and twelve feet thick. Josephus records that the entire facade was covered with gold plates, while the temple was made of pure white marble.[13] On a clear day, the sun reflecting off the structure was blinding and could be seen for miles. If the temple were still standing, it would legitimately be considered the eighth wonder of the world.

Jesus' response to John's observation must have come as a shock. Without hesitation, he predicted the complete destruction of the temple. The disciples were silenced by Jesus' words. How could such a horrific prophecy be true?

Olive trees on the Mount of Olives

How could Jesus continue to speak such doom about the future — his death and the destruction of Israel?

When they arrived at the Mount of Olives, they asked three questions: "Tell us, [1] when will this happen, and [2] what will be the sign of your coming and [3] of the end of the age?" (Matt. 24:3). The disciples assumed the temple had to be destroyed before Jesus could return to inaugurate his kingdom.

Luke recorded Jesus' answer to this first question: "When you see Jerusalem being surrounded by armies, you will know that its desolation is near" (Luke 21:20). Looking back today on history, we can see that the destruction of Jerusalem by Titus in AD 70 fulfilled that promise.

Matthew recorded Jesus' answer to the other two questions in Matthew 24:4–35. Jesus began by describing the signs of this age. Many will come in Jesus' name claiming to be the Messiah. There will be wars and rumors of wars; nation will strive against nation; the world will experience famines and earthquakes.[14]

The use of the figure of speech "birth pangs" often refers to Israel's time of tribulation. The tribulation will continue for seven years in order for the gospel of the kingdom of God to be preached in the whole world. Then the end of the present age will come. The Lord will appear in the sky, and the nations of the earth will mourn because the Messiah will come with great power and glory. But as for the day or the hour of Jesus' coming, no one knows.

Jesus concluded his remarks with a warning for those living at that time to be watching and to be prepared for the kingdom of heaven[15] by being good stewards of their property and talents. When the Son of Man comes, he will sit on his throne in heavenly glory and will issue righteous judgment on all his subjects.

The disciples had no follow-up questions. Jesus had given them enough to think about. And in the wake of the lessons they just heard, Jesus' band of followers probably slept little that night.

Wednesday:[16] Day of Rest and Meditation

The traditional view suggests that Jesus, after two exhausting days of battling in Jerusalem, spent Wednesday with his disciples resting in the home of Martha and Mary in Bethany in anticipation of the Passover.

Thursday: Passover and Christian Manifesto

(Matthew 26:21 – 26:35; Mark 14:12 – 42; Luke 22:21 – 22:46; John 13:1 – 18:1; T&G 145 – 52)

On Thursday morning, Jesus wasted no time before beginning to teach. He reminded the disciples of the approaching Passover and his arrest that would lead to his crucifixion. He knew the chief priests and elders were gathering in the court of the high priest Caiaphas to plot his arrest. The only question that remained was how they could take him into custody without his supporters interfering.

Plans for their plot were under discussion when Judas came forward to offer his services. He was willing to betray the friend who brought him into his inner circle, treated him with respect, and trusted in him. For thirty pieces of silver, Judas helped Israel's leaders identify Jesus in the dark so the temple police could capture him before his followers could react.

The motives for Judas's actions are a source of debate among scholars.[17] Was he trying to hasten Jesus' kingdom; was he about to be caught for

Qumran Cave 1 from below

Scriptorium at Qumran. On the basis of ink-wells and "writing benches" that were found in the second-story room of this building, archaeologists have suggested that this was where scrolls were copied. The benches are wooden desks that were covered with a plaster coating. Some of these were destroyed in fighting during the 1967 war while stored at the Rockefeller Museum. No scrolls were found in this room or in the ruins of the site itself. However, the same type of unique pottery was found both on-site and in the caves with the scrolls. The pottery has helped to connect the caves with the site.

Cave 4 was among those looted by the Bedouins during the free afternoons on the days they were in the employ of the Qumran archaeologists. It lies adjacent to the Qumran settlement. This most famous of the Dead Sea Scroll caves boasts of the most significant finds. More than fifteen thousand fragments from over two hundred books were found in this cave. One hundred twenty-two biblical poorly preserved (not in jars) scrolls (or fragments) were found in this cave.

Cave 1 from inside looking out. The scrolls found in Cave 1 were well preserved because they were stored in jars. The practice of paying "per piece" led to the creation of multiple fragments from single pieces by the Bedouins. The seven scrolls found in this cave were the *Manual of Discipline, War of Sons of Light*, the *Thanksgiving Scroll, Isaiah A* and *B, Genesis Apocryphon*, and *Habakkuk Commentary*.

THE ESSENE COMMUNITY

According to Josephus, the Essenes did not have a city of their own but lived in many places and considered Jerusalem to be their sacred city. According to the *Damascus Document*, the faithful Essenes fled in 104 BC from a Hasmonean ruler to various parts of the empire. Many settled in Qumran until an earthquake occurred in 31 BCE, prodding many to migrate to Jerusalem. Because of the Essenes' long-standing opposition to the Hasmonean priesthood and Herod the Great's bitter attitude toward the Hasmonean dynasty, Herod granted the Essenes sanctuary in Jerusalem.[18]

Archaeological remains of Essene Gate in Jerusalem from the north

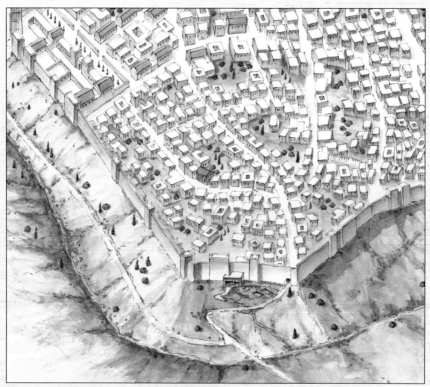

Essene community (southwestern Jerusalem)

Original artwork by Ron Waalkes

The Qumran community of Essenes was located in the southwestern part of the City of Jerusalem. Interestingly, a ritual bath[19] was located outside the city walls with steps leading to a garden. Deuteronomy 23:10–11 says that when a man was unclean because of a nocturnal emission, he was to go outside the camp and stay there. But as evening approached he was to wash himself and then

Essene *mikvah* (ritual bath) in Protestant cemetery on Mount Zion

return to the camp at sunset. Bargil Pixner excavated a gate in this area of the city (outside the southern old city walls, still visible today) that today is called the "Essene Gate."[20]

Modern view of Mount Zion. An ancient Essene community inhabited this area (today it is outside the city walls, but in Jesus' day the walls incorporated this area.

pilfering the treasury; or was he simply interested in the cash payoff? Did the priests place doubts in Judas's mind about Jesus' messianic claim? Did they recruit him for the shameful deed? Judas, who was the only disciple not from Galilee, lived in Judea. Did he feel a sense of estrangement from the others? In addition, Jesus' public rebuke of Judas a few days earlier at the feast in Bethany may have angered him (John 12:1–8). These and other questions remain unanswered. Whatever Judas's motives, he was the lynchpin in the most hideous act of treason in history.

Jesus Entered the Essene Community for the Passover Feast
(Matthew 26:17–35; Mark 14:12–31; Luke 22:7–38; T&G 143–51)

The Passover feast drew near, and Jesus sent Peter and John to a private location to prepare the meal where Jesus would passionately communicate his final message. Little did Jesus' disciples know this night would change the world and provide new standards that would far exceed the old covenant's Ten Commandments.

The Master issued a request for his disciples to find and follow a man carrying a pitcher of water. They were to tell him the Teacher wanted a guest room to eat the Passover (Luke 22:10–11). But the instructions bewildered the disciples. The only place they could find men carrying water pots was in the old Essene community in the southern section of Jerusalem. As a celibate community of men, the Essenes performed routine chores usually reserved for women in other Jewish communities. Jesus' words may have indicated that the location for the Last Supper was in the area of the Essene community and they were going to use an Essene guest room for the Last Supper.[21]

THE UPPER ROOM

The modern location of the upper room on Mount Zion has one of the longest standing traditions of any of the sites connected to Jesus' life. The upper room shown today by tour guides is a building from the Crusader period, but it is located on the traditional area of the first-century upper room. During the Passover celebration, Jesus and the disciples would have been challenged to find a room large enough to host a group of their size. A room in the Essene community, where "God-fearing Jews" (Acts 2:5; perhaps a reference to Essenes), would most likely have been available for the disciples' use.

Just prior to the fall of Jerusalem in AD 70, Christians fled the city for Pella in the north, where they waited the return of the Lord. By AD 73, with hopes of the second coming fading, Christians returned to Jerusalem and rebuilt a Jewish Christian synagogue. The foundation stones are still visible today. The location in Acts 1:13, "they went upstairs to the room where they were staying," may identify the place of the events described in Acts 2.[23]

The Christian manifesto spoken by Jesus in the Upper Room Discourse was given following a Passover meal. James Fleming introduced the seating chart of the twelve apostles around a triclinium to me in the late 1970s. Since then, many scholars have followed his hypothesis regarding the seating arrangement.

Rather than the traditional Last Supper table as painted by Leonardo da Vinci, Fleming suggests the table seating followed the Roman custom of dining at a triclinium. Predetermined

Place of the upper room. The upper room is located just below the Dome of the Rock on the far left. This photograph offers a unique vantage point no longer possible today because of the construction of the Dormition Abbey.

Modern view of the building housing the traditional upper room. The stones on the right center in photo are perhaps from the first century.

seating around the table identified the guests.

The host was always seated second on the left side of the three-sided table, which was considered the head table. The server normally occupied the left end of the right side of the table. Jesus would have sat in the middle of the left side of the table, leaning on his left elbow, with John positioned to lean on Jesus' breast on his right side on the end (John 13:23). Judas, as the guest of honor, sat on Jesus' left. It was important that he be seated in close proximity to Jesus. As Jesus identified his betrayer, he handed Judas a piece of bread. When Peter entered the room and saw Judas seated in the place of honor and John seated on Jesus' right,[24] perhaps Peter impetuously stormed off to the servant's seat in a childlike act of defiance.

Because he sat directly across from John, Peter could get John's attention to ask Jesus to identify his betrayer. Peter's rebellious spirit surfaced when Jesus came to wash the server's feet; in this case, Peter occupied the server's position. Typical of Peter's impetuous character, he refused the Master's gesture and then later felt shame for his act of defiance.

(1) Host Jesus, middle left side of table; (2) the disciple John on Jesus' right side (John 13:23); (3) Jesus offering bread to Judas, third on left; (4) Peter attempting to get Jesus' attention first on the right side of triclinium.

The Last Supper took place Thursday evening as the traditional Passover feast (Luke 22:15). At the end of a Passover meal, custom dictated a conversation that rehearsed the significance of the exodus story. Jesus took the opportunity to expand on the real meaning of the redemption of the Israelites in the

Judas

Jesus

Peter

John

Original artwork by Ron Waalkes

exodus account. Some scholars suggest the teachings of Jesus here could be called the "second exodus."

Jesus instituted a new rite. Speaking of his mission, he focused on the aspect of the kingdom that instituted the new covenant—forgiveness and redemption. Jesus charged believers to practice this institution, known as Communion or Eucharist, and to continue until his return, at the inauguration of the future kingdom.

The long evening ended as the small band of men made their way back to Bethany for a much-needed night's sleep. But the night would reveal God's plan for the redemption of his people through the gift of his Son to the world. The surprising means by which God would accomplish this was about to unfold.

City of Jerusalem in the first century AD.[25]

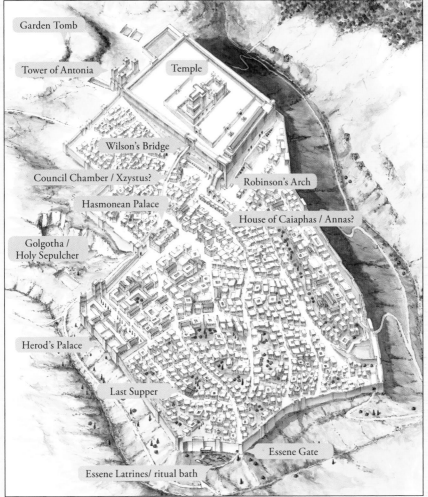

Garden Tomb

Tower of Antonia

Temple

Wilson's Bridge

Council Chamber / Xzystus?

Robinson's Arch

Hasmonean Palace

House of Caiaphas / Annas?

Golgotha /
Holy Sepulcher

Herod's Palace

Last Supper

Essene Gate

Essene Latrines/ ritual bath

Original artwork by Ron Waalkes

CHAPTER 12

MESSIAH FROM CHRISTIAN MANIFESTO TO THE CROSS: MISSION ACCOMPLISHED

PASSOVER WEEK AD 33
Matthew 26:30 – 27:26; Mark 14:26 – 15:15; Luke 22:39 – 23:25; John 18:1 – 19:16 (T&G 152 – 61)

UPON COMPLETING THE UPPER ROOM DISCOURSE, the largest body of teaching recorded in the Gospels, Jesus led the disciples to the garden of Gethsemane. Here he wrestled with the unimaginable sacrifice that faced him: laying down his sinless life for the sins of all humankind.

The emotional, spiritual, and physical agony Jesus suffered in the hours before his arrest is beyond our ability to comprehend. We do know that his soul was overwhelmed with sorrow to the point of death. He pleaded with the Father to provide another way.[1] Jesus was so distressed that he fell to the ground and sweat bloodlike drops.

Jesus was not a stoic hero fearlessly facing and inviting death. He feared death, knowing that it meant far more than his physical demise—that he would face a God whose wrath must be satisfied and who could not look upon sin. Jesus feared the agony of bearing the weight of God's wrath for the

Traditional rock in the garden of Gethsemane where Jesus's sweat was like great drops of blood on the night before his crucifixion (Luke 22:44).

world. He was about to *become* sin and give his life "as a ransom for many" (Matt. 20:28; Mark 10:45). Jesus was made sin (2 Cor. 5:21) and became "a curse for us" (Gal. 3:13). Bearing our sins in his body (1 Peter 2:24), he freely offered himself. The amazing grace of Jesus' obedience to the Father is that he chose to suffer for the sins of people once and for all (Heb. 7:27) and to say, "Not as I will, but as you will" (Matt. 26:39). With those words, Jesus slowly rose. His work lay before him, and it was time to go.

LATE THURSDAY OR EARLY FRIDAY: THE ARREST
(Matthew 26:47 – 56; Mark 14:43 – 52; Luke 22:47 – 53; John 18:2 – 12; T&G 153)

When Jesus returned to the spot where he had left Peter, James, and John waiting for him, he was disappointed to find the men sleeping. After all, had he not pleaded for them to keep watch with him? Knowing the agony of abandonment from the Father that would come as an inevitable consequence of his sacrifice, Jesus went away a second time to pray and pleaded for another solution. Again Jesus returned to seek the comfort of his friends, and again he found them sleeping. A third and final time he turned away and implored his

Father, "My Father, if it is not possible for this cup to be taken away unless I drink it, may your will be done" (Matt. 26:42).

Jesus returned to the disciples a final time and wakened them as he identified his betrayer with the temple police. Judas approached Jesus and gave him the customary kiss of greeting, the signal that would identify Jesus to the soldiers. They all knew what Jesus looked like, but his popularity with the crowds prevented them from arresting him. Judas arranged to take them to Jesus in private. By virtue of being his disciple, Judas was able to get close to Jesus. The kiss may have helped to identify Jesus in the darkness and amid the small band of disciples, but it also may have been a way of "closing the deal." When Judas kissed Jesus, he fulfilled his end of the bargain.

With the words, "Do what you came for, friend" (Matt. 26:50), Jesus willingly identified himself to the soldiers. But Peter was immediately incensed. He unsheathed his sword and swung wildly, cutting off the ear of the high priest's slave.[2] Jesus quickly rebuked the brave and overzealous Peter, reminding him that Jesus could call more than twelve legions of angels to fight his battle if he desired.

We can imagine that Jesus' rebuke crushed Peter's spirit — that he felt hurt and rejected. *Why wouldn't Jesus let me defend him? Is he not going to establish the kingdom now? Must he really die?* The questions reflect the same struggles we would have faced if we had been with Jesus that night. And we are left to wonder if Jesus' reprimand played a part in Peter's thoughts as he denied the Lord only a few hours later. As for all of us, Peter's struggle with questions regarding Jesus' role in his life would be fought on a battlefield within his heart but played out in the moment-by-moment choices of his life.

Traditional spot of Jesus' betrayal on the Mount of Olives

EARLY FRIDAY: JESUS' FIRST JEWISH TRIAL BEFORE ANNAS[3] (John 18:13 – 24; T&G 154)

The gospel accounts of Jesus' trial before Annas and Caiaphas presents a challenge. John records a trial before Annas, and the gospels of Matthew, Mark, and Luke mention two trials: one before Caiaphas and one before the Sanhedrin. Peter seems to warm himself twice at a fire in the courtyard and possibly denied Jesus four times not three. While these issues cry out for a solution, perhaps the understanding of the relationship of Annas and Caiaphas to the Jews and Romans and their common residences present a possible harmony.

In the 1970s, the elaborate first-century structure known today as the Palatial Mansion was discovered. It may be the house of the high priest[4] mentioned in the Gospels and the scene of Jesus' religious trials.[5]

Jesus' first trial convened before Annas,[6] the high priest whose authority the Jewish leaders recognized. However, Herod appointed Caiaphas, whom the Jews did not consider to be their official high priest — only a political figure.

As the temple police led the prisoner from the Mount of Olives, Peter and John[7] followed the mob from a comfortable distance. As they approached the house of the high priest, the gatekeeper denied Peter entry. Fortunately, the high priest knew John, and he gained access for Peter. The rest of the disciples slipped away, perhaps making their way to the safe confines of the compound of Martha and Mary in nearby Bethany.

The events of that horrifying night began with Jesus' interrogation before Annas.[8] As Avigad made his archaeological discoveries in the 1970s, he devoted most of his attention to the well-preserved Palatial Mansion.[9] However, he noted finding another building with a similar floor plan butted up against the Palatial Mansion.[10] It was less preserved and difficult to excavate the ruins of this building.

Jesus was escorted first to the house of Annas (Palatial Mansion) and into the "council chamber" and then later before Caiaphas[11] in the "high priest's courtyard"[12] (John 18:15). John was most likely known among those associated with Annas rather than with the politically appointed Caiaphas. A great deal of activity seemed to have centered around the courtyard. A central courtyard was common to most residences, even in poorer communities.

The slave girl, keeper of the door, asked Peter, "You aren't one of this man's disciples too, are you?" Peter wasted no time in denying it: "I am not" (John 18:17).

Peter's emphatic answer marked his first denial of his Master. This occurred at the entrance to the vestibule (John 18:16 – 17). John followed

Jesus and his captors more closely while Peter disappeared to warm himself in the center of the courtyard, which provided a fire to counter the chilly spring night air (John 18:18).

As John witnessed the proceedings, he could read the handwriting on the wall. This trial would end in disaster. Jesus did not cooperate as he stood before Annas. He curtly reminded Annas that he had done his miracles openly, and the law gave the high priest the duty to investigate. After questioning Jesus, the officials struck him in the face, then sent him to Caiaphas.

JESUS' SECOND JEWISH TRIAL BEFORE CAIAPHAS[13]
(Matthew 26:57–68; Mark 14:53, 55–65; Luke 22:54–65; T&G 155)

In order for the Roman authorities to carry out the sentence desired by the religious community, Caiaphas, the high priest appointed by Rome, also had to agree to condemn Jesus. Jesus' captors ushered him into the large reception room across the entryway to meet Caiaphas. Peter followed the party from the council chamber where Jesus had appeared before Annas (Matt. 26:58).

The night passed slowly as the leaders sought to indict Jesus. It was, perhaps, between midnight and 2:00 a.m. The law required the proceedings to be conducted in broad daylight. By getting an indictment from the high priest late at night, the Jewish hierarchy could send their recommendation to the full council of the Sanhedrin for judgment by daybreak, or at least before Jesus' loyal followers found out about the trial.

In spite of his best efforts during the interrogation, Caiaphas could get no false witness to testify against Jesus. Finally, someone stepped forward and accused Jesus of threatening to destroy the temple of God and to rebuild it in three days (Matt. 26:61). The high priest responded, "Tell us if you are the Messiah, the Son of God" (v. 63).

Jesus often refused to answer foolish questions or questions he'd already clearly answered. But this time he stated his answer unequivocally: "You have said so. But I say to all of you: From

Caiaphas's ossuary

Wikimedia Commons / Israel Museum

now on you will see the Son of Man sitting at the right hand of the Mighty One and coming on the clouds of heaven" (v. 64). By identifying himself as the divine figure whom Daniel saw in his vision, Jesus instantly sparked the wrath of Caiaphas. Caiaphas tore his robes, not in a fit of rage, but in a public display of judicial pronouncement to a person who admitted his guilt. Showing no empathy, Caiaphas allowed Jesus to be slapped and beaten as he issued his final pronouncement: Guilty.

Wikimedia Commons

Caiaphas's ossuary with inscription. This ossuary contained human remains. An Aramaic inscription read, "Joseph son of Caiaphas." Archaeologists believed the bones of a sixty-year-old man (other bones were also in the box) possibly belonged to the high priest Caiaphas.

With those words, a chorus of protestors shouted, "He is worthy of death" (Matt. 26:66). Bystanders watched as history's greatest travesty of justice unfolded and Jesus was led away to face death on the cross.

PETER'S DENIALS (Luke 22:55 – 65; T&G 156)

Model of high priest

Woven amid the tapestry of the events of Jesus' trial were Peter's statements of denial. He had once pledged that he was ready to go with Jesus to prison and to death (Luke 22:33). Yet as events unfolded, Peter's words proved to be hollow.

Peter crossed the courtyard near the entryway to the reception hall where Jesus was held in order to take his place undetected among the "officers" to witness the outcome of the trial.[14] A servant girl sitting outside the reception hall in the courtyard confronted Peter as he passed and accused him of being with Jesus. Peter snapped at her, "Woman, I don't know him" (Luke 22:57). A second time a woman confronted him, saying, "This fellow was with Jesus of Nazareth" (Matt. 26:71). Peter lashed back, "I don't know the man!" (v. 72). At Peter's words, Jesus

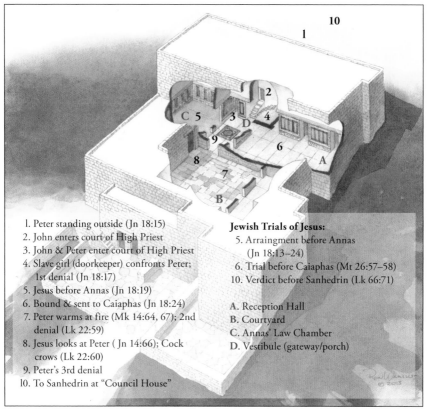

1. Peter standing outside (Jn 18:15)
2. John enters court of High Priest
3. John & Peter enter court of High Priest
4. Slave girl (doorkeeper) confronts Peter; 1st denial (Jn 18:17)
5. Jesus before Annas (Jn 18:19)
6. Bound & sent to Caiaphas (Jn 18:24)
7. Peter warms at fire (Mk 14:64, 67); 2nd denial (Lk 22:59)
8. Jesus looks at Peter (Jn 14:66); Cock crows (Lk 22:60)
9. Peter's 3rd denial
10. To Sanhedrin at "Council House"

Jewish Trials of Jesus:
5. Arraingment before Annas (Jn 18:13–24)
6. Trial before Caiaphas (Mt 26:57–58)
10. Verdict before Sanhedrin (Lk 66:71)

A. Reception Hall
B. Courtyard
C. Annas' Law Chamber
D. Vestibule (gateway/porch)

Palace of Annas/Caiaphas with possible locations of Jewish trials of Jesus. Dimensions: A: 21 by 36 feet; B: 24 by 24 feet; C: 16 by 12 feet; and D: 21 by 11 feet.

turned and looked straight at him, reminding Peter of his words of warning (Luke 22:61).[15]

At Peter's third denial of any association with Jesus (Mark 14:71), the cock crowed a second time (v. 72). Within a space of a few hours, Peter had denied the Lord three times. Unable to face what he had done, he fled, weeping, as he contemplated the enormity of his actions.

JESUS' THIRD JEWISH TRIAL BEFORE THE SANHEDRIN
(Matthew 27:1–10; Mark 15:1; Luke 22:66–71; T&G 157–58)

As the morning sun broke through the darkness of night, soldiers led Jesus from the high priest's house and brought him before the Sanhedrin, which met in the Hall of Hewn Stones (council house)[16] in the temple area.[17] The Sanhedrin consisted of seventy members plus the high priest.[18]

The full Sanhedrin, as well as the Lesser Council, with a quorum of twenty-three, was informed of the findings of Caiaphas. The Sanhedrin likewise questioned Jesus about his claim to be the Son of God. Jesus, exhausted from lack of sleep and feeling the effects of a night of mistreatment, once again spoke clearly: "I am." The verdict was the same: guilty. Early in the morning, the chief priests and the elders of the people made their plans for how to accomplish Jesus' execution. They never questioned their guilty verdict; the purpose behind the verdict was to produce charges that would persuade Pilate to pronounce Jesus guilty. A charge of blasphemy would not be enough.

Defensive towers of Herod's palace. Herod the Great built three large defensive towers at the northern end of his palace. The towers were named after important people in Herod's life: Hippicus (a friend), Phasael (his brother), and Mariamne (his wife). The Roman general Titus destroyed the entire city but decided to save Herod's three towers and a section of the western city wall because he wanted to show Jerusalem's former strength, and he had soldiers stationed there who used it as living quarters.[19] After destroying Jerusalem, the Tenth Roman Legion was stationed here for two hundred years.

As the council was deliberating, Judas's guilt from his treacherous act finally surfaced. In a gesture of remorse, he confessed that he had betrayed an innocent man and threw the thirty pieces of silver into the sanctuary. Then he fled to commit suicide. The chief priests, who did not want responsibility for the "blood money" on their hands, used it to buy a burial site for foreigners. The man whose name became synonymous with treachery left this world in disgrace.[20]

After Archelaus fell in AD 6, the Sanhedrin lost its authority as a political force. Josephus notes that the authority of the Sanhedrin did not extend to the implementation of the death penalty.[21] A Roman trial was necessary because the Sanhedrin lacked legal authority to execute the death penalty. However, since the resurrection of Lazarus, the Jews had been looking for an excuse to put Jesus to death.

JESUS' FIRST ROMAN TRIAL BEFORE PILATE
(Mathew 27:2; Mark 15:1 – 5; Luke 23:1 – 5; John 18:28 – 38; T&G 159)

The temple police led the tired and battered Jesus to the Praetorium to be judged by Pilate.[22] In response to Jewish pressure,[23] Pilate came out of the palace to the porch to judge Jesus outside. Jews who entered the defiled Praetorium would disqualify themselves from observing the Passover. The trumped-up charge of treason, tax evasion, and claims to be Messiah and King threatened Pilate. A charge of blasphemy, however, would not challenge a Roman prefect's power.

Jesus' route to the Last Supper and return to the Mount of Olives; arrest; trials before Annas, Caiaphas, the Sanhedrin, Pilate, and Herod Antipas; and back to Pilate.

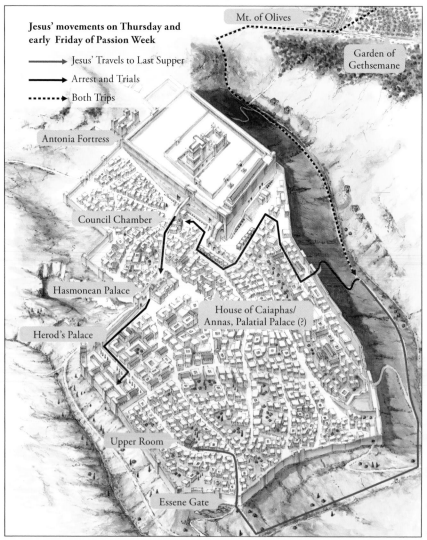

Original artwork by Ron Waalkes

Pilate was concerned about the challenge to his throne. He had questioned Jesus about his identity, and Jesus had declared his kingdom was not of this world but insisted he was born to be King. Unlike the Jewish authorities, Pilate was unconvinced by the evidence against Jesus and pronounced him not guilty of the charges. But as he heard people cry out against the Galilean, he quickly seized the opportunity to send Jesus to Herod Antipas, the Galilean authority who could take responsibility for this rebel.

While Judas and Peter clearly failed Jesus during the arrest and trial, the other disciples abandoned Jesus as well. They may have been cowering in the home of Martha and Mary. The women seem to have been the brave ones during this period. They were at Jesus' side all the way — never denying their Master nor running from danger.

JESUS' SECOND ROMAN TRIAL BEFORE HEROD ANTIPAS (Luke 23:6 – 12; T&G 160)

The change of venue brought Jesus face-to-face with Herod, the man who had brutally beheaded Jesus' cousin and forerunner, John. Herod, the Galilean tetrarch, made his way to Jerusalem for the Passover festivities, and as usual, he quartered at the Hasmonean palace.[24]

Silver tetradrachmas found at Gamala

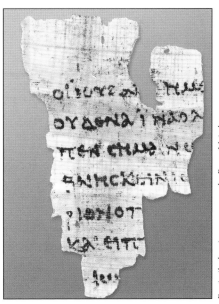

Facsimile drawing on papyrus by Rusty Maisel

John Ryland's P52 (c. AD 116–138). The oldest known manuscript fragment of the New Testament records Pilate's encounter with Jesus (portions of John 18:31 – 33). Bold italic letters indicate in English the Greek letters preserved:

the Jews, "For us it is not lawful to kill
no one [anyone]," *that the* word of Jesus might
be fulfilled, which he sp-
oke signifying by what sort of death he was
about to
die. Entered then again into the Praeto-
rium Pilate and called Jesus
*and said t*o him, "Are you the king of the
Jews?"

Model of Herod's palace, now at the Israel Museum; the place of Jesus' trial before Pilate

Model of Hasmonean palace, now at the Israel Museum. Western Wall of Temple Mount in background

Herod was happy to see Jesus. The news of Jesus' miracles in Galilee had reached him months before, and Herod was eager to see one of Jesus' miracles for himself. So it is not surprising that when Jesus was brought into his presence, Herod commanded, "Do a miracle, Jesus." Jesus, however, did not intend to perform a miracle to titillate Herod's curiosity and so remained closed-mouthed. The chief priests and scribes surrounding Herod vehemently screamed accusations as Herod ridiculed his prisoner and dressed him in an elegant robe to mock him. Irritated, he finally stated that Jesus was not his problem and that he be sent back to Pilate, who could settle the issue once and for all.

JESUS' THIRD ROMAN TRIAL BEFORE PILATE (Matthew 27:15 – 26; Mark 15:6 – 15; Luke 23:13 – 25; John 18:39 – 19:16; T&G 161)

Once again Pilate was disappointed with the outcome of his efforts. Almost sheepishly he spoke these words: "I have examined him in your presence and have found no basis for your charges against him" (Luke 23:14). Perhaps he

PONTIUS PILATE

Pontius Pilate's title (ruled AD 26 – 36) was traditionally thought to have been procurator. However, an inscription on a limestone block discovered in 1961 reads: [...]S TIBERIVM ... [PON]TIVS PILATVS ... [PRAEF]ECTVS IVDA[EA]. Apparently Pilate dedicated a public structure to Tiberias Caesar in honor of him. Whatever the occasion, the inscription mentions Pontius Pilate as the prefect (governor) of Judea. The position included military authority

A replica of the Pilate inscription

and administrative responsibilities. For centuries Christians have quoted the Apostles' Creed acknowledging Pilate's historicity: "I believe in God the Father Almighty.... And in Jesus Christ, his only Son, our Lord: who was conceived by the Holy Spirit, born of the Virgin Mary, suffered under Pontius Pilate, was crucified, dead, and buried." Yet, the Pilate stone is the first mention of Pilate in an ancient inscription.

took seriously his wife's warning from a troubling dream she had the night before, to have nothing to do with this righteous man.

Jesus' last Roman trial before Pilate ended in a not guilty verdict. However, at the last minute, Pilate appealed to the court of popular opinion. He desperately tried to appease the crowds and religious leaders by offering amnesty to either Jesus or Barabbas, a common Jewish practice during Passover. Pilate mistakenly thought the Jews would pardon Jesus in favor of the known insurrectionist and murderer Barabbas. But when Pilate discovered he had misjudged the crowds, he relented and delivered Jesus over to his tormentors for execution. As he washed his hands in a symbolic gesture, Pilate heard the exclamation from the people: "His blood is on us and on our children" (Matt. 27:25).[25] Pilate scourged Jesus, stripped him, placed a crown of thorns on his head, and draped a scarlet robe around him as the people continued to mistreat him.

The cheering mob began their evil and sadistic march to Golgotha. Clad in scarlet and a crown of thorns, Jesus made his way to fulfill his destiny.

St. Peter in Gallicantu alleged prison. The church includes a rock-cut crypt, known traditionally as the prison where Jesus stayed the night of his trial. That which was identified as the prison of Christ was obviously a ritual bathing installation (*mikveh*) in the Second Temple Period. (Ritual baths had not been identified archaeologically when the church was excavated in the early twentieth century.)

IDENTITY OF BIBLICAL SITES OF HOLY WEEK

A number of sites in Jerusalem can be identified today as witnesses to the footprints of Jesus during "Holy Week."

Location of House of the High Priest[26]

Three sites have traditional support as the house of the high priest.

1. *House of Annas/Caiaphas at St. Peter in Gallicantu (place where the cock crowed).* Halfway down the eastern slope of Mount Zion sits a modern church that retains the traditional claim of being built over the site of the house of the high priest Caiaphas. Under the church is a cave that early pilgrims believe to be the place where Jesus

Ancient steps, perhaps climbed by Jesus from AD 12–14. Modern scholars, however, believe they are actually from the Byzantine period.

was detained. Archaeological excavations undertaken around 1930 uncovered the remains from the Second Temple period (Herodian period). However, it is more likely that the church commemorates the place where Peter went to weep in contrition for his denial of Jesus.

2. *Annas's/Caiaphas's house in Armenian Quarter.* The Armenian Orthodox Church places the house of Caiaphas near the Dormition Abbey near the modern Armenian cemetery on Mount Zion. Magen Broshi excavated the area in 1971–72 and concluded that the site was a late Herodian structure.[27] The unimpressive rooms would suggest the house of a less observant Jew. The close proximity of a bitter enemy, the high priest, to the site of the upper room (about 25–30 yards) would seem strange for holding the Last Supper and possibly the gathering for assigning Matthias as the new apostle after Jesus' resurrection. It would also place the house of Caiaphas in the Essene Quarter, an unlikely location.[28]

3. *Annas's/Caiaphas's house in the Palatial Mansion.* During Nahman Avigad's excavations in the Jewish Quarter of the Old City from 1971 to 1974, he uncovered the first physical remains of the destruction of the city of Jerusalem. The occupation of the Jewish Quarter after the Six-Day War enabled

Armenian church under construction (over the proposed site of the house of Caiaphas) just outside modern Old City walls on Mount Zion.

the archaeologists to do a salvage dig. The Romans completely destroyed the city and temple. The aftermath of the Roman conflagration could be seen everywhere. In addition to the many finds, the archaeologists discovered a large Palatial Mansion on the western hill opposite the Temple Mount. A fully equipped residence with ritual baths, pools, bathrooms, and plenty of cisterns for water storage gave evidence of a very wealthy family. The remains support a most impressive complex rivaling any elaborate structure in the Roman period. The architectural design, fine wall frescos, and intricately formed floor designs suggest the work of highly skilled craftsmen.

The mansion is laid out with a large open-air central courtyard surrounded by various rooms, ritual baths, and chambers. The two-story structure has a main floor for living and a basement for ritual bathing, storing water in cisterns, and carrying out other services. From the central courtyard, one could access the various quarters. Occupants entered the ground floor through a west side set of steps leading down from a southern street. A large stucco reception hall off the vestibule with walls of ashlar-type masonry and, perhaps, carpets on the floors, provided space for entertaining or meetings. A room directly outside the vestibule contained the largest area of frescos.[29]

A study of the plan of the mansion and the consideration of other evidence suggests this was the house of the high priest Annas and/or Caiaphas under whom the religious authorities tried Jesus.[30] Avigad first suggested the possibility of this as the house of the high priest, especially in light of the "Burnt House"[31] in the same neighborhood.[32]

In the early stages of the Jewish revolt in AD 66, a group of rebels seized the temple area to prevent strangers from sacrificing. They attacked the

Upper City and set it ablaze. Josephus wrote, "The leading men, encouraged by these additions with the chief priests and all who have peace, occupied the upper city. The revolutionaries took control of the lower city and temple."[33] This suggests that the palace of Agrippa and the house of Annas were in close proximity and certainly conforms to the location of the Palatial Mansion.

An inscription reading "of bar Kathros" was found in the Burnt House, another discovery in the area. This inscription may be a reference to a powerful priestly family by the name of "Kathros."[35] The proximity of the house of Kathros to the Palatial Mansion suggests that priestly families inhabited the area. Josephus referred to the priests of this time period as being quite wealthy.[36] The Burnt House displays evidence of a kitchen sufficient for priests when preparing showbread, incense, and oil.

The location directly across from the Temple Mount, the quantity and elaborate nature of ritual baths, and the ornately decorated living quarters supply evidence of a community of wealthy priests. The finest of these homes would undoubtedly belong to the high priest.

The Roman Praetorium: Herod's Palace or Fortress of Antonia

For centuries the location of Jesus' trial before Pilate and Herod Antipas was identified as the Antonia Fortress situated north of the Temple Mount over-

Ron Waalkes's concept of the house of Annas/Caiaphas (Palatial Mansion?) based on Wohl Museum's model.[34]

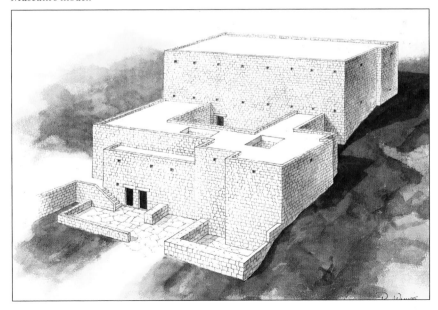

Herod's palace from southwest, now at the Israel Museum

looking the temple area. It functioned as a watchtower for any possible Jewish insurrection. Support for this site is at least as early as Theodosius (AD 530). Christian tradition begins the Via Dolorosa (Way of the Cross/Sorrow) from the Fortress of Antonia.

Modern archaeological remains from the area of Herod's palace

D. Brake

Considerable evidence exists that the true location of the Praetorium is Herod's palace near the Jaffa Gate where the modern Armenian Orthodox Seminary stands. Today the Citadel, the Kishleh compound (area of a prison built by Ottoman Turks in the mid-1800s near the Jaffa Gate in Jerusalem's Old City), and the Israeli police station are built over the space once occupied by the barracks and courtyard of the Praetorian Guard.

Place of execution outside walls of Jerusalem, now at the Israel Museum

Josephus identifies a palace in the Upper City (built by Herod in 25–24 BCE in the western portion of the Old City of Jerusalem) used by the procurators, which Pilate used for his own quarters.[37] The judgment seat was placed in front of the building for the practice of justice. This was probably located somewhere near or in the compound of St. James Cathedral of the Armenian Orthodox Church down the street southward.

Hasmonean Palace

Jesus walked only a short distance when he was brought before Herod Antipas in the Hasmonean palace. Herod was happy to see Jesus because he wanted to see a miracle, but his desire was not satisfied. In frustration, Herod's soldiers mistreated Jesus and sent him back to Pilate. Josephus mentioned the palace several times in his accounts. It was located high above the other buildings so that it was possible to see into the inner court of the temple. The Jews built a high wall within the court to block the view. No remains of the palace were found, and no excavations have been attempted due to its location in a heavily populated area. Based on Josephus's description, it is most likely located in the northeastern corner of the Jewish Quarter. It stood above the bridge (Wilson's Arch) that connected the Upper City to the Temple Mount.[38]

Model of the City of David with the temple in the background, now at the Israel Museum

The Via Dolorosa (The Way of Sorrow)

The traditional Via Dolorosa provides a walk of faith rather than a path supported by historical and archaeological evidence. Fourteen stations represent various events that occurred on Jesus' walk carrying his cross from his trial

Traditional beginning of Via Dolorosa

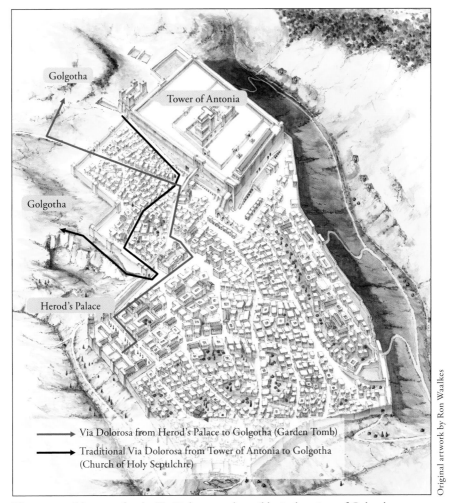

Golgotha

Tower of Antonia

Golgotha

Herod's Palace

→ Via Dolorosa from Herod's Palace to Golgotha (Garden Tomb)

→ Traditional Via Dolorosa from Tower of Antonia to Golgotha
(Church of Holy Sepulchre)

Original artwork by Ron Waalkes

The two possible routes for the Via Dolorosa and possible site locations of Golgotha.

to the place of his execution. These events include scriptural references and events linked to tradition. The pilgrims' traditional Via Dolorosa begins at the Antonia Fortress close to the Ecco Homo Arch inside St. Stephen's Gate.

The current route of the Via Dolorosa was established during the Crusader period. Some stations were added as late as the nineteenth century. The authenticity of this processional rests on where Pilate was residing the day of Jesus' crucifixion. According to this tradition, Pilate stayed at the Antonia Fortress.

The journey today taken daily by the Franciscans includes fourteen stations: (1) Jesus is condemned; (2) Jesus carries his cross; (3) Jesus falls the first time; (4) Jesus meets Mary; (5) Simon the Cyrene takes the cross; (6)

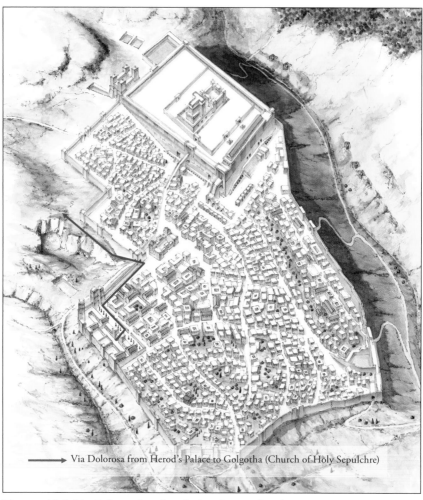

Via Dolorosa from Herod's Palace to Golgotha (Church of Holy Sepulchre)

The most likely Via Dolorosa based on the best historical evidence.

Veronica wipes his face; (7) Jesus falls the second time; (8) Jesus meets the women of Jerusalem; (9) Jesus falls the third time; (10) Jesus is stripped of his garments; (11) Jesus is nailed to the cross; (12) Jesus dies; (13) Jesus is taken down from the cross; and (14) Jesus is laid in the tomb.

The modern Via Dolorosa as defined by recent archaeological discoveries begins near the Armenian Orthodox Cathedral of St. James Church in the Armenian Quarter.[39] This represents the place where the crowds took Jesus after Pilate condemned him. From here it is difficult to trace the exact route, but a possible route may be constructed. St. James and el-Arman Streets probably preserve the basic west-to-east direction from the Praetorian and intersect the north/south Suq el-Hussor and Mundalin Streets. Jesus began

D. Brake

Modern picture of possible revised Via Dolorosa

by heading eastward on the street of St. James and then turned left on Suq el-Hussor (extension of Hadran's *Cardo*) northward toward David Street/ Tariq Bab es-Silsileh (following Josephus's "first wall") passing through el-Bashurah (Old Testament period, Corner Gate and New Testament, Garden Gate) and possibly the place where Jesus received help with the cross from Simon Cyrene. From here it is a short distance to Golgotha (modern Church of the Holy Sepulcher) where he was crucified.[40]

While the exact route eludes modern knowledge, archaeologists have uncovered Roman period pavements and identified the area as the palace of Herod. This solution to the Via Dolorosa explains the text, history, and archaeological evidence available now. [41]

Traditional tomb in Church of the Holy Sepulcher[42]

CHAPTER 13

MESSIAH'S SURPRISE: "HE IS ALIVE!"

PASSOVER WEEK AD 33

Matthew 27:27 – 28:20; Mark 15:16 – 16:20; Luke 23:26 – 24:53;
John 19:16 – 21:25 (T&G 162 – 84)

THE CRUCIFIXION (Matthew 27:31 – 60; Mark 15:16 – 46;
Luke 23:26 – 54; John 19:16 – 42; T&G 162 – 67)

Thousands of modern pilgrims delight in walking where Jesus walked. During Easter week, that walk begins with the Via Dolorosa (Way of Sorrows), from the place of his trial, to Golgotha, "the place of the skull." It is here where humanity's tragedy became God's greatest victory — the reconciliation between a holy God and sinful man.

The pagan Roman soldiers at the foot of the cross were unaware of the eternal drama playing out before their eyes as they gambled to win the dying man's clothes — especially his seamless tunic. Abandoned by most of his disciples and soon his heavenly Father, Jesus counted out the moments of his agonizing death. He was innocent, yet he willingly chose to hang on one of the cruelest execution devices ever created as he paid the price for the most heinous crimes, sins, and perversions ever devised by humanity throughout the span of history.

As he hung on the cross, two criminals who were hours from paying the ultimate price for their sins flanked Jesus. Their hearts mirrored the response of the world to Jesus' authority. As they awaited the end of their earthly existence, one thief jeered at him while the other confessed Jesus as Lord.

At the foot of the cross, Mary, Jesus' mother, knelt. She could get no closer to the Son of her womb. The woman who had birthed him and nourished him now awaited his tortured end. Beside her, Mary, the wife of Clopas, Mary Magdalene, and one lone disciple, John, stood with her as Jesus spoke from the cross.

Jesus offered the believing thief pardon and charged John with the care of his mother, Mary. He also offered his executioners forgiveness. For himself, Jesus requested only water. With his ministry and mission accomplished, Jesus uttered his final words, "It is finished" (John 19:30), in reference to the prophecy of Isaiah 53:5: "He was pierced for our transgressions, he was crushed for our iniquities; the punishment that brought us peace was on him, and by his wounds we are healed."

"It is finished."

Artwork by Ron Waalkes

The Place of Execution

The city of Jerusalem is not only a holy place for Jews and Muslims, but for Christians as well. The holiest place for Christians worldwide is the area where Jesus Christ, our Savior, King, and Lord, was crucified, buried, and resurrected. Christian pilgrims desire to be confident that the sites of these monumental events be verified properly. Identification of these holy sites brings Christians to grips with the reality of the one they worship. They come face-to-face with a real man, living in a real culture, facing the challenges of real people.

The Garden Tomb

Many Protestants believe that the Garden Tomb (Gordon's Calvary) is the location of Golgotha. The quiet, tranquil beauty of the garden sets it apart from the hustle and bustle of the city, and the serene location seems appropriate as a place for worship and drawing close to God. Visitors can reflect and meditate in the beautifully kept garden, with a large tomb nearby identified as the burial place of Jesus. However, evidence for the authenticity of the Garden Tomb is sparse.

Otto Thenius first suggested the rocky escarpment as the location of Jesus' crucifixion in 1842. In 1867 a peasant who wanted to farm the land found a rock-hewn tomb on the northwestern side of this hill. Conrad Schick explored it soon after and published a report in 1874. During the centuries following Jesus' burial, the tomb filled in with debris and human bones. After Schick's visit, the owner cleared the cave. Charles Warren and C. R. Condor (nineteenth-century archaeologists) described the tomb in their work based on their 1875 excavations.[1] They concluded that their finds confirmed mostly Crusader period remains.

British General Charles Gordon identified the Garden Tomb as the place of crucifixion and burial in 1883. It met the basic biblical and customary criteria because it was located outside the city walls. Gordon's typological argument was based on Leviticus 1:11, "You are to slaughter it at the north side of the altar before the LORD, and Aaron's sons the priests shall splash its blood against the sides of the altar." Gordon argued that if a particular direction was given by God about where the types were to be slain, then it must be deduced that the prototype would be slain in the same direction. The Garden Tomb is north of the Temple Mount rather than west, the direction of the Church of the Holy Sepulcher.

Gordon's Calvary (Golgotha, or "Place of the Skull")

The shape of a skull can be seen in this rock escarpment. The two holes in the center are the "eyes" of the skull, with the "bridge of a nose" coming down in between them. Erosion in the last one hundred years has made the skull shape more difficult to discern.

Gordon also noted the shape of the skull (eyes, nose, and mouth) behind the tomb facing southward. If the skull is important enough to be mentioned in all four gospels, then the torso must be found, Gordon reasoned. The city of Jerusalem became the form of a giant skeleton. The skull at the Garden Tomb, the chest at Solomon's quarries, the pelvis at the Dome of the Rock, and the legs extending down into the old City of David. The British general's enormous popularity for his heroic deeds in the Sudan gave the view popular acceptance. The Garden Tomb site is still managed by the British Anglican Church.

While many disagree with the site as authentic, the Garden Tomb is venerated by many Christians as the site of Jesus' tomb. It meets many of the criteria for authenticity. It is outside the walls of the Old City as suggested

Gordon's Calvary, today (above) and in the early twentieth century (below)

LC-matpc-06671-t/www.LifeintheHolyLand.com

Inside the Garden Tomb

by John 19:20; it is near a hill that would be a place for crucifixions; and has been revered since the late 1800s. Certainly its peaceful demeanor provides a place for quiet piety. The discovery of a cross carved in its walls gave some the satisfaction it was remembered by early Christians as the place of the burial of Jesus. Regardless of its claim to authenticity, it is a great place to meditate on the life and death of Jesus.

The Garden Tomb today

The Christian community has celebrated the identity of the Church of the Holy Sepulchre as the authentic place since the fourth century. In AD 41–43, Herod Agrippa incorporated the area by enclosing it within his city walls. In AD 135, the second Jewish revolt was brutally crushed by Roman emperor Hadrian, who banned the Jews from the city. This began a period of Jewish exile.[2] While a small number of Jews returned a short time later, Jewish

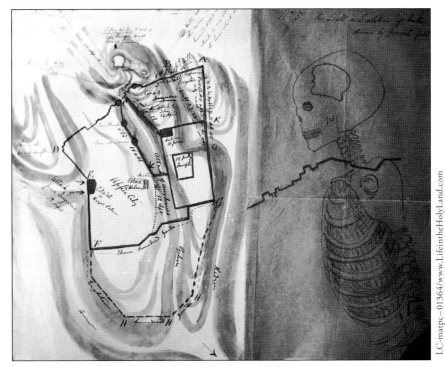

Gordon's drawing justifying the Garden Tomb as the authentic Golgotha

Church of the Holy Sepulchre

First-century tomb in Church of the Holy Sepulchre

Tombs inside Church of the Holy Sepulchre

LC-matpc–05017/www.LifeintheHolyLand.com

independence in 1948 was a major turning point for the return of Jews to the land.

To remove all memories of Jewish history, Hadrian rebuilt Jerusalem into a Roman city, renamed it Aelia Capitolina, and changed the name of the country from Judea to Palestine. On the site of Golgotha, Hadrian built a huge platform and filled in a retaining wall. On top of the platform, he built a pagan temple to Jupiter. Modern archaeologists have uncovered remnants of this platform and retaining wall.

In AD 326, Constantine's mother, Queen Helena, visited Jerusalem and concluded that the site was authentic. Ironically, the Roman emperor's efforts to eliminate memory of the Christian holy place only served to preserve it. Queen Helena ordered that the remains of the pagan temple be destroyed and a rotunda be built around Jesus' tomb. In addition, Constantine ordered that a basilica be constructed between the rotunda and the place of crucifixion. It appears likely that Constantine built the rotunda on the exact spot of the tomb.

In AD 1009 the Egyptian Muslim ruler Al-Hakim destroyed the entire complex. Remains of the rotunda alone stood as a marker for the site of the tomb. The Crusaders conquered Jerusalem in AD 1099 and fashioned the church in the essential appearance it is today. The entire complex was enclosed from the hill of Golgotha to the tomb. It no longer had the appearance of a peaceful garden or the eerie feel of a cemetery. It now contained all the religious trappings many today find objectionable.

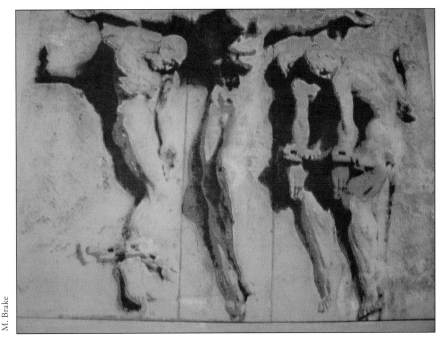

Three crosses

Jerome Murphy-O'Connor described the disappointment Christian pilgrims experienced with their first encounter with the Church of the Holy Sepulcher as the place of Jesus' death:

> One expects the central shrine of Christendom to stand out in majestic isolation, but anonymous buildings cling to it like barnacles. One looks for numinous light, but it is dark and cramped. One hopes for peace, but the ear is assailed by a cacophony of warring chants. One desires holiness, only to encounter a jealous possessiveness: the six groups of occupants — Latin Catholics, Greek Orthodox, Armenians, Syrians, Copts, Ethiopians — watch one another suspiciously for any infringement of rights.[3]

Could this be the place of Christ's death and burial? The evidence suggests the affirmative.

The Via Dolorosa ends at the Church of the Holy Sepulcher. John writes, "So the soldiers took charge of Jesus. Carrying his own cross, he went out to the place of the Skull (which in Aramaic is called Golgotha). There they crucified him, and with him two others — one on each side and Jesus in the middle. Pilate had a notice prepared and fastened to the cross. It read: JESUS OF NAZARETH, THE KING OF THE JEWS" (John 19:16 – 19).

Rolling stone tomb at Khirbet Midras

The Empty Tomb, the Hope of Humankind
(Matthew 28:1 – 15; Mark 16:1 – 8; Luke 24:1 – 43; John 20:1 – 31; T&G 169 – 79)

The anticipated Messiah who had promised the kingdom and stirred the hopes and imaginations of a nation was dead. His followers' sorrow, his mother's heartbreak, and his disciples' disappointment seem to suggest a story of ultimate tragedy. The disciples were left afraid of being arrested by the Roman guard. The women languished and fell into a routine of menial chores. Feelings of shame, fear, and failure overwhelmed Jesus' followers as he lay in a tomb on Saturday, the hopes and dreams of those who had loved him, dead with him.

The world descended into a nightmare until an angel spoke from Jesus' tomb on Sunday morning: "He has risen" (Matt. 28:6). The eternal God became man, died, was buried, and rose again to satisfy God's justice to reconcile humans to himself.

Men and women have scrutinized and debated what happened in those hours on that historic day. Jesus' resurrection has been doubted, disregarded, ridiculed, believed, and fanatically proclaimed. Believers in Jesus Christ regard the resurrection as the greatest triumph of human history. The apostle Paul summarizes the significance of Jesus' victory over death: If Jesus didn't rise from the dead and defeat death, our faith is worthless (1 Cor. 15:13 – 19). No matter what critics say, the gospel narratives are clear: "Once he was dead; now he lives." Jesus' human, frail cadaver became a glorious, resurrected body.

When compared to the men who betrayed, denied, and hid during Passion Week, women played heroic roles. They anointed Jesus at Bethany, confronted Peter regarding his commitment, warned Pilate to have nothing to do with the innocent Jesus, stood by the cross in Jesus' greatest hour of need, and were the first witnesses of the risen Christ, the greatest event ever recorded.[4]

The Sunday morning of Jesus' resurrection began like any other, as men and women throughout Israel rose to greet a new day. But some rose to what they thought was a day of broken promises and shattered dreams. They believed the promised Messiah lay dead in a tomb and that God had failed them.

The Sabbath behind them, Mary Magdalene, Salome, and Joanna quickly moved through the dark, predawn streets of Jerusalem as they headed toward the cemetery where Jesus lay in a fresh tomb donated by Joseph of Arimathea, a prominent member of the Sanhedrin.[5] Jesus' promise of resurrection had found fertile ground in the minds of the Pharisees, and they had asked Pilate to guard the tomb for fear that Jesus' disciples would steal his body in an attempt to trick people into believing he had risen from the dead.

But the women, who were unaware that Herod had assigned guards, believed they could somehow gain access to Jesus' tomb to anoint his body. They knew a heavy stone covered the doorway and wondered how they would move it, but faith moved them forward in spite of their question, "Who will remove the stone from the doorway?"

But upon their arrival, they found the stone rolled away and the tomb empty. Stunned, they began to weep as two men dressed in dazzling white appeared to

The Resurrection, HE LIVES.

Original artwork by Ron Waalkes

them. One spoke directly: "Do not be afraid, for I know that you are looking for Jesus, who was crucified. He is not here; he has risen, just as he said"
(Matt. 28:5–6). The angel instructed them to go tell Jesus' other followers.
The women, in fear and shock but with renewed excitement, ran to tell the
others what they saw and heard.

With the startling news of Jesus' resurrection, Peter and John rushed in
disbelief to the tomb. Were the women telling the truth? Was it possible that
he really was not in the tomb? They argued with each other as they ran, both
certain that if the body was missing, it surely had been stolen. The disciples
who entered the tomb found Jesus' grave clothes lying discarded. Indeed, he
was nowhere to be found!

> They saw the linen grave clothes in two parts: the main linen bands lying
> flat, pressed down by the eighty-pound weight of the spices, and the separate
> napkin, which covered Jesus' head, in a bunched-up, rolled condition at the
> end of the stone slab on which his body had lain, retaining its shape because
> of the smaller size.... it seemed as if the body simply vanished from its grave
> wrappings, leaving them exactly in place except for gravity flattening the
> main shroud.[6]

The disciples were confused. "Why didn't Jesus tell us this was going
to happen?" they asked. Their minds raced as they tried to make sense of
these events. The evidence was obvious. He was not where they thought he
would be.

Jerusalem was in turmoil. Rumors spread throughout the city that the
rabbi from Galilee was not in his grave. Both the believers and unbelievers
were stunned. What had happened? They knew a man had been crucified.
And some believed the recent earthquakes had been a divine response to
his death. Moreover, something strange had occurred in the temple: it was
rumored that the heavy curtain separating the Most Holy Place had ripped
from top to bottom. And now this man's followers proclaimed him resurrected. How could it be?

Shortly afterward, two disciples, one who was called Cleopas, were likely
fleeing toward Emmaus to avoid possible arrest. They had heard the rumors,
and panic ruled their every step. As they moved quickly and with purpose,
a stranger approached them. Who was he? Was he seeking to find out their
relationship to Jesus, in hopes of informing on them? To their surprise, the
stranger gave them an explanation of what was happening. While listening
to the stranger rehearse Jesus' message on his death and resurrection, the disciples suddenly recognized that the man was Jesus himself. Questions flooded

their minds and were about ready to spill over to fill the identified stranger's ears when suddenly he vanished.

John and Peter's skepticism also quickly vanished when Jesus appeared to them.[7] Then on Sunday evening, he appeared to the ten disciples (Luke 24:36). A week later (John 20:26), he appeared to Thomas and the other disciples. In spite of Thomas's former doubts about Jesus, his mood changed from disbelief to radiant joy as he confessed, "My Lord, and my God!" (John 20:28). Up to this moment in time, no one — including any of the other disciples — had addressed Jesus as God.[8] "Doubting Thomas," as he so often has been called, made the ultimate confession of Jesus as Lord and as God.

Morning's daybreak brought the sun in all its splendor. Fresh hope permeated the air. But what would the new future bring? The disciples still were not sure. But they placed their hope in a risen Lord as they walked into the new day.

POST-RESURRECTION AND ASCENSION
(Matthew 28:16 – 20; Mark 16:9 – 20[9]; Luke 24:44 – 53; John 21:1 – 25; T&G 180 – 84)

Jesus continued to appear in his resurrection body for forty more days, but his earthly ministry to the disciples and others was near completion.[10] It was time to return to the Father. After speaking to the disciples, Jesus ascended into a cloud. Two men who stood nearby in white clothing promised that he would come again. "This same Jesus, who has been taken from you into heaven, will come back in the same way you have seen him go into heaven." But until that day, Jesus' followers are instructed to proclaim the gospel message and to go into all the world and make disciples (Acts 1:1 – 11).

Hope for this cruel and troubled world hinges on the resurrection. God showed his limitless love on the cross and his approval of Jesus' work in the resurrection. Through simple faith in a risen Savior, all are offered the free gift of eternal life. Believe on Jesus and know the hope of your eternal destiny and a relationship with a living Lord.

"I am the resurrection and the life. The one who believes in me will live, even though they die; and whoever lives by believing in me will never die."
John 11:25 – 26

HISTORICAL AND GEOGRAPHICAL LIFE OF JESUS

		BIRTH AND EARLY LIFE OF JESUS		
Date	**Location**	**Event**	**Reference**	**Page**
		Jesus' lineage	Luke 3:23–38	31
6/5 BC	Jerusalem	John's birth foretold	Luke 1:5–25	23
6/5 BC	Nazareth	Jesus' birth foretold to Mary	Luke 1:26–38	25
6/5 BC	Hill country of Judea	John's birth	Luke 1:57–66	23
Winter 6 or 5/4 BCE[1]	Bethlehem	Birth of Jesus	Luke 2:1–7	27
Winter 6 or 5/4 BC	Bethlehem (shepherds' field)	Visit of shepherds	Luke 2:8–20	31
8th Day	Bethlehem	Circumcision	Luke 2:21	52
After 40 days	Jerusalem	Presentation in temple	Luke 2:22–38	33
Before Herod died 5/4 BC	Bethlehem	Visit of magi	Matt. 2:1–12	34
4 BC	Egypt by way of Ashkelon	Flight to Egypt	Matt. 2:13–18	40
After Herod died 4 BC	Nazareth	Return to Nazareth	Matt. 2:19–23	40, 43
Passover AD 9	Jerusalem	First Passover visit to Jerusalem	Matt. 3:1–6	45
AD 29 – 28	Wilderness of Judea	Commencement of John's ministry	Matt. 3:1–6; Luke 3:16	45

AD 26	Judea	Arrival of Pilate		
Summer or Autumn 29	Bethany beyond Jordan	Baptism of Jesus	Matt. 3:13–17; Mark 1:9–11; Luke 3:21–2; John 1:29–39	49, 63
	Wilderness of Judea	Temptation of Jesus	Matt. 4:1–11; Mark 1:12–13; Luke 4:1–13	63
	Bethany beyond Jordan	John's witness to Jesus Messiah	John 1:29–34	48
	From Bethany beyond Jordan	To Galilee	John 1:43	48
	Cana of Galilee	Jesus' first miracle	John 2:1–11	53
	Capernaum	First visit to Capernaum	John 2:12	42

EARLY JUDEAN MINISTRY

Date	Location	Event	Reference	Page
Passover AD 30	Jerusalem	First cleansing of temple	John 2:13–22	58, 63
30 (April?)	Jesus departs from Judea	To Galilee after John's imprisonment	Matt. 4:12; John 4:1–3	65

SAMARITAN MINISTRY

Date	Location	Event	Reference	Page
Jan/Feb 31 (late 30?)	Jacob's well and Sychar	Dialogue with woman in Sychar	John 4:5–42	63

GALILEAN MINISTRY: PASSOVER AD 31 TO PASSOVER 32

Date	Location	Event	Reference	Page
Spring– Autumn 31	From Samaria	Jesus went to Galilee	John 4:43–45	58
Spring– Autumn 31	Cana of Galilee	Healing of the nobleman's son	John 4:46–54	63, 66, 83
Spring– Autumn 31	Nazareth	First rejection at Nazareth	Luke 4:16–31	67

Spring? 31 (30)	Tabgha	Call of disciples	Matt. 4:18–22; Luke 1:16–20	48
	Move to Capernaum	Capernaum-home	Matt. 4:13–16	69
	Capernaum	Call of four disciples	Matt. 4:18–22; Mark 1:16–20	69, 83
31	Galilee, Jesus' second Passover	Plucking grain on Sabbath	Matt. 12:1–8; Mark 2:23–28	79
	Capernaum	Healing Peter's mother–in–law	Matt. 8:14–17; Mark 1:29–34	79, 83
Spring 31	Mountain near Tabgha	Sermon on the Mount	Matt. 5–7; Luke 6:20–49	85
Summer 31	Galilee	Leaders' accusation of blasphemy	Matt. 12:22–45; Mark 3:20–30	91
Summer 31	On shore near Capernaum (Sower's cove)	Parables by the sea	Matt. 13:1–35; Mark 4:1–34; Luke 8:4–18	93
	Sea of Galilee	Stilled storm	Mark 4:35–41; Matt. 4:35–41; Luke 8:22–25	101
	Near harbor of Gadara	Demoniacs healed	Matt. 8:28–34; Mark 5:1–20; Luke 8:26–39	103
	Capernaum/ "over the other side"	Jairus' daughter raised	Matt. 9:18–26; Mark 5:22–43; Luke 8:40–56	105
Late summer? 31	Nazareth	Last visit to Nazareth	Mark 6:1–6; Matt. 13:54–58	109
	Jerusalem	Healing at pool of Bethesda	John 5:1–47	79
	Galilee	Twelve commissioned	Mark 6:6–13; Matt. 9:35–11:1; Luke 9:1–6	100
	Nain	Raising of widow's son	Luke 7:11–17	100
31 or 32	Machaerus	Death of John the Baptist	Matt. 14:1–2; Mark 6:14–29; Luke 9:7–9	109

TRAINING OF THE TWELVE IN GALILEE

Date	Location	Event	Reference	Page
April 13–14, AD 32	Near Bethsaida, Jesus' third Passover	First withdrawal; five-thousand fed	Matt. 14:13–21; Mark 6:32–44; Luke 9:10–17; John 6:1–14	116
	Bethsaida to Gennesaret	Jesus walks on Sea/Peter takes leadership	Matt. 14:22–32; Mark 6:45–53; Luke 6:16–21	112
	Land of Tyre	Healing of daughter of Syro–Phoenician	Matt. 14:21–28; Mark 7:24–30	115
After Passover 32	From Sidon to Decapolis	Fourth withdrawal	Matt. 15:21,29; Mark 7:31	116
	Decapolis: Tell Hadar? or HaOn?	Feeding four-thousand	Matt. 15:32–38; Mark 8:1–9	116, 124
	Magdala/ Dalmanutha	Sign of Jonah given	Matt. 15:39–16:4; Mark 8:10–12	134
	Bethsaida	Healing of blind man	Mark 8:22–26	136
Spring (?) 32	Region of Caesarea Philippi	Confession of Peter	Matt. 16:13–20; Mark 8:27–30; Luke 9:18–21	118
	Region of Caesarea Philippi	First prediction of crucifixion and resurrection	Matt. 16:21–26; Mark 8:31–37	119
	Mount Hermon	Transfiguration	Matt. 17:1–8; Mark 9:1–13; Luke 9:28–36	120
	Capernaum	Temple tribute paid	Matt. 17:22–27	107
Spring–December 32 (Feast of Tabernacles to Feast of Dedication)	Luke's record of Journeys:[2] Journey to Jerusalem, first account	He set out to Jerusalem	Luke 9:51–13:21	125, 246
Winter 32?	Journey to Jerusalem, second account	Continues toward Jerusalem; raising Lazarus	Luke 13:22–17:10	150, 143
Winter 32?	Journey to Jerusalem, third and last account	Raising Lazarus to Passover	Luke 17:11–19:28	143

LATER JUDEAN AND PEREAN MINISTRY

Date	Location	Event	Reference	Page
September 32	To Jerusalem	To feast of Tabernacles	John 7:2–10	125
September 32	Jerusalem, Temple	Feast of Tabernacles	John 7:11	128
	Judea	Sending of seventy-two	Luke 10:1–16	157, 259
December 32	Jerusalem	Feast of Dedication	John 10:22–39	136
	Judea	Good Samaritan	Luke 10:25–37	29, 132
32–33?	Bethany	Visit with Mary and Martha	Luke 11:1–12:3	133
December 32 (Feast of Dedication)	Jerusalem	Healing man born blind	John 9:1–7	136
	Jerusalem	Good Shepherd	John 10:1–18	137
	To Perea	Ministry in Perea	John 10:40–42; Luke 13:22–17:10	150
Winter 32/Spring 33	Bethany near Jerusalem	Raising of Lazarus	John 11:1–44	143
	Ephraim	Sanhedrin decides to put Jesus to death	John 11:45–54	145

THE FINAL JOURNEY TO JERUSALEM AD 33

Date	Location	Event	Reference	Page
Spring 33	Bethany to Jerusalem	Jesus to Jerusalem for Passover	John 11:55–12:1	189
Spring 33	Border of Galilee and Samaria	Healing of 10 lepers	Luke 17:11–21	150, 152
	Thru Perea to Jerusalem	On to Passover	Matt. 19; Mark 10; Luke 17	189
	Jericho	Blind Bartimaeus healed	Matt. 20:29–34; Mark 10:46–52	150

	Herodian Jericho	Ministry to Zacchaeus	Luke 19:1 – 10	150
	Ascent to Jerusalem	Kingdom delayed	Luke 19:11 – 28	95, 136

PASSION WEEK IN JERUSALEM AD 33 (LAST PASSOVER)

Date	Location	Event	Reference	Page
Saturday March 28, 33	Bethany	Anointing of Jesus	John 12:1 – 8; Matt. 26:6 – 13	248
Sunday March 29, 33	Bethany	Crowd came to see Jesus	John 12:9 – 11	248
Sunday (March 30, 33)[3]	Jerusalem	Triumphal entry and visit to temple	Matt. 21:1 – 11; John 12:12 – 19	243
	Bethany	Stayed in Bethany	Matt. 21:17	247
Monday (March 31, 33)	From Bethany–Jerusalem	Cursing of fig tree	Matt. 21:18 – 19; Mark 11:12 – 14	194
	Temple	Second cleansing of temple	Mark 11:15 – 17; Matt. 21:12 – 13	262
	Bethany	Stayed in Bethany	Mark 11:18 – 19	262
Thursday (April 1, 33).	From Bethany–Jerusalem	Fig tree seen	Mark 11:20 – 25	194
	Jerusalem	Controversy with religious leaders	Matt. 21:23 – 23:39; Mark 11	195
	Mount of Olives	Olivet discourse	Matt. 24:1 – 25:46	248
Thursday April 2, 33	Jerusalem	Preparations for Passover	Matt. 26:17 – 19	199
	Upper Room	Passover meal discourse	Matt. 26:20 – 30; John 13 – 14	200
	Way to Garden of Gethsemane	Discourse on the way	John 15:1 – 18:1	204
	Garden of Gethsemane	Prayer, betrayal and arrest	Matt. 26:36 – 56; Mark 14:32 – 15:15; Luke 22:40 – 23:25; John 18:19 – 23	209

	House of Caiaphas	Trial before Caiaphas and Annas	John 18:13–27	211, 212
Friday April 3, 33	Palace of Herod	Trial before Pilate and Antipas	John 18:28–19:16	216, 219
9:00 am–3:00 pm	Golgotha	Crucifixion of Jesus	Matt. 27:31–60; John 19:16–42	230
Saturday April 4, AD 33	Tomb at Golgotha	Tomb guarded by Roman soldiers	Matt. 27:61–66	237, 249
Sunday April 5, 33	Tomb at Golgotha	Jesus resurrected	Matt. 28:1–15	237
	Road to Emmaus	Appearance to two disciples	Luke 24:13–33	240
	Jerusalem	Appearance to ten disciples	John 20:13–25	240
Sunday April 12, 33	Jerusalem	Appearance to eleven disciples	John 20:26–31	240
Post–resurrection period	Sea of Galilee	Appearance to seven disciples	John 21:1–22	240
Thursday May 14, 33 AD	Mount of Olives	Ascension of Jesus	Acts 1:9–12	241

NOTES

A Word. . .

1. Determining original sources for the gospel accounts is a complex and difficult subject. The issues of priority, dependence, and interdependence have occupied scholars for many years. For the purpose of this volume, the subject of source criticism will be left to authors majoring on the subject: Eta Linnemann, *Is There a Synoptic Problem? Rethinking the Literary Dependence of the First Three Gospels*, trans. Robert W. Yarbrough (Grand Rapids: Baker, 1992); Robert L. Lindsey, *The Jesus Sources: Understanding the Gospels* (Tulsa: Hakesher, 1990); John Wenham, *Redating Matthew, Mark, and Luke* (Downers Grove, IL: InterVarsity, 1992); and Robert Stein, *The Synoptic Problem: An Introduction* (Grand Rapids: Baker, 1994).
2. Alfred Edersheim, *The Life and Times of Jesus the Messiah* (New York: Longmans, Green, 1912), 2:127–28.

Introduction

1. The land is often referred to as Israel (Jews prefer *Erets Yisrael*) or Palestine (Arabs' preference). The term *Palestina* was first used by the Romans to expunge the name Israel/Judea. The designation became popular after the failure of the second Jewish revolt under Bar Kokhba in AD 132–35.
2. When the Maccabean king John Hyrcanus conquered Idumea in 140–130 BCE, he required the Idumeans to accept Jewish law. At this time, many converted to Judaism, and perhaps Antipater did as well.
3. An Idumean was someone from Edom, an area near the Dead Sea. (In the first century BCE, Idumeans lived in the Negev and southern Shephelah.)
4. In 2007 the tomb and sarcophagus of King Herod the Great was found at the Herodium by archaeologist Ehud Netzer who had been excavating the area since 1972. While most scholars suspected Herod was buried in or around Herodium, discovery had eluded them. The Herodium is located on the top of a desert mountain about 6–7 miles south of Jerusalem.
5. While Herod attempted to befriend the Jewish population, his cruelty betrayed his intentions. He executed forty-six leading members of the Sanhedrin for upholding the law of Moses, tortured men and women who condemned his pagan practices, and slaughtered infants at the time of Jesus' birth (Matt. 2:16–18). Josephus wrote, "He [Herod] had not the least suspicion that any trouble could arise in his kingdom, because he kept his people obedient, as well by the fear they stood in of him, for he was implacable in the infliction of his punishments" (*Antiquities of the Jews* 15.326). Later Roman emperors openly persecuted Christians with relentless cruelty.
6. *Ethnarch* was a term used in the first century for a governor of a town or country by a person of a different race or people. *Tetrarch* referred to a ruler over a larger territory, with authority just below a king.

7. The knowledge of the events of the Roman siege at Masada comes from Josephus. While he had access to Roman records, his account of the suicide of the men and women the last night of the attack is in question. It was Passover, and a full moon suggests there was insufficient time for a mass suicide. Instead, Jerome Murphy-O'Connor proposes that some of the defenders killed their families, burnt their possessions, and finally committed suicide, while others fought to the death and still others tried to hide and escape but were dispatched out of hand when they were discovered. Josephus invented a speech of Eleazar Ben Yair to blame the war, not on the Jewish people, but on a minority of violent revolutionaries, the Sicarii. Jerome Murphy-O'Connor, *The Holy Land: An Oxford Archaeological Guide*, 5th ed. (Oxford: Oxford University Press, 2008), 380.
8. Yadin Yigael, *Masada: Herod's Fortress and the Zealots' Last Stand* (London: George Weidenfeld and Nicolson, 1966), 15.

CHAPTER 1

1. Offering the incense wasn't limited to the Abijah course, but it was during their period of service (two weeks a year) that Zechariah was performing the duty.
2. Late tradition suggests Zechariah and Elizabeth lived in Ein Kerem, a village in Judea. Today it is a suburb of Jerusalem in a branch of the Sorek Valley. A mosaic in a church there depicts John's birth.
3. This tradition is preserved by the Sisters of Anna, an Italian order that operates an orphanage near Sepphoris. A Crusader church preserves a Byzantine mosaic that indicates the site of Mary's home.
4. George Berry, *The Classic Greek Dictionary* (Chicago: Wilcox & Follett, 1945), 516. Berry defines it as "a house for the reception of strangers, an inn."
5. There is no conclusive evidence that eliminates December 25 as a date for Jesus' birth.
6. Jeremiah 22:30 reads, "This is what the LORD says: 'Record this man [Jeconiah/Jehoiachin] as childless, a man who will not prosper in his lifetime, for none of his offspring will prosper, none will sit on the throne of David or rule anymore in Judah.'" The description here seems to curse the kingly line of Jeconiah.
7. While this is a common explanation, there is another way of understanding it. Jesus' legal right to the throne comes through the line of kings, given by Matthew. And, regardless of Mary's genealogy, Jesus' right to the throne comes through Joseph, and thus the Jeconiah (Jehoiachin) curse may not be avoided. There are a number of possibilities but one possible explanation is: (1) None of Jeconiah's children succeeded him on the throne; the passage isn't talking about grandchildren or future descendants; and/or (2) the curse was reversed. This seems hinted at in the very next chapter (Jer 23:5–6) and then made more explicit in Haggai's promise to Zerubbabel, the grandson of Jeconiah (Hag 2:23).
8. Some suggest this bright star was the *shekinah* glory, a rabbinic description of God's awesome presence. It must also be noted that the appearance of the magi may have taken place up to two years after Jesus' birth. Some suggest that the bright light in the sky was an aligning of the stars and therefore not a miracle. This view, however, would require a miracle in itself.
9. The Hasmoneans were Israel's legitimate line of kings. While they were more "legitimate" than Herod, they were not of the kingly line of David or even of the tribe of Judah. Nor were they appointed by God as kings of Israel.
10. Harold Hoehner has an excellent treatment of dates for the life of Christ. For the most

part, I have followed his dates throughout this work. Harold W. Hoehner, *Chronological Aspects of the Life of Christ* (Grand Rapids: Zondervan, 1977).

11. Hoehner concludes that Jesus had to be born in late 5 BCE or early 4 BCE. *Chronological Aspects*, 25.

12. Some Old Testament events were in fact commemorated by placing a stone (*massebah*) in a certain location to remind the Israelites of significant events, but generally New Testament events were not so marked.

13. Josephus's actions at Jotapata, where he tricked survivors into suicide and then failed to follow with his own suicide, and his later action of joining the Romans brought suspicion from the Jews that led to their contempt for him.

14. J. J. Scott, s.v. "Josephus," *Dictionary of Jesus and the Gospels* (Downers Grove, IL: InterVarsity, 1992), 391–92.

Chapter 2

1. The new appointment was not viewed positively. Josephus reports that Archelaus ordered three thousand to be killed at the time of a Passover. *Antiquities of the Jews* 17.218.

2. The Gospels relate the story of Jesus at the temple at the age of twelve.

3. It is assumed that Joseph died before Mary moved to Capernaum. He is not mentioned after the events in Jerusalem.

4. Josephus, *Wars of the Jews* 1.167.

5. Ibid. 1.304.

6. Josephus, *Antiquities* 18.26.

7. The word traditionally translated "carpenter" in the Gospels is actually a more generic Greek word that means "builder" and can refer to working with stone as well as wood.

8. Josephus, *Wars* 3.29.

9. This is the event that brings Josephus's credibility into question. His account of Masada sounds eerily like Sepphoris.

10. These three cities received most of Jesus' teaching and witnessed the most miracles. It was for this reason that they were without excuse; Matt 11:20–24

11. Ray Pritz argues convincingly of this relationship between "Nazarenes" and netzer. Ray A. Pritz, *Nazarene Jewish Christianity* (Jerusalem: Magnes, 1988), 11–18.

12. A case can be made that to be called a Nazarene was a fulfillment of the prophecies that the Messiah would be despised (e.g., Isa. 53:2).

13. Bargil Pixner, *With Jesus through Galilee according to the Fifth Gospel* (Rosh Pina, Israel: Chorazin, 1992), 16.

14. A Nazirite refers to one who voluntarily took a vow as described in Numbers 6.

15. Pixner, *With Jesus through Galilee*, 14–15.

16. The established Jewish ritual of ceremonial cleansing was washing in a bath-like structure called a *mikveh*.

17. Hershel Shanks, "John the Baptist's Cave?" *Biblical Archaeology Review* 30, no. 6 (November–December 2004): 18–19. The article suggests the cave may have been a simple water system.

18. Some translations read, "Bethany beyond the Jordan." The King James Version, following the Textus Receptus Greek text, reads, "Bethabara."

19. Day 1, John 1:19–28; day 2, 1:29–34; day 3, 1:35–42; day 4, 1:43–51. In Jewish reckoning, the "third day" of Jesus' ministry was the end of the week. "If this reckoning of days is correct, then the Cana miracle takes place on the seventh day and mirrors a work of new creation." Darrell L. Bock, *Jesus according to Scripture* (Grand Rapids: Baker Academic, 2002), 424n2.

20. If John were baptizing near the Dead Sea and then on the next day called his first disciples, he would have had to travel seventy-five to eighty miles from the Bethabara area to Capernaum in a short period of time—a challenge by foot.

21. William Schlegel, *Satellite Bible Atlas* (Israel: BiblePlaces.com, 2012), 9–3. Josephus mentions the province of Batanea (Judea beyond the Jordan, *Wars of the Jews* 3.51–58; Josh. 19:34 also suggests Judah extended beyond the Jordan) in Philip's dominion. *Wars* 2.94–95, *Antiquities* 18.106. The nineteenth-century explorer C. R. Condor places Bethabara just south of the Sea of Galilee, not as far south as the Dead Sea. Charles Wilson et al., *The Survey of Western Palestine* (London: Committee of the Palestine Exploration Fund, 1881), 134.

22. Pixner argues that "Bethany beyond the Jordan" refers to the area of Batanea in the territory of Bashan. John's baptism was in the Yarmuk River—beyond the Jordan. Its location would be associated with Kochaba and Bethany/Echtane on the Yarmuk River. Today it is located in the southwest corner of Syria. Pixner, *With Jesus through Galilee*, 20–21.

23. Rami Khouri, "Where Jesus Baptized: Bethany beyond the Jordan," *Biblical Archaeological Review* 31, no. 1 (2005): 34–43.

24. John undoubtedly had been baptizing in association with his ministry prior to his baptism of Jesus (Luke 3:2–3).

25. J. Carl Laney reminds us of the difficulty in identifying "beyond the Jordan." It is possible that the ruins of Bethany beyond the Jordan will never be found, but an abundance of evidence indicates that cartographers should place it east of the Jordan River near the Hajlah ford in the vicinity of Wadi el-Kharrar (just east of the Jordan and near the Dead Sea). J. Carl Laney, "Selective Geographical Problems in the Life of Christ," doctoral diss. (Dallas Theological Seminary, 1977), 69.

26. Laney, "Selective Geographical Problems," 67. Laney has an excellent discussion on the other possible sites as well.

Chapter 3

1. Most observant Jews took ceremonial baths to cleanse themselves from ritual impurity. The Essenes took ritual baptism to another level. John came baptizing others for repentance unto the remission of sins. Even Josephus recognized that John's baptism did not provide forgiveness for sins but merely signified repentance. Josephus, *Antiquities of the Jews* 18.116–18.

2. Luke's account adds the element, "And all people will see God's salvation" (3:6). Throughout the book, Luke places emphasis on the inclusion of Gentiles.

3. Hebrews 7:11–28 associates Jesus' priesthood with the eternal priesthood of Melchizedek. The implication is that the Levitical priesthood was imperfect because all of its priests and subjects were responsible to the law as sinners and faced condemnation.

4. Harold Hoehner, *Chronological Aspects of the Life of Christ* (Grand Rapids: Zondervan, 1977), 30–37.

5. Three passages that are helpful in this discussion are John 3:2; Acts 2:22; and Hebrews 2:3–4.

6. Cana may also be spelled Qana, Kenna, and Kanah.

7. J. Carl Laney, "Selective Geographical Problems in the Life of Christ," doctoral diss. (Dallas Theological Seminary, 1977), 90–107.

8. A triclinium is a table arrangement in the form of a square horseshoe.

9. John McRay, *Archaeology and the New Testament* (Grand Rapids: Baker, 1991), 110.

10. A Tyrian shekel had a value of 4 dinars (drachma). One dinar could purchase a large meal, two gallons of flour, and twelve loaves of bread, or pay the wages of a vineyard worker. An ox cost 100–200 dinars, a newborn donkey foal cost 2–4, and a Roman soldier's annual salary was 50 dinars. Miriam Feinberg Vamosh, *Daily Life at the Time of Jesus* (Herzlia, Israel: Palphot, 2004), 98.

11. John 3:23, after Jesus' encounter with Nicodemus, places John's baptizing at "Aenon near Salim." This location is still in question. Presumably John moved from baptizing in the Jordan (where he baptized Jesus, just north of the Dead Sea) on to Bethany, on the other side of the Jordan (east of the Sea of Galilee), in Herod Philip's territory. See Josephus, *Antiquities* 17.23–26, 317–20.

CHAPTER 4

1. Some historians believe Jesus lived in the home of Peter while in Capernaum. However, evidence is sparse.

2. Stanislao Loffreda, *Recovering Capharnaum* (Milan, Italy: Edizioni Custodia Terra Santa, 1985), 11–12.

3. Ibid., 12.

4. An *insula* is a self-contained block of rooms forming units of living space surrounding a common courtyard. As the family grew, additional rooms were added. Perhaps Jesus (and his family) occupied one or more of these rooms.

5. Loffreda gives a full description in his book *Recovering Capharnaum* (Milan, Italy: Edizioni Custodia Terra Santa, 1985), 52ff.

6. Dennis Bratcher, "Introduction to a Christian Seder: Recovering Passover for Christians," *The Voice*, November 8, 2011, http://www.crivoice.org/seder.html.

7. Earlier in his ministry, Jesus had delivered a man possessed by a demon in the synagogue in Capernaum (Luke 4:31–37) but was not charged with violating the Sabbath. Capernaum theologically accommodated the school of Hillel, a moderate division of the Pharisees. Laws concerning loving neighbors and attending to the welfare of livestock took precedence over the stricter interpretation of the law.

8. Jesus quickly defended his actions. David's eating of the priests' showbread was a necessity, and as such it was not a violation of the law (1 Sam. 21:6). Works of worship were permitted on the Sabbath as well (Num. 28:9–10). Moreover, "the Sabbath was made for man, not man for the Sabbath" (Mark 2:27), for Jesus is Lord of the Sabbath.

CHAPTER 5

1. While Jesus knew he was God and had all the divine privileges necessary to control his environment, during his earthly mission on earth, housed in a human body, he limited his power and authority on most occasions. He experienced fatigue, human emotions, hunger and thirst, and pain. He was truly a man.

2. Bargil Pixner, *With Jesus through Galilee according to the Fifth Gospel* (Rosh Pina, Israel: Chorazin, 1992), 37.

3. John was probably not faltering in his faith but had grown impatient in light of his own predicament. The necessity of Jesus' death on the cross was not yet in Jesus' preaching (see Matt. 16:21).

4. Jesus, the King of the kingdom of God, offered the kingdom, but it was rejected. Today believers benefit from aspects of the covenants, but the Davidic kingdom will be inaugurated later.

5. Hoehner dates the founding of Tiberias to AD 23. Harold Hoehner, *Herod Antipas*

(Grand Rapids: Zondervan, 1980), 94. However, the more commonly accepted view is AD 19, as argued by Hirschfeld. Yizhar Hirschfeld, *Roman, Byzantine, and Early Muslim Tiberias: A Handbook of Primary Sources* (Ann Arbor: University of Michigan Press, 2005).

6. It may have offended some Jews who thought it sacrilegious to inhabit sites on ancient Jewish graveyards.

7. Hoehner, *Herod Antipas*, 223.

8. Anson F. Rainey and R. Steven Notley, *The Sacred Bridge: Carta's Atlas of the Biblical World* (Jerusalem: Carta, 2006), 355.

9. J. Carl Laney, "Geographical Aspects of the Gospel," *Essays in Honor of J. Dwight Pentecost* (Chicago: Moody, 1986), 85.

CHAPTER 6

1. The Sea of Galilee is also called Sea of Tiberias (John 6:1), Lake of Gennesaret (Luke 5:1), and "the lake" (Mark 3:7).

2. The discovery of the "Jesus Boat" (for twelve to fifteen occupants) may shed some light on the boats on the Sea of Galilee. The traffic of boats from the fishing industry on the sea must have been intense. Many boats were small, designed for one or two fishermen. The size of the "Jesus Boat" may suggest that a few larger boats were used to transport people across the sea. The smaller fishing boats turned back because of the impending storm. The larger boats, with a capacity of twelve to fifteen passengers, could face the stormy waters.

3. The demand for Jesus to leave them in spite of his heroic deed seems strange. Perhaps his Jewish message in a Gentile community created the fear. Or perhaps they may have been overwhelmed by the power Jesus displayed, and rather than submit to him, they preferred to avoid him.

4. The Greek text known as the Textus Receptus, and hence the King James Bible, reads in Matthew 8:28, "Gergesenes," and in Mark 5:1 and Luke 8:26, "Gadarenes."

5. Mendel Nun, *Sea of Galilee: Newly Discovered Harbours* (Ein Gev, Israel: Kinnereth Sailing Co., 1989), 17.

6. Ibid.

7. Perhaps the greatest expert on the Sea of Galilee during the biblical and Second Temple Period, as well as an accomplished fisherman himself, the late Mendel Nun (d. 2010) was a lecturer and writer on fish and fishing in the Sea of Galilee for decades. For a detailed list of the fish in the Sea of Galilee see his many works including *The Sea of Galilee and Its Fishermen in the New Testament* (Ein Gev, Israel: Kinnereth Sailing Co., 1989); *The Land of the Gadarenes* (Ein Gev, Israel: Sea of Galilee Fishing Museum, 1996); *Gergesa (Kursi)* (Kinnereth Sailing Co., 1989); *ha-Dayig ha-Ivri ha-kadum* (ha-Kibuts ha-me'uhad, 1963); *Susita ve En-gev* (Maarakhot); *Ancient Stone Anchors and Net Sinkers from the Sea of Galilee* (Kibbutz Ein Gev Tourist Department and Kinnereth Sailing Co., 1993); *Ma'aganim u-nemalim kedumim ba-Kineret* (Ariel, 1987); *Der See Genezareth und die Evangelien. Archäologische Forschungen eines jüdischen Fischers* (Brunnen-Verlag: Gießen, 2001).

8. Nun, *Sea of Galilee*, 34–35.

9. Some suggest this event is the same as that recorded in Luke 4:16–31. However, the differences and placement would seem to mitigate against it being the same event.

10. J. W. Shepherd, *The Christ of the Gospels* (Grand Rapids: Eerdmans, 1968), 256–59. Shepherd gives an extensive account of the beheading of John.

11. Most of those seeking Jesus sought him for his teaching rather than to get healed. The

feeding of the five thousand represents the high point of Jesus' popularity with the masses.

12. Nun, *Sea of Galilee*, 51.

13. While this was a simple act of compassion, the implications were that they were "like sheep without a shepherd." In the messianic kingdom, the people will experience a Shepherd who will lead them. This miracle, along with the sermon on the Bread of Life, is reminiscent of the wilderness wanderings of the Old Testament.

14. Tabgha is a form of the Greek word *heptapegon*, meaning "seven springs." These warm water springs filled with minerals are rich with fish, especially in the winter months.

15. In Matthew 14:22, after the feeding of the five thousand, Jesus commanded the disciples to "go on ahead of him to the other side." They were certainly intending to go back to the western side. Matthew wrote, "They landed at Gennesaret" (14:34), which is on the western side of the lake. Jesus started from Capernaum and crossed over to Bethsaida (Luke 9:10), where they went to a "remote place" (v. 12). There were villages in the surrounding places. The feeding of five thousand men plus women and children took place near Bethsaida. The one verse that indicates a feeding on the western side at Tabgha is Mark 6:45, as recorded in the NASB. "Immediately Jesus made His disciples get into the boat and go ahead of Him to the other side to Bethsaida, while He Himself was sending the crowd away." This suggests they got in the boat from Tabgha (five thousand fed) and went to Bethsaida. The NIV reads, "Immediately Jesus made his disciples get into the boat and go on ahead of him to Bethsaida, while he dismissed the crowd." The miracle took place near Bethsaida, in a "solitary" (v. 32) or "remote" (v. 35) place, and Jesus told the disciples to go ahead of him to the nearby city of Bethsaida.

16. Scriptures do not reveal the occupations of all the disciples. Some certainly were fishermen; perhaps most of them were. They were all from Galilee. Judas's occupation is unknown, but because he was from Judea, he may not have been a fisherman.

17. The term "disciples" often refers to men and women who are simply inquirers. At other times, the term refers to those who are convinced of who Jesus is, and of course, it refers to those committed to him.

18. Jesus' message of the kingdom of God was given exclusively to the Jews. Gentiles would be a part of the kingdom, but that was not yet clear to hearers.

19. Some scholars prefer the feeding of the four thousand taking place near the kibbutz HaOn or En Gev south of Kursi. The area south of Kursi is deep in the Gentile Decapolis, and a large mountain range provides a context for the feeding of the four thousand. Crowds may have been a result of the notice taken at Jesus' multiple healings. It is perhaps a more "remote place" than the Kursi area.

20. Bargil Pixner, *With Jesus through Galilee according to the Fifth Gospel* (Rosh Pina, Israel: Chorazin, 1992), 83. See mosaic in photo depicting a pannier design (basket) on the floor at Kursi.

21. Another small mosaic tile at Kursi has its center eradicated, but the remains appear to picture two fish tails, perhaps another indication of Kursi (or nearby Tel Hadar) as the place commemorating the feeding of the four thousand.

22. Mendel Nun, "Fish, Storms, and a Boat," *Jerusalem Perspective* 3, no. 2 (March–April 1990): 3.

23. This is the first time the disciples confess Jesus as the Messiah.

24. Darrell L. Bock, *Jesus according to Scripture* (Grand Rapids: Baker Academic, 2002), 231.

25. It is noteworthy that Jesus' ministry centered around the smaller villages in Galilee. Most of his work centered in what is called the "Evangelical Triangle": Bethsaida, Chorazin, and Capernaum. There is no mention of him ministering in the major cities of Tiberias, Hippos, Sepphoris, Scythopolis, or even Caesarea-Philippi proper. Perhaps

as an observant Jew he refrained from entering cities known for their uncleanness or just to keep a low profile while avoiding Herod Antipas or religious authorities.

26. Matthew 8:19–22//Luke 9:57–62 may actually follow Luke 9:51–56//John 7:10. In Luke's gospel, Luke 9:51–56 precedes Luke 9:57–62, and Luke 9:57 notes that the group was on a journey, the beginning of which had already been indicated in Luke 9:51. Robert L. Thomas and Stanley N. Gundry, *The NIV Harmony of the Gospels* (New York: Harper Collins, 1988), 127.

CHAPTER 7

1. The typical route from Capernaum to Jerusalem crossed the Jordan River and passed along the eastern side of the river. This time Jesus set his face directly toward Jerusalem by way of Samaria. This trip did not go directly to Jerusalem. For an extended period he ministered in Samaria, Perea, and Judea (perhaps Batanea?).

2. Luke's account from 9:51–19:48 is called "Luke's Jerusalem travel narrative." Section 9:51–13:21 details Jesus' journey as he set out for Jerusalem through Samaria. In 13:22–17:10 he continues on his way to Jerusalem, and in 17:11–19:48 he travels between Samaria and Galilee and concludes his trip to Jerusalem. Scholars are quite certain he did not leave Galilee and go straight to Jerusalem. He traveled between Galilee and Jerusalem but always with the final destination of Jerusalem. Much of Luke's material is unique to Luke, so the chronology is a bit of a question. Perhaps Luke is simply presenting the teachings of Jesus from his later ministry and recounting them together in this section with little thought of chronology. Bailey insists the narratives form a literary device and must be interpreted as such. See Kenneth E. Bailey, *Poet and Peasant and Through Peasant Eyes: A Literary-Cultural Approach to the Parables in Luke*, combined ed. (Grand Rapids: Eerdmans, 1976), 85ff. The record does not suggest three trips to Jerusalem but three parts of the same journey to Jerusalem that resulted in Jesus' death. The period covers several months, so a great deal of travel was taking place. Since Luke was not so concerned with the chronology or geography of his account, it is unknown whether Jesus ever returned to Capernaum during this period. Some scholars believe Luke got his unique material while in Jerusalem in AD 57–58 as suggested by Acts 21:17ff., perhaps from personal interviews. Following are passages unique to Luke's travel narrative: journey through Samaria (Luke 9:51–56), parable of the good Samaritan (10:29–37), at the home of Mary and Martha (10:38–42), parable of the friend at midnight (11:5–8), declaration of blessedness of Mary (11:27–28), parable of the rich fool (12:13–21), punishment of disobedient servants (12:47–48), Jesus' warning to repent or perish (13:1–9), healing of crippled woman (13:10–17), warnings of Herod's intentions (13:31–33), parable of the prodigal son (15:11–31), Pharisees' hypocrisy (16:14–15), parable of the rich man and Lazarus (16:19–31), warnings to disciples (17:7–10), healing of the ten lepers (17:11–19), and parable of the persistent widow (18:1–8).

3. Josephus, *Antiquities of the Jews* 18.310–17; *Wars of the Jews* 1.62.

4. Thomas and Gundry point out that the events in this section likely happened during the Feast of Dedication rather than the Feast of Tabernacles. They list these reasons among others: The Jews would not have attempted to stone Jesus on the sacred "Sabbath." Elapsed time was required after the attempt to stone Jesus (John 8:59) to allow antagonism to die down before another public encounter. The tone is different from the turmoil and debate that dominated the Feast of Tabernacles. Robert L. Thomas and Stanley N. Gundry, *The NIV Harmony of the Gospels* (New York: Harper Collins, 1988), 134.

5. Given the strong opposition from the Jewish leaders, Jesus may not have remained

in the area continuously for the three-month period. The gospel accounts, however, suggest he did, but given the height of tensions, he may have moved around. One major advantage of going during the feasts (but not otherwise) was that the crowds of pilgrims, many from Galilee, were there, and Jesus' popularity with them would have protected him from the evil designs of Jerusalem's leaders. Judea was large enough for him to minister throughout the province.

6. Suetonius, *Divus Claudius* 25.4. Quoted in F. F. Bruce, *Jesus and Christian Origins outside the New Testament* (Grand Rapids: Eerdmans, 1974), 21.

7. Tacitus, *Annales* 15.44. Quoted in Bruce, *Jesus and Christian Origins*, 22.

8. Josephus, *Antiquities* 18.63.

9. This section does not appear in modern critical Greek texts, and most modern translations cite it only as a Christian tradition but not as the original writing of John's gospel. The King James Version and the Byzantine text-type include the reading as authentic.

10. The King James Version in Luke 10:1, 17 has "seventy" while the NIV has "seventy-two." Textual evidence is divided.

11. It is here that Jesus spoke the famous words "I and the Father are one" (John 10:29).

CHAPTER 8

1. John 10:40: "Then Jesus went back across the Jordan to the place where John had been baptizing in the early days." Is this to be equated with "Bethany on the other side of the Jordan" (John 1:28)? If so, perhaps this last journey toward Jerusalem includes ministry in the region of Batanea on the east side of the Sea of Galilee (see n. 6).

2. Herod was watching Jesus closely; he suspected he was John the Baptist come back to life. Herod as "the fox" was suspicious of popular figures that had the attention of large crowds. He was concerned about the threat of rebellion.

3. In the context of Jesus' ministry, his challenge was not idle, for he was at that time telling the disciples that he was going to die; and generally speaking, disciples follow the path of their master.

4. The gospel of John is the only gospel that records this event making it difficult to know exactly where this event occurred in the chronology.

5. Jewish tradition suggests that the soul remains in the body for three days before departing. This may be hinted at in Talmud tractate *Semahot* 8.1: "One goes out to the graveyard and visits the dead until three days [to see signs of death] and one does not suspect at all the ways of the Amorites [pagan practices]. A story of one whom they [invested parties] visited [and found him alive], and he lived for twenty-five years thereafter he died." The visits, then, are to assure the one is actually dead.

6. Pixner has an interesting approach to the location of this "region of Judea to the other side of the Jordan" (Matt. 19:1). Perea was in the jurisdiction of the "fox" Herod Antipas, a man seeking Jesus' death. The region of Judea beyond the Jordan is never referred to as Perea. At this time, Judea included Galilee, Gaulanitis, and Batanea according to Josephus. Leaving Galilee, Jesus entered the Jewish region on the other side of the Jordan where Jews who returned from the Babylonian exile (the clan of Nazarenes at Batanea) were established. Large followings, including children, came to him in a region not controlled by Herod Antipas (Mark 10:1; Matt. 19:2). This period of Jesus' ministry was not in Perea but in the region east of the Sea of Galilee. Bargil Pixner, *With Jesus through Galilee according to the Fifth Gospel* (Rosh Pina, Israel: Chorazin, 1992), 108.

7. Additional information is revealed in Mark's account: "to give his life as a ransom for many" (10:45).

8. The meaning is perhaps interpreted as "in your midst." The King is present. Ultimately, however, the kingdom is spiritual, even though its manifestation will be physical.

9. The kingdom was clearly in mind in Zechariah's day, as the offices of priest and king would fall to one person (a picture of the Messiah-King, 6:11). The royal crowning of the high priest was necessary for the messianic King-Priest. Realization of the kingdom of the King-Priest was dependent on the requirement of "if you diligently obey the LORD our God" (6:15). Israel did not obey, so the kingdom could not be realized, yet Zechariah continued to describe the kingdom that awaited its inauguration under the King-Priest-Messiah in an undetermined number of years in the future (Zech. 14:9). Zechariah was prophesying that Jesus would fulfill the kingdom promises — yet we now know it did not happen in the first century at Jesus' first coming but is still awaited.

10. This could be a reference to the destruction of Jerusalem in AD 70 by the Romans.

11. The Davidic kingdom was not given to the church. The church benefits from the new covenant and is the fundamental guardian of God's saving promises.

12. Acts 1:3–8 suggests the kingdom was still a possibility. The kingdom awaits a generation of obedient believers.

CHAPTER 9

1. Jews refer to this area as the West Bank.

2. *Intifada* means "shaking off" — that is, shaking off the yoke of Israeli rule.

3. The Likud Party led a political revolution in 1977. The Labor Party had ruled Israel since independence in 1948. The formal action taken by Knesset vote occurred on July 22, 1980. The annexation signaled Israel's determination that Jerusalem would not be open for negotiations.

4. Martin Gilbert, *Jerusalem in the Twentieth Century* (New York: John Wiley, 1996), 327.

5. There had been a number of incidents prior to December 1987: Israeli soldiers killed, a Dutchman murdered, a secret service agent killed by jihadists, and more, but the riot on December 9 is viewed as the beginning, when Israeli soldiers opened fire on some youths. The violence grew and spread rapidly to the West Bank. Thomas L. Friedman, *From Beirut to Jerusalem* (New York: Anchor Books, 1989), 370–71.

6. David Dolan, *Holy War for the Promised Land* (Nashville: Thomas Nelson, 1991), 173.

7. Quoted in Gilbert, *Jerusalem*, 358.

8. The Ophel refers to an elevation or fortified area that lies on the southern slope extending from the Temple Mount to the City of David.

9. Assyria ultimately failed because it returned home without conquering Jerusalem.

10. Nahman Avigad, *Discovering Jerusalem* (Jerusalem: Shikmona, 1980), 55–56.

11. Ibid., 54.

12. Dan Bahat and Chaim T. Rubinstein, eds., *The Illustrated Atlas of Jerusalem* (New York: Palgrave Macmillan, 1990), 34.

13. Ibid., 37.

14. Ibid., 38.

15. Josephus, *Wars* 5.136–88. Josephus was a first-century historian from whom we have received much valuable information about life in Israel during that period. While he may have exaggerated at times, he is nevertheless considered the best primary source from that period.

16. Recent excavations of Warren's Shaft by Ronny Reich and Eli Shukron date the earliest part of Warren's Shaft to about 1800 BC.

17. Randall Price reports that the claim by Jerusalem to be the third holiest place for Muslims has objections from Iraq, Iran, Turkey, and Syria who each claim that distinction.

In fact, Jerusalem is not mentioned at all in the Qur'an. Randall Price, *The Coming Last Days Temple* (Eugene, OR: Harvest House, 1999), 171, 181.

18. Today both passageways are used by the mosques.

19. Josephus gave the name of the valley running through the Old City the Valley of Cheesemakers (Cheesemongers) (*Wars* 5:14). Its common name is Tyropoeon Valley, a Greek name derived from the words "cheese" and "makers," presumably named for the business activity of making cheese in the area. The valley separated the Temple Mount from the Western City and ultimately emptied into the Hinnom Valley. Over the centuries, the valley filled up with debris and is barely noticeable today.

20. Eilat Mazar and Benjamin Mazar, "Excavations in the South of the Temple Mount. The Ophel of Biblical Jerusalem," in Lee I. Levine, *Qedem, Monographs of the Institute of Archaeology* (Jerusalem: Institute of Archaeology, Hebrew University of Jerusalem, 1989).

CHAPTER 10

1. Following the Six-Day War in 1967, Israel had agreed to Muslim administrative control of the Temple Mount. The Jews continued to pray at the Western Wall.

2. Martin Gilbert, *Jerusalem in the Twentieth Century* (New York: John Wiley, 1996), 343.

3. Ibid.

4. Bahat and Rubinstein, *Illustrated Atlas of Jerusalem* (New York: Macmillan, 1990) 39.

5. Josephus, *Wars* 1.141.

6. Bahat and Rubinstein, *Illustrated Atlas of Jerusalem*, 41.

7. Ibid.

8. Josephus, *Antiquities of the Jews*, 15.380.

9. Ibid. 20.219–23.

10. James Fleming, "The Undiscovered Gate beneath Jerusalem's Golden Gate," *Biblical Archaeology Review* (January/February 1983), 24–30.

11. *Middot* 2:4.

12. Leen Ritmeyer, *The Quest: Revealing the Temple Mount in Jerusalem* (Jerusalem: Carta and the Lamb Foundation, 2006), 146ff. Ritmeyer writes an authoritative and extensive argument for a square Temple Mount and the ark of the covenant resting in a square indentation on the Kubbat as-Sakhra.

13. Ibid, 167.

14. Ibid., 241–49. Ritmeyer has a good discussion of the various theories placing the site of the Holy of Holies in nontraditional locations.

15. John L. Esposito, ed., *The Oxford History of Islam* (Oxford: Oxford University Press, 1999), 216.

16. Qur'an 4:171; Abdullah Yusuf Ali, trans., The Holy Qur'an (Hertfordshire: Wordsworth Limited Editions, 2000).

17. Eyal Merion, *Jerusalem, A Walk through Time* (Jerusalem: Yad Izhak Ben-Zvi Publications, 1999), 154.

CHAPTER 11

1. Bethphage marked the outer limits of the city, and today a Franciscan chapel commemorates the site.

2. Evidence indicates Jesus had been in the vicinity prior to the triumphal entry and made

arrangements ahead of time for the donkey (perhaps Lazarus did it for him). There is no indication that Jesus' supernatural knowledge played a part.

3. Harold Hoehner has been a worthy advocate of a Monday triumphal entry. His position rests on an intricate chronology beginning with Daniel's words, "From the time the word goes out to restore and rebuild Jerusalem until the Anointed One, the ruler, comes, there will be seven 'sevens,' and sixty-two 'sevens'" (9:25). However, the traditional view makes good sense and sets up the narrative: Jesus arrived in Bethany on Friday afternoon just before the Sabbath began. The crowds he was traveling with from Jericho continued on into the city. Word spread that night and throughout the Sabbath that Jesus was coming on Sunday morning when the Sabbath ended. That would explain the large crowds that were present at his entry.

4. The resurrection of Lazarus was a direct threat to the Pharisees. Ever since the Sabbath controversy in Galilee, the Pharisees were seeking a way to arrest Jesus (Mark 3:6), but with the raising of Lazarus, the Jewish leaders felt that Jesus was an immediate threat who needed to be removed (John 11:46–53).

5. Other scholars would suggest the Holy One was cut off at his death.

6. Editorial staff, Zondervan, *NIV Archaeological Study Bible* (Grand Rapids: Zondervan, 2005), 1600.

7. Ed. R.H. Charles, "I Maccabees" *The Apocrypha and Pseudepigrapha of the Old Testament* (London: Oxford University Press, 1973), note on I Maccabees 2:42, 73.

8. Robert H. Stein, *Jesus the Messiah: A Survey of the Life of Christ* (Downers Grove, IL: IVP Academic, 1996), 191–192. Stein points out that the cleansing of the temple is sandwiched in the middle of the account of the cursing of the fig tree: Mark 11:12–14 (cursing), Mark 11:15–19 (cleansing), Mark 11:20–24 (cursing). By sandwiching the cleansing event in this manner, Mark suggests the judgment is upon the nation Israel and Judaism's symbol, the temple, for not bearing fruit.

9. Jesus' act of driving out the money changers in Matthew 21:12–13 probably included the sons of the high priest Annas. Many of these priestly families were corrupt. Money changing business normally took place in the Royal Stoa in the southern area of the Temple Mount. Perhaps at this time the market spilled over from the legal area of the stoa into the Court of the Gentiles and so profaned it. The Court of the Gentiles extended as far as the soreg, which was a low wall surrounding the temple. The soreg displayed signs in a number of languages warning of the dire consequences for Gentiles who passed beyond the wall. When Jesus quoted Isaiah 56:7 and Jeremiah 7:11, "My house will be called a house of prayer, but you are making it a 'den of robbers'" (Matt. 21:13), he may have been angered by the fact that the area of worship for Gentiles was profaned by the business activities of the Jewish leaders. Jesus' accusation that the merchants had turned the area into "a den of robbers" reflects the evidence confirming the exorbitant prices charged for sacrificial animals and money changing for paying the temple taxes. See Leen Ritmeyer, "The Palace of Annas the High Priest," *Ritmeyer Archaeological Design*, August 28, 2012, http://www.ritmeyer.com/2012/08/28/the-palace-of-annas-the-high-priest/.

10. This probably took place near the Hulda Gates on the southern steps leading up to the Temple Mount, a place where many of the scribes, Pharisees, and chief priests held open court.

11. A "woe" is a reaction to a serious statement expressing deep suffering from misfortune, grief, regret, or distress: "Woe is me" or "Woe! Woe!"

12. The King James Version follows the Byzantine text that includes an additional woe for devouring widows' houses and making long prayers.

13. While it was Josephus who described the marble stones of the temple, he was undoubt-

edly wrong. No marble stones have been found in Jerusalem from this time; they created fake marble by means of plaster.

14. Some believe Matthew 24:4–6 represents conditions in this present age; others believe verses 4–14 occur in the first half of the Jewish tribulation (Daniel's seventy weeks prophecy (Dan. 9:20–27) and the events in verses 15–28 occur in the second half of the tribulation period.

15. Perhaps because of the possible Jewish sensitivity to the use of the name of "God," Matthew prefers the term "kingdom of heaven" (although "kingdom of God" is used twice in Matt. 19:16, 24). The other gospels prefer the expression "kingdom of God."

16. Harold Hoehner's view places the events normally considered to have happened on Tuesday on Wednesday. The problem presented by the traditional view is that there are no events recorded for Wednesday.

17. A popular notion has surfaced with public awareness of a series of books published on the *Gospel of Judas*, in which the Gnostic author attempts to rehabilitate Judas. In this heretical work, Judas is transformed into the hero of the disciples. No evidence exists to support such a theory.

18. Pixner conducted extensive excavations in the area of Mount Zion and discovered the Essene Gate. His article gives evidence of a community of Essenes living in the southern area of Jerusalem. Bargil Pixner, "Jerusalem's Essene Gateway," *Biblical Archaeology Review* 23, no. 3 (May–June): 23–30.

19. This *mikva* (ritual bath) is the same style as those found at Qumran. However, archaeologist Gabriel Barkay pointed out to the author in a private conversation that other baths of this style are found in various places in Jerusalem.

20. Frederick Jones Bliss, "Third Report on the Excavations at Jerusalem," *Palestinian Exploration Fund Quarterly Statement* 27, no.1 (Jan. 1895): 9–25. Archibald Campbell Dickie, "Fifth Report on the Excavations at Jerusalem," *Palestinian Exploration Fund Quarterly Statement* 27, no.3 (July 1895): 235–248.

21. The word for "guest room" is used only here and in Luke 2:7, referring to the "inn" in Bethlehem, Jesus' place of birth.

22. Leen Ritmeyer advances the theory that the upper room was located directly south and close to the Temple Mount, because the man carrying the water pitcher would be near the Water Gate in the Lower City above the Gihon Spring. He acknowledges he cannot prove it. Ritmeyer, *Jerusalem in the Year 30 A.D.* (Jerusalem: Carta, 2004), 71.

23. Some suggest this event in Acts 2 took place in the temple precincts (see Acts 1:13 and Luke 24:53).

24. The disciples were constantly jockeying for the best position (see Mark 9:34; Luke 22:24).

25. The extent and direction of the Second Wall is difficult to determine. Some scholars suggest the wall of the city extended north from the Tower of Antonia to the present Old City wall, incorporating the Damascus Gate, and then south, just skirting the area of the garden of the Holy Sepulcher. See Eliat Mazar, *The Complete Guide to the Temple Mount Excavations* (Jerusalem: Shahom Academic Research and Publication, 2002), 16ff.; and Dan Bahat, *Carta's Historical Atlas of Jerusalem* (Jerusalem: Carta, 1973), 12. Others have the Second Wall as depicted by the artist here. See Jerome Murphy-O'Connor, *The Holy Land: An Oxford Archaeological Guide*, 5th ed. (Oxford: Oxford University Press, 2008), 10, 15; Norman Kotker, *The Holy Land in the Time of Jesus* (New York: Harper and Row, 1967), 118; and Jack Finegan, *The Archaeology of the New Testament* (Princeton: Princeton University Press, 1969), 109, 136–37.

CHAPTER 12

1. Some have suggested that Jesus' prayer was to avoid eternal death as a payment for sin.

2. Some suggest the soldier's helmet, pointed at the crown, caused Peter's blow to glance off the helmet and strike the ear.

3. The trial before Annas was not a formal trial, but an interrogation seeking evidence to make formal charges.

4. Some have identified the house of the high priest, here referred to as the Palatial Mansion, as either the house of Annas or Caiaphas. Ritmeyer argues for identifying it as the home of the Jewish high priest Annas (see below). Additionally, it could be the residence of both.

5. The only evidence that the Palatial Mansion may be the house of Annas and/or Caiaphas is its location and the fact that the layout of the house closely matches the description of movements and events at Jesus' trial. It is the site archaeologist Nahman Avigad first suggested could possibly be identified with the high priest's house. Since then the well-respected scholars Arthur Rupprecht and Leen Ritmeyer have argued for the possible identification. Others have joined the speculation that the findings could possibly be identified with the house of Annas and/or Caiaphas.

6. Annas was the recognized Jewish high priest from AD 6–15. He was certainly the power behind the Jewish leaders. Priests were generally wealthy landowners and had a monopoly on the trade of sacrificial animals. Their excessive wealth led to powerful priestly families (Acts 4:5–6). Josephus says Annas was a "great hoarder of money" (Josephus, *Antiquities of the Jews* 9.3).

7. Some have suggested that the man running away naked at the time of Jesus' arrest was John Mark. Mark 14:51–53 mentions a man who "fled naked."

8. Leen Ritmeyer argues extensively that the Palatial Mansion is the house of the high priest Annas rather than Caiaphas. See www.ritmeyer.com/2012/08/28/the-palace-of-annas-the-high-priest/.

9. Nahman Avigad, *Discovering Jerusalem* (Jerusalem: Shikmona, 1980), 95.

10. Leen Ritmeyer and Kathleen Ritmeyer, *Jerusalem in the Year 30 A.D.* (Jerusalem: Carta, 2004), 44. The Ritmeyers refer to a structure just across the alleyway.

11. It is possible that within the large structure of Annas's mansion Caiaphas also had his residence.

12. There is some question whether the structure was a palace or living quarters.

13. In 1990, while constructing a water park on the slope south of the Old City in Jerusalem, excavators uncovered a burial cave. In it was a first-century ossuary that bore the Aramaic name "Joseph son of Caiaphas." The remains of a sixty-year-old man were identified as the high priest Caiaphas of the gospel accounts. This was the first ever confirmation of Caiaphas as the one described in the Gospels. Ronny Reich, "Caiaphas Name Inscribed on Bone Boxes," *Biblical Archaeology Review* 18 (September–October 1992), 28–44.

14. Avigad allows for a second floor above the western section of the mansion. This could give support to the descriptions recorded in Mark 14:66 and Luke 22:61. The mansion, as it is laid out, certainly accommodates such a view. Avigad, *Discovering Jerusalem*, 97, 99. However, it may have been only one story with stairs leading to the roof. The building is constructed on a slope, and Jesus' looking down could be explained by viewing the building's physical location.

15. Jesus' eyesight was in a direct line with Peter's location in the courtyard. If Peter moved from the fire to the corner of the courtyard, Jesus, standing in the middle of

the floor, could look down and see Peter (Mark 14:66: "While Peter was below in the courtyard").

16. Originally the seventy-one members of the Sanhedrin sat in the Hall of Hewn Stones, and two courts of twenty-three sat, one at the entrance of the Temple Mount and one at the door of the temple court. However, they did not always retain this place of meeting. According to Josephus, the council house was in the vicinity of the *xystus* (Josephus, *Wars* 5.142–44). Some have identified the council house with the *xystus*, a covered colonnade in the gymnasium, in an area connecting the temple with the Upper City. It is debated whether the Sanhedrin met in the *xystus* or in the confines of the temple area itself. Titus met Jewish leaders in the *xystus* to negotiate the surrender of the city in AD 70. Josephus gave the location as the first wall on the north, beginning at the southern tower of Hippicus, extending to the xystus, then skirting the council house and ending at the western cloister of the temple.

17. If the houses of Annas and Caiaphas were both in the same building, the room identified in the Palatial Mansion for this trial could be the reception hall, but the size of the room suggests it was not large enough to accommodate the entire Sanhedrin, a large crowd of priests, accusers, and onlookers. So it seems unlikely. It is possible that this interrogation took place in a hall on a second floor if it did have a second floor. However, it seems best that they took Jesus to the regular assembly of the Sanhedrin.

18. In some cases, it was only necessary for a twenty-three-member panel to convene. The full panel of seventy-one members convened only in cases of national significance. Paul Maier suggests two of the Sanhedrin were not present—Joseph of Arimathea, whose family tomb was given to bury Jesus, and Nicodemus, who was a secret follower of Jesus. Paul L. Maier, *In the Fullness of Time* (Grand Rapids: Kregel, 1991), 144.

19. Josephus, *Wars* 7.1–2.

20. The recent exploitation of the Gnostic writing *The Gospel of Judas* attempts to rehabilitate the character and actions of Judas Iscariot, history's greatest traitor. Books like Rodolphe Kasser, Marvin Meyer, and George Wurst's *The Gospel of Judas* and Bart D. Ehrman's *The Lost Gospel of Judas Iscariot* suggest Judas was actually a secret hero accomplishing God's purpose.

21. Josephus, *Wars* 2.117.

22. *Praetorium* is a general term referring to a place for administrative and juridical functions. It could refer to the Antonia Fortress on the north side of the Temple Mount or Herod's palace near the Jaffa Gate. As Josephus and Philo both state that Pilate resided in Herod's palace when he visited Jerusalem, most scholars today locate the Praetorium at Herod's Palace.

23. Pilate often accommodated the Jews because of his fear they would riot and get him in trouble with Rome.

24. While the authors prefer to support the idea that this trial before Herod took place in the Hasmonean palace, it is quite possible Pilate could have made guest quarters for Herod at his own palace. However, their animosity toward each other would seem to preclude such hospitality.

25. This statement has been the basis for anti-Semitism for many years. Jesus was a Jew, his disciples were Jews, and the early church was primarily Jewish. There is no room in these words to warrant anti-Semitism. The ultimate cause of Jesus' death was the sins of *humankind*. We are all guilty of Jesus' death—and praise God for his willingness to die for us.

26. As we have discussed, the house of the high priest seems to be the house of Annas. However, traditionally the house is generally referred to as the house of Caiaphas.

27. Magen Broshi, "Excavations of Mt. Zion, 1971–1972, Preliminary Report," *Israel Exploration Journal* 26 (1976): 81–88.

28. Bargil Pixner and Shlomo Margalit excavated the Essene Gate in the Protestant cemetery on Mount Zion in 1977–78. They identified a lower-level gate as that which Josephus called "the Essene gate." Pixner theorized that the southwestern section of the walled city was inhabited by an Essene community. The gate faces the direction of the Essene community at Qumran. Since that time many have embraced his theory.

29. A detailed description with accompanying diagrams and pictures can be seen in Avigad, *Discovering Jerusalem*, 95–120.

30. Early scholars believed the wealthy and members of the priesthood lived farther south on Mount Zion. Josephus, however, helps identify the location of the homes of the high priests in the area where the Palatial Mansion was discovered. *Wars*, 2.422; 4.426 (mention of the house of the high priest Annas).

31. The so-called "Burnt House" was discovered under layers of ashes beneath the paving stones in the Jewish Quarter of the Old City of Jerusalem. It was the first evidence discovered to illustrate the Roman destruction of the Upper City in 70 AD. Archaeologists uncovered a wealth of material culture associated with priestly activity.

32. Avigad, *Discovering Jerusalem*, 120. I first became aware of the many correlations between the Gospels' accounts and the plan of the mansion in an article by Arthur Rupprecht. Arthur Rupprecht, "The House of Annas-Caiaphas," *Archaeology in the Biblical World*, Spring 1991, 4–17.

33. Josephus, *Wars* 2.422. William Whiston's translation of Josephus with commentary by Paul Maier incorrectly identifies the upper city with Mount Zion, which Maier puts in brackets, indicating what he believes Josephus meant rather than an actual translation. Flavius Josephus, *The New Complete Works of Josephus*, trans. William Whiston, commentary by Paul Maier (Grand Rapids: Kregel, 1999), 759.

34. Nahman Avigad, *The Herodian Quarter in Jerusalem* (Jerusalem: Keter, 1989), 75. Leen Ritmeyer designed the model.

35. The house of the high priest Annas and his five sons and son-in-law Caiaphas overtook the powerful priestly family Boethus. The power struggle of high priestly families can be seen in a lament describing the fall of the new hierarchy family prior to AD 70. "Woe unto me because of the house of Boethus.... Woe unto me because of the house of Qathros." Joachim Jeremias, *Jerusalem in the Time of Jesus* (Philadelphia: Fortress, 1969), 195.

36. Josephus, *Antiquities* 20.205.

37. Josephus, *Wars* 2.9, 14, 16, 18.

38. Avigad, *Discovering Jerusalem*, 65. It is interesting that Avigad describes a residence called "Herodian Residence" that fits much of what is thought to be true of the Hasmonean palace. Unlike most finds on the western hill, it did not continue until AD 70; nor was it sacked at that time. No traces can be found of fire or debris. A large amount of coins, the majority from Alexander Jannaeus's (Hasmonean) and Herod's time, along with pottery of the Hasmonean period was found. It was a large dwelling that spread over 200 square meters, with rooms arranged around a central courtyard. Avigad, *Discovering Jerusalem*, 83, 84. Is it possible that this is a part of the Hasmonean palace complex?

39. Herod scourged Jesus at the Roman Praetorian, where the modern police barracks (citadel) are. From there the crowd took Jesus back to the public square (perhaps where the Armenian Orthodox Seminary is today). This is where Jesus began his path to Golgotha.

40. Richard M. Mackowski, *Jerusalem, City of Jesus* (Grand Rapids: Eerdmans, 1980), 109, 111.
41. John Wilkinson, *The Jerusalem Jesus Knew* (Nashville: Thomas Nelson, 1978), 144–59. Wilkinson has a well-reasoned section on the Via Dolorosa as the revised "Way of the Cross."
42. Pilgrims come to Jerusalem primarily to see the site where Jesus died, was buried, and rose again. The Church of the Holy Sepulcher was constructed over this authentic site—and has seen numerous renovations. Today the site is so cluttered with religious paraphernalia that to envision it as Golgotha is difficult. A 3-D video has been made that shows those changes in the structure up to the Crusader period. See it at http://www.youtube.com/watch?v=7JrtcvNUK6Y.

Chapter 13

1. Charles Warren and C. R. Condor, *Survey of Western Palestine, Jerusalem* (London: Committee of Palestine Exploration Fund, 1884), 8–120, 321–31.
2. Jews were exiled after AD 135, but they were back living in Jerusalem already by the Middle Ages, if not before. I suspect that the exile didn't last very long and that Jews have had a pretty continuous (though small) presence throughout all of the centuries.
3. Jerome Murphy-O'Connor, *The Holy Land: An Oxford Archaeological Guide*, 5th ed. (Oxford: Oxford University Press, 2008), 43.
4. Paul L. Maier, *In the Fullness of Time* (Grand Rapids: Kregel, 1991), 86.
5. Mary from Magdala in Galilee is the only woman named in all four gospels. Perhaps Mary arrived first before sunrise (John 20:1) and the others got there after sunrise (Mark 16:2).
6. Maier, *In the Fullness of Time*, 184–85. Maier gives a wonderfully creative account of the process of the resurrection.
7. The appearance to Peter (1 Cor. 15:5) must have happened shortly after his appearance to the disciples on the road to Emmaus.
8. The disciples earlier confessed Jesus as the "Son of God" (Matt. 14:33), and Peter confessed Jesus as the "Son of the living God" (Matt. 16:16). Undoubtedly acknowledging his deity, Thomas called Jesus "God."
9. Modern Greek New Testaments and most modern translations do not include Mark 16:9–20. The Greek New Testament (Textus Receptus) and the King James Version include it in their readings.
10. Jesus continued to minister to the disciples for forty days (including the restoration of Peter in John 21), and he continues to minister to his disciples now at the Father's right hand (Heb. 1).

Chart

1. While some suggest the birth of Jesus could be as early as 6 BCE, Hoehner argues for a birth in 5 BCE or early 4 BCE. *Chronological Aspects*, 25.
2. Luke's account from 9:51–19:48 is called Luke's Jerusalem Travel Narrative; 9:51–13:21 is his journey as he set out for Jerusalem through Samaria; in 13:22–17:10 he continues his way to Jerusalem; and in 17:11–19:48 he travels between Samaria and Galilee and then concludes his trip to Jerusalem. Much of Luke's material is unique to Luke so the chronology is a bit awkward. Apparently there are not three trips to Jerusalem but each account describes the same journey to Jerusalem with the purpose to die. The period covers several months so a great deal of travel was taking place.
3. Tradition places the Triumphal Entry on Sunday and Hoehner places it on Monday.

BIBLIOGRAPHY

Aland, Kurt, ed. *Synopsis of the Four Gospels.* 8th ed. Stuttgart, Germany: German Bible Society, 1987.

Ali, Abdullah Yusuf, trans. *The Holy Qur'an.* Hertfordshire, UK: Wordsworth Limited Editions, 2000.

Andrews, Samuel J. *The Life of Our Lord upon the Earth.* New York: Scribner, 1892.

Avigad, Nahman. *Discovering Jerusalem.* Jerusalem: Shikmona, 1980.

———. *The Herodian Quarter in Jerusalem: Wohl Archaeological Museum.* Jerusalem: Keter, 1989.

Bahat, Dan. *Carta's Historical Atlas of Jerusalem.* Jerusalem: Carta, 1973.

Bahat, Dan, and Chaim T. Rubinstein, eds. *The Illustrated Atlas of Jerusalem.* New York: Palgrave Macmillan, 1990.

Baretz, Julie. *Our Pilgrimage to Israel.* Jerusalem: Julie Baretz, 1993.

Batey, Richard A. *Jesus and the Forgotten City.* Pasadena, CA: Century One Media, 2000.

———. "Sepphoris—An Urban Picture of Jesus." *Biblical Archaeology Review* 18, no. 3 (May/June 1992): 50.

Ben-Dov, Meir. "Herod's Mighty Temple Mount." *Biblical Archaeology Review* 12, no. 6 (Nov/Dec 1986): 40–49.

———. *In the Shadow of the Temple.* Jerusalem: Keter, 1985.

Ben-Yehuda, Nachman. "Where Masada's Defenders Fell." *Biblical Archaeology Review* 24, no. 6 (Nov/Dec 1998): 32–39.

Blomberg, Craig L. *Jesus and the Gospels.* Nashville: Broadman and Holman, 1997.

Bock, Darrell L. *Jesus according to Scripture.* Grand Rapids: Baker Academic, 2002.

Bolen, Todd. "The Byzantine Church of Khirbet el-Maqatir." *Bible and Spade* 12, no. 3 (1999): 91–94.

———. "Jesus and the Sea of Galilee." *Bible and Spade* 16, no. 4 (2003): 116–119.

———. *Pictorial Library of Bible Lands.* Revised and Expanded Edition, 2012. BiblePlaces.com.

———. "The Samaritan Passover." *Bible and Spade* 14, no. 2 (2001): 41–42.

Boochny, Etty. *The Holy Land: Follow the Steps of Jesus.* Jerusalem: Steimatzky, 1999.

Bratcher, Dennis. "Introduction to a Christian Seder: Recovering Passover for Christians." *The Voice.* November 8, 2011. http://www.crivoice.org/seder.html.

Cohen, Abraham. *Everyman's Talmud: The Major Teachings of the Rabbinic Sages.* New York: Dutton, 1949.

Connolly, Peter. *Living in the Time of Jesus of Nazareth.* Tel Aviv: Steimatzsky, 1983.

Demsky, Aaron. "When the Priests Trumpeted the Onset of the Sabbath." *Biblical Archaeology Review* 12, no. 6 (Nov/Dec 1986): 72–73.

Dolan, David. *Holy War for the Promised Land.* Nashville: Thomas Nelson, 1991.

Dudman, Helga. *Tiberias.* Jerusalem: Carta, 1992.

Dyer, Charles H. *Thirty Days in the Land with Jesus.* Chicago: Moody, 2012.

Dyer, Charles H., and Gregory A. Hatteberg. *The New Christian Traveler's Guide to the Holy Land*. Chicago: Moody, 2006.

Esposito, John L., ed. *The Oxford History of Islam*. Oxford: Oxford University Press, 1999.

Finegan, Jack. *Archaeology of the New Testament*. Princeton: Princeton University Press, 1978.

———. *The Archaeology of the New Testament: The Life of Jesus and the Beginning of the Early Church*. Princeton: Princeton University Press, 1992.

Fleming, Jim. *The World of the Bible Gardens*. Ein Karem, Jerusalem: Biblical Resources, 1999.

Friedman, Thomas L. *From Beirut to Jerusalem*. New York: Doubleday, 1989.

Geva, Hillel. "Jerusalem: The Early Periods and the First Temple Period: Recent Discoveries within the City." In *The New Encyclopedia of Archaeological Excavations in the Holy Land*, edited by E. Stern. New York: Simon and Schuster, 1993.

———. "Jerusalem: Second Temple Period: The Temple Mount and Its Environs." In *The New Encyclopedia of Archaeological Excavations in the Holy Land*, edited by E. Stern. New York: Simon and Schuster, 1993.

Gilbert, Martin. *Jerusalem in the Twentieth Century*. New York: John Wiley, 1996.

Gonen, Rivka. *Biblical Holy Places: An Illustrated Guide*. New York: Macmillan, 1987.

Green, Joel B., Scott McKnight, and I. Howard Marshall, eds. *Dictionary of Jesus and the Gospels*. Downers Grove, IL: InterVarsity, 1992.

Greenhut, Zvi. "Burial Cave of the Caiaphas Family." *Biblical Archaeology Review* 18, no. 5 (Sept/Oct 1992): 29–36.

Gulston, Charles. *Jerusalem: The Tragedy and the Triumph*. Grand Rapids: Zondervan, 1978.

Hoehner, Harold. *Chronological Aspects of the Life of Christ*. Grand Rapids: Zondervan, 1977.

Hudson, Christopher D., David Barrett, and Todd Bolen. *Bible Atlas & Companion*. Uhrichsville, OH: Barbour, 2008.

Jeremias, Joachim. *Jerusalem in the Time of Jesus*. Philadelphia: Fortress, 1969.

Johnson, Paul. *A History of the Jews*. New York: Harper and Row, 1987.

Kaiser, Walter C. Jr., and Duane A. Garrett, *NIV Archaeological Study Bible: An Illustrated Walk through Biblical History and Culture*. Grand Rapids: Zondervan, 2006.

Kauffmann, Joel. *The Nazareth Jesus Knew*. Nazareth: Nazareth Village, 2005.

Kim, Stephen S. *The Miracles of Jesus according to John*. Eugene, OR: Wipf & Stock, 2010.

Klausner, Joseph. *Jesus of Nazareth: His Life, Times, and Teaching*. Translated by Herbert Danby. New York: Macmillan, 1953.

Kotker, Norman. *The Holy Land in the Time of Jesus*. Horizon Caravel. New York: American Heritage, 1967.

Laney, J. Carl. *Concise Bible Atlas: A Geographical Survey of Bible History*. Peabody, MA: Hendrickson, 1999.

———. "Geographical Aspects of the Gospel." In *Essays in Honor of J. Dwight Pentecost*, 75–88. Chicago: Moody, 1986.

Loffreda, Stanislao. *Recovering Capharnaum*. Studium biblicum Franciscanum Guides. Milan, Italy: Edizioni Custodia Terra Santa, 1985.

Mackowski, Richard M. *Jerusalem: City of Jesus*. Grand Rapids: Eerdmans, 1980.

Maier, Paul L. *In the Fullness of Time: A Historian Looks at Christmas, Easter, and the Early Church*. Grand Rapids: Kregel, 1991.

———. ed. *The New Complete Works of Josephus*. Translated by William Whiston. Grand Rapids: Kregel, 1999.

Martin, James C., John C. Beck, and David G. Hansen. *A Visual Guide to Gospel Events*. Grand Rapids: Baker, 2010.

Mazar, Benjamin. "Excavations Near the Temple Mount Reveal Splendors of Herodian Jerusalem." *Biblical Archaeology Review* 6, no. 4 (Jul/Aug 1980): 44–50.

———. "Herodian Jerusalem in the Light of Excavations South and South-West of the Temple Mount." *Israel Exploration Journal* 28 (1978): 230–37.

———. *The Mountain of the Lord*. Garden City, NY: Doubleday, 1975.

———. "The Temple Mount." *Biblical Archaeology Today: Proceedings of the International Congress on Biblical Archaeology Jerusalem, April 1984.* Jerusalem: Israel Exploration Society, The Israel Academy of Sciences and Humanities in cooperation with the American Schools of Oriental Research, 1985, 463–68.

Mazar, Eilat. *The Complete Guide to the Temple Mount Excavations*. Jerusalem: Shahom Academic Research and Publications, 2002.

———. "Royal Gateway to Ancient Jerusalem Uncovered." *Biblical Archaeology Review* 15, no. 3 (May/June 1989): 38–51.

———. "The Royal Quarter of Biblical Jerusalem: The Ophel." In *Ancient Jerusalem Revealed*, edited by Hillel Geva, 64–72. Jerusalem: Israel Exploration Society, 1994.

Mazar, Eilat, and Benjamin Mazar. "Excavations in the South of the Temple Mount." *The Ophel of Biblical Jerusalem*. 29 (1989): Jerusalem.

McRay, John. *Archaeology and the New Testament*. Grand Rapids: Baker, 1991.

Metzger, Paul Louis. *Consuming Jesus*. Grand Rapids: Eerdmans, 2007.

———. *The Gospel of John*. Downers Grove, IL: InterVarsity, 2010.

Meyers, Eric M., ed. *The Oxford Encyclopedia of Archaeology in the Near East.* Vol. 5. Oxford: Oxford University Press, 1997.

Meyers, Eric M., Ehud Netzer, and Carol L. Meyers. *Sepphoris*. Winona Lake, IN: Eisenbrauns, 1992.

Miller, Stephen M. *The Jesus of the Bible*. Uhrichsville, OH: Barbour, 2009.

Murphy-O'Connor, Jerome. *The Holy Land: An Oxford Archaeological Guide*. 5th edition. Oxford: Oxford University Press, 2008.

Nun, Mendel. *Gergesa (Kursi): Site of a Miracle Church and Fishing Village*. Ein Gev, Israel: Kinnereth Sailing Co., 1989.

———. *Sea of Galilee: Newly Discovered Harbours from New Testament Days*. Ein Gev, Israel: Kinnereth Sailing Co., 1989.

———. *The Sea of Galilee and Its Fishermen in the New Testament*. Ein Gev, Israel: Kinnereth Sailing Co., 1989.

Page, Charles R. II. *Jesus and the Land*. Nashville: Abingdon, 1995.

Pentecost, J. Dwight. *The Words and Works of Jesus Christ*. Grand Rapids: Zondervan, 1981.

Perowne, Stewart. *The Life and Times of Herod The Great*. New York: Abingdon, 1956.

Pixner, Bargil. *An Essene Quarter on Mount Zion*. Jerusalem: Franciscan Printing Press, 1976.

———. "Jerusalem's Essene Gateway." *Biblical Archaeology Review* 23, no. 3 (May/June 1997): 23–31.

———. "The Miracle Church at Tabgha on the Sea of Galilee." *Biblical Archaeologist* 48, no. 4 (Dec. 1985): 196–206.

———. *With Jesus in Jerusalem*. Rosh Pina, Israel: Chorazin, 1996.

———. *With Jesus through Galilee according to the Fifth Gospel*. Rosh Pina, Israel: Chorazin, 1992.

Price, Randall. *The Coming Last Days Temple*. Eugene, OR: Harvest House, 1999.

Pritz, Ray A. *Nazarene Jewish Christianity*. Jerusalem: The Hebrew University, 1992.

Raney, Anson F., and R. Steven Notley. *The Sacred Bridge*. Jerusalem: Carta, 2006.

Reed, Jonathan L. *Archaeology and the Galilean Jesus*. Harrisburg, PA: Trinity Press International, 2000.

Reich, Ronny. *The Jerusalem Archaeological Park*. Jerusalem: Israel Antiquities Authority, 1999.

Richman, Chaim. *The Holy Temple of Jerusalem*. Jerusalem: Carta, Israel Map and Publishing Company, 1997.

Ritmeyer, Kathleen, and Leen Ritmeyer. *Reconstructing Herod's Temple Mount in Jerusalem.* Washington, DC: Biblical Archaeology Society, 1990.

———. "Reconstructing Herod's Temple Mount in Jerusalem." *Biblical Archaeology Review* 15, no. 6 (Nov/Dec 1989): 23–42.

———. "Reconstructing the Triple Gate." *Biblical Archaeology Review* 15, no. 6 (Nov/Dec 1989b): 49–53.

———. *Secrets of Jerusalem's Temple Mount.* Washington, DC: Biblical Archaeology Society, 1998.

Ritmeyer, Leen. "The Palace of Annas the High Priest." Ritmeyer Archaeological Design. August 28, 2012. http://www.ritmeyer.com/2012/08/28/the-palace-of-annas-the-high-priest/.

———. "Quarrying and Transporting Stones for Herod's Temple Mount." *Biblical Archaeology Review* 15, no. 6 (Nov/Dec 1989): 46–48.

———. *The Quest: Revealing the Temple Mount in Jerusalem.* Jerusalem: Carta, 2006.

———. *The Temple and the Rock.* Harrogate, UK: Ritmeyer Archaeological Design, 1996.

Ritmeyer, Leen, and Kathleen Ritmeyer. *Jerusalem in the Year 30 A.D.* Jerusalem: Carta, 2004.

———. *Secrets of Jerusalem's Temple Mount.* Washington, DC: Biblical Archaeological Society, 1998.

Rousseau, John J., and Rami Arav. *Jesus and His World.* Minneapolis: Fortress, 1995.

Rupprecht, Arthur. "The House of Annas-Caiaphas." *Archaeology in the Biblical World* (Spring 1991): 4.

Schlegel, William. *Satellite Bible Atlas: Historical Geography of the Bible.* BiblePlaces.com.

Shanks, Hershel. "John the Baptist's Cave." *Biblical Archaeology Review* 30, no. 6 (Nov–Dec 2004): 18–19.

Shenhav, Dodo Joseph. "Loaves and Fishes Mosaic Near the Sea of Galilee Restored." *Biblical Archaeology Review* 10, no. 3 (May/June 1984): 22–31.

Shepard, J. W. *The Christ of the Gospels.* Grand Rapids: Eerdmans, 1939.

Smith, George A. *The Historical Geography of the Holy Land.* 25th ed. Jerusalem: Ariel, 1966.

Stalker, James M. *The Trial and Death of Jesus Christ.* Grand Rapids: Zondervan, 1961.

Stein, Robert H. *Jesus the Messiah: A Survey of the Life of Christ.* Downers Grove, IL: IVP Academic, 1996.

Sterling, John. *An Atlas of the New Testament.* 4th edition. London: George Philip & Son, 1966.

Thomas, Robert L., and Stanley N. Gundry. *The NIV Harmony of the Gospels.* New York: Harper Collins, 1988.

Vamosh, Miriam Feinberg. *Daily Life at the Time of Jesus.* Herzlia, Israel: Palphot, 2004.

Walker, Peter. *In the Steps of Jesus.* Grand Rapids: Zondervan, 2006.

Ward, Kaari, ed. *Jesus and His Times.* Pleasantville, NY: Reader's Digest Association, 1987.

Warren, Charles, and C. R. Condor. *Survey of Western Palestine Jerusalem.* London: Committee of Palestine Exploration Fund, 1884.

Wilkinson, John. *The Jerusalem Jesus Knew.* Nashville: Thomas Nelson, 1978.

Wright, Paul H. *Greatness, Grace & Glory.* Jerusalem: Carta, 2008.

———. *Understanding the New Testament: An Introductory Atlas.* Jerusalem: Carta, 2007.

Yadin, Yigael. *Masada: Herod's Fortress and the Zealots' Last Stand.* London: Sphere, 1975.

———. *The Story of Masada.* New York: Random House, 1966.

SCRIPTURE INDEX

SUBJECT INDEX